# Evolving Dynamics: From Revenue Management to Revenue Strategy

THE STUDY GUIDE FOR
THE CERTIFIED REVENUE
MANAGEMENT EXECUTIVE
(CRME) CERTIFICATION

## 3RD EDITION

*By Kathleen Cullen, CRME*

Published by:

Publishing Partner:

Dear Hospitality Colleagues,

As the global leader in hotel performance benchmarking, analytics and insights, STR is proud to once again sponsor this resource. A true testament to the mission of HSMAI, the publication continues to cultivate knowledge, provide insight into the future of our business, and inspire revenue and marketing professionals worldwide.

Like HSMAI, STR understands that the hospitality industry plays a vital role in the global economy. In March 2018, STR celebrated the 10th anniversary of its international entity, which was launched to enhance the capabilities of revenue professionals around the globe.

Today, STR maintains the world's largest hotel performance data sample, which comprises 63,000 hotels and 8.4 million hotel rooms in 180 countries.

Throughout STR's more than 30 years of service, we have been a collaborative partner in the evolution and success of the revenue optimization discipline through thought leadership, dedicated service and product development. Continuing in that tradition, we remain committed to our company's foundation and legacy of providing the industry with confidential, accurate and actionable data and insights.

On behalf of STR and its more than 300 employees around the world, we thank HSMAI for the opportunity to sponsor this significant contribution to the advancement of the global hospitality industry. STR's growing network of representatives is invested in the success of its partners. To learn more about our team and our data-driven solutions, please visit www.str.com

*Amanda Hite*

Amanda Hite
President and CEO, STR

str

34 years

63,000 hotels

8.4 million
hotel rooms

180 countries

STR maintains
a presence in
15 countries
with a corporate
North American
headquarters in
suburban Nashville
and an international
headquarters
in London.

Dear Colleagues,

This book is the study guide for the Certified Revenue Management Executive (CRME) designation (www.hsmai.org/crme). We hope you will learn more about the CRME and what it can bring to you and your organization. As you read and use this book, you will understand why every hotel professional needs a copy of it!

As part of our mission to provide hospitality professionals with the most up-to-date and forward-looking information on revenue optimization principles, practices, and strategies, we are proud to deliver this industry-leading book. It has been made possible in terms of content and production by many industry professionals, business partners, and HSMAI's global advisory boards who have contributed their best thinking and experience.

We believe this book not only delivers high-quality educational content, but industry-leading insights and best practices. With practical and relevant information along with a comprehensive roadmap for hotel owners and operators to establish and enhance revenue optimization and revenue strategy at their properties, we hope you see this book as giant step toward meeting our mission.

We promise to continue to provide resources and information that will help you and your company increase your performance. Even as we send this book to the printer, the industry is changing with impacts on the revenue optimization discipline as we know it. Increasingly, industry leaders are thinking about and talking about Revenue Strategy in hotels as a distinct specialty that ties together revenue optimization, marketing, sales, distribution, and analytics in a disciplined way with a focus on enterprise profitability. Learn more, and understand how revenue professionals, owners, and operators can prepare for the future throughout this book (especially by reading chapters 1, 13, 15, and 16).

As you read and use this book in your work, remember: Hotel executives will get the most out of revenue optimization within their organizations if they heed the following advice.

- Create an optimal organization for success including having appropriate resources and executive alignment.

- Ensure adequate support and the resources needed to execute the revenue strategies.

- Commit to staying focused on long-term strategies, employ tactical short-term solutions only when necessary, and be sure that the short-term solutions do not conflict with the long-term strategies.

- Commit to understanding the difference between a budget and a revenue forecast and be willing to work with both. Contrary to popular opinion, a revenue forecast should not be created to meet or exceed the budget. Instead, it should be created based on market conditions.

- Embrace change and be proactive to stay ahead of the curve and competitors.


Please see the page vi for a roster of all advisory board members.

# Additional Revenue Optimization Resources & Education from HSMAI

HSMAI, with its advisory boards, provides leading education, a best practices exchange, thought leadership, and networking for revenue professionals, other sales and marketing professionals, and senior leaders in the hospitality industry. Learn more about these and other resources and educational opportunities at www.hsmai.org.

**ROC conferences** — In all regions where HSMAI operates, these annual gatherings of revenue professionals address the most critical trends affecting hotels today.

**Certified Revenue Management Executive (CRME)** — This certification, for which this book is the study guide, offers revenue professionals the opportunity to confirm their knowledge, experience, and capabilities.

**Certified Revenue Management Analyst (CRMA)** — This certification recognizes students for their understanding of the application of revenue optimization concepts.

**CRME Review Course** — This one-day event is designed to assist those taking the CRME exam with their final preparations.

**Revenue Ready "Certificate of Revenue Management (Hospitality)"** — An online course for people just starting in the revenue discipline, and hotel staff who would like to move into a revenue role.

**RO2Win** — An online course specifically designed for those not currently working as a revenue professional (for instance, sales, marketing, and operations professionals). It teaches the power of revenue optimization, and how the discipline interacts with and influences others in the hotel.

## AMERICAS REVENUE OPTIMIZATION ADVISORY BOARD

Chair: **Tim Wiersma**
*Vice President, Revenue Management*
Red Roof Inns, Inc.

Vice Chair: **Nicole Young, CRME**
*Corporate Director of Revenue Management*
Rosewood Hotel Group

**Chris K. Anderson, PhD**
*Academic Director*
Cornell University

**Veronica Andrews, CRME**
*Director, Digital Data Solutions*
STR

**Vivek Bhogaraju**
*Director, Revenue Management Solutions*
Expedia Group

**Christopher Biondo**
*Corporate Director of Distribution & Product Development*
Standard International

**Christian Boerger, CRME, CHDM, CHBA**
*Revenue Strategist and Digital Marketing Expert*

**Denise Broussard, CHDM**
RVP – CENTRAL, Travelclick

**Dana Cariss**
*Vice President, Revenue Strategy*
CoralTree Hospitality

**Tammy Farley**
*Co-Founder*
Rainmaker

**Monte Gardiner**
*Managing Director, Revenue Management Services*
Best Western Hotels & Resorts

**Eric Gravelle, CRME**
*Vice President of Revenue Management, North America*
Diamond Resorts International

**Linda Gulrajani, CRME**
*Vice President, Revenue Strategy & Distribution*
Marcus Hotels

**Renee Haddad, CRME**
*Director, Revenue Account Management*
Preferred Hotels & Resorts

**Adam Hayashi, CRME**
*Vice President of Revenue Management*
Accor Hotels

**Brian Hicks**
*Vice President, Global Revenue Strategy*
IHG

**Jennifer Hill, CRME**
*VP, Client Engagement*
Kalibri Labs

**Erich Jankowski**
*Vice President, Revenue Management*
Host Hotels & Resorts

**Michael Klein**
*Executive Director, Revenue Performance Strategy*
MGM Resorts International

**Michael Maher, CRME, CHDM**
*Director of Strategic Accounts*
IDeaS - A SAS COMPANY

**Chris Nixon, CRME, CHDM**
*VP Revenue Optimization*
Ashford Group of Companies

**Breffni Noone, PhD**
*Associate Professor*
Pennsylvania State University

**Julie Abou Nohra**
*Regional Director of Revenue Management, The Americas*
Mandarin Oriental Hotel Group

**Heather Richer**
*Chief Marketing Officer*
RedAwning

**Corey Stanley, CRME, CHDM**
*Corporate Director of Revenue Management*
Seneca Gaming Corporation

**David Warman**
*Senior Vice President Hotel Marketing and Revenue Management*
Four Seasons Hotels & Resorts

**Hunter Webster, CHDM**
*SVP, Revenue Strategy*
Interstate Hotels & Resorts

**Monica Xuereb**
*Chief Revenue Officer*
Loews Hotels & Co.

## ASIA PACIFIC REVENUE ADVISORY BOARD

**Devdutta Banerjee**
*VP Revenue Management*
Millennium & Copthorne Hotels

**Bilal Chamsine**
*Passionate Revenue Guru*
President, HSMAI Indonesia

**Limin Cheng**
*Director of Revenue & Distribution Management*
Marina Bay Sands, Singapore

**Jackie Douglas**
*President*
HSMAI Asia Pacific

**Heidi Gempel**
*Managing Partner & Founder*
HGE International
Facilitator, HSMAI Asia Pacific Revenue Advisory Board

**Tony Gothard**
*Senior Director Revenue, Sales & Marketing*
Wyndham Hotel Group

**Dr. Basak Denizci Guillet**
*Associate Professor of Hospitality Business Analytics*
School of Hotel and Tourism Management
The Hong Kong Polytechnic University

**Rita Jiang**
*Head of Commercial Performance, Greater China*
IHG

**Suneet Kumar**
*VP Revenue Performance & Distribution*
Pan Pacific Hotels Group

**Andrew Lau, CRME**
*Corporate Director of Revenue Management*
Rosewood Hotel Group

**Puneet Mahindroo**
*Senior Director of Hotel Marketing and Revenue Management*
Four Seasons Hotels and Resorts

**Luke Moran**
*Executive Director Revenue, Sales*
Mantra Group Hotels & Resorts

**Pallavi Nirula Nath**
*Director,*
Revmax Technologies Pte Ltd

**Liz Perkins**
Head of Revenue Management-
Europe, Asia, Middle East, Africa and Australasia
IHG

**Dr. Detlev Remy**
*Associate Professor*
Singapore Institute of Technology

**C.S. Ramachandran, CRME**
*Director Revenue Management - South Asia, Middle East and Africa*
Preferred Hotels & Resorts

**Fanie Swanepoel**
*SVP Revenue*
Marina Bay Sands

**Jeffrey Young, CRME**
*Director of Revenue Management Development*
Minor Hotels

## EUROPE REVENUE ADVISORY BOARD

Chair: **Paul Van Meerendonk, CRME**
*Director Global Advisory Services*
IDeaS

Vice Chair: **Steven Dow, CRME**
*Vice President of Revenue Management – Europe*
Diamond Resorts International

**Thomas Adler**
*Vice President Global Revenue Strategy*
Melia Hotels International

**Scott Dahl**
*Senior Lecturer*
Ecole Hôtelière, Lausanne

**Lennert De Jong**
*Chief Commercial Officer*
citizenM

**Gino Engels**
*Co-Founder and Chief Commercial Officer*
OTA Insight

**Etienne Faisandier, CRME**
*VP Revenue Management & Business Intelligence*
Moevenpick Hotels & Resorts

**Philip Gardner**
*Vice President, Commercial*
Intercontinental Hotels Group (IHG)

**Stan Josephi**
*Senior Lecturer Hotel Management*
Breda University

**Jan Lundborg**
*Chief Commercial Optimization Officer*
Scandic Hotels

**Michael McCartan**
*Managing Director, EMEA*
Duetto

**Bela Nagy**
*Global SVP Revenue Management & Pricing*
Accorhotels

**Perra Pettersson**
*Founder & Owner*
Benchmarking Alliance

**Joanna Schröder, CRME**
*Vice President Revenue Management*
Deutsche Hospitality

**Chinmai Sharma, CRME**
*Executive Vice President and Chief Revenue Officer*
Taj Hotels Resorts and Palaces

**Stan Van Roij, CRME**
*VP Hospitality Solutions and Program Management*
Infor

# TABLE OF CONTENTS

# TABLE OF CONTENTS

# INTRODUCTION

**While the foundational concepts of hotel revenue optimization largely remain the same since the last edition of this book was published in 2015, new dynamics have come into play and are disrupting the traditional landscape.**

In addition to providing detailed education on the fundamentals, this edition gives significant attention to the evolution of, and the new entrants and disruptors impacting, the critical discipline of hotel revenue optimization. Additionally, this edition shifts the focus from traditional rooms revenue management to a more holistic approach of total asset optimization.

Traditionally, hoteliers have primarily focused on *rooms* — the costs of distribution, understanding the differing costs by channel, and how this plays a role in optimizing room revenues. With more and more attention being paid to optimizing the total asset, applying revenue optimization techniques outside of guest rooms to other revenue centers is largely what many revenue professionals are working toward, if they are not already there. And their focus is shifting toward managing the increasing costs of acquisition and their impact on profits.

At the same time, hotel revenue management has historically been a highly tactical discipline. The industry's need has evolved from being tactically-focused to a much broader and more strategic approach concentrating on future strategies across all revenue-generating areas.

The revenue professional, and revenue discipline, are universally recognized as key pieces to the puzzle of driving success for the total hotel asset. All revenue centers can be optimized today, and the expectation from owners and operators is to ensure optimal profitability throughout all revenue centers.

With a broader scope in responsibility or a broader scope in applying revenue optimization techniques outside of guest rooms, and moving towards optimizing the total asset, it is more appropriate to think in terms of "hospitality revenue optimization" versus the more traditional "hotel revenue management."

These shifts in focus have implications for those in leadership roles in hotels and hotel companies today. As the demands on revenue grow, leaders need to adjust and evolve according to the need, and those supporting and/or working in conjunction with the revenue optimization discipline must also adjust and evolve with this new way of doing business.

The intent of this book is to help revenue professionals, as well as operators and owners, understand revenue optimization in today's complicated and ever-changing landscape. We'll answer important questions including:

- What are the criteria for a successful revenue optimization operation?
- What changes need to be embraced to be successful in today's world?

Today's world is far more complicated than in times past, making revenue optimization a true mix of art and science. Supported by appropriate talent and leadership, business intelligence, and technology tools, your revenue strategy can achieve your hotel's optimal business mix.

## A Special Note to Owners and Operators

There is no question that today's owners and operations executives understand what revenue optimization can do for the bottom line. However, it is crucial that owners and operators understand the resources — human, technology, and other — that are needed to create and maintain a strategic focus and timely execution.

Unfortunately, when times are tough, too many owners and operators fall back on the all-too comfortable tactic of cutting costs instead of investing in and optimizing top line revenue. If that is not properly optimized, then the bottom line will be negatively impacted, the hotel's long-term revenue optimization will be negatively impacted, and the hotel will lose its ability to attract and retain top revenue professionals to the team.

On the other hand, those who invest in ongoing training and relevant tools, unify the entire organization around profitability goals, and trust their revenue teams to act quickly (and stay out of "analysis paralysis") will lead the revenue optimization discipline and will win the best talent — all of which leads ultimately to optimal profits.

# PART ONE: THE FUNDAMENTALS

**A hotel has a finite number of guest rooms and a finite number of seats in its restaurant, making those rooms and seats perishable items.**

When a sleeping room is not priced right, or the seating configuration in a restaurant is not optimal or not flexible, or perishable inventory of any type is mismanaged, that is lost revenue that can never be realized.

Revenue optimization is focused on balancing and managing demand by setting appropriate pricing for each usage pattern by customer segment. Those usage patterns differ depending on the revenue center.

For guest rooms, it is the stay pattern; for restaurants it is the length of time in the seat or at the table; for golf it can be the amount of time in between tee-times. Each revenue center must understand its own inventory options, demand patterns, and customer segments in order to set pricing and optimize the profitability.

At the same time, there are many dynamic variables involved in hospitality revenue optimization. Without an understanding of them, it is virtually impossible to deploy strategies. In addition to usage patterns, other variables impacting the optimization of revenue and profit decisions include:

- Supply and Demand
- Product Offering
- Inventory
- Booking Pace
- Booking Window
- Market Position
- Usage Patterns
- Competitor Pricing
- Unconstrained Demand
- Customer Segments
- Optimal Business Mix
- Demand Drivers (negative and positive)
- Consumer Lifetime Value

Many of these variables, and more, will be explored throughout this book.

# CHAPTER 1
## FROM REVENUE MANAGEMENT TO REVENUE STRATEGY

### Learning Objectives
- To understand the history of revenue optimization in hotels, and how it has evolved
- To understand the increasingly complex nature of revenue optimization in hotels

### What is Revenue Optimization?

Revenue optimization is a discipline that is used in many industries, but the application and implementation can vary greatly from sector to sector. In an industry like hotels, where perishable goods and services are involved, revenue optimization provides a significant competitive advantage to companies that practice it effectively.

It is the science of managing a limited amount of supply to maximize revenue and profits, by dynamically controlling the price and quantity offered by distribution channel.

Other ways to think about revenue optimization in hospitality include:
- It is the art and science of predicting real-time customer demand at the micro market level and optimizing the price and availability of products to match that demand.
- It allows for the offering of room rates and the control of inventory through a variety of channels that are most appropriate for the anticipated demand.

Revenue optimization can be applied to restaurants: selling the right seat to the right customer at the right price for the right duration.

Total hotel revenue optimization (THRO) is the "consideration of multiple revenue sources, a deep understanding of customer value, and a shift [from top-line metrics to bottom-line measures to take] into consideration distribution and operating costs."[1]

All of these definitions boil down to the simple essence of what revenue optimization is all about: selling the right amount of inventory at the right pricing levels based on the customer's willingness to pay.

Robert Cross, one of the earliest experts in the discipline, and a recipient of HSMAI's Vanguard Award for Lifetime Achievement, described the timeless principles of the discipline: "The application of revenue management principles is limitless and the potential in terms of revenue return is impressive. Firms employing revenue management techniques have seen revenues increase between 3% and 7% without significant capital expenditures, resulting in a 50% to 100% increase in profits!"[2]

Bill Marriott, Jr. was quoted in Cross's book, "Revenue management has contributed millions to the bottom line, and it has educated our people to manage their business more effectively. When you focus on the bottom line, your company grows."

### The History and Evolution of Revenue Optimization

Revenue optimization in hotels and hotel companies is not an independent business process or system. It is a discipline that has evolved significantly over time, and has become intimately intertwined with others including sales, marketing, and distribution.

Its origins as revenue management were very descriptive, describing historical results: "Here is what happened last night…." In its next evolution, it became predictive, predicting future results: "Here is what we think is going to happen, and what we're going to do about it…." Today, powered by data and analytics which fuel AI and machine learning, the discipline is becoming more and more prescriptive, recommending or even automating decisions that will achieve the overall goals for the hotel: "Here is how we will achieve our goals…."

The resulting automation can help a hotel company move forward significantly faster. It will be like in Star Wars when R2-D2 is at the controls of the Starfighter taking care of the routine functions of flight, leaving Luke Skywalker free to focus on the strategy and more complex tasks at hand.[3]

#### The Beginning

It all started with revenue management in the airline industry. It wasn't until the late 1980s that revenue management made its way into hotels with Marriott officially introducing revenue management in its business strategies.

Early on, all revenue management practices were deployed manually, which meant that data analytics (although it was not referred to as data analytics at that time), pricing, inventory controls, demand generators, and more were tracked in some type of manual format such as an inventory control book.

The manager, typically the reservations leader at that time (or front office manager or even general manager for a smaller hotel), manually counted room availability to know how many rooms were available to sell for a given date. Reservations were manually recorded — usually handwritten on a standard form — and then entered into the inventory control book to get accurate house-counts. Cancellations were tracked manually in the same book. Calculations for all days into the future had to be counted and recounted on a regular basis to know availability for each day and how many rooms were left to sell. Guest folios were handwritten or typed on a typewriter and then put into a "bucket" based on day of arrival.

The approach to pricing was static, and far from as dynamic as it is today. Typically, a small range of rates were set based on room type and seasonality — think High Season, Shoulder Season, and Low Season. There was typically one rate per room type during a given season. It did not change by day nor was it based on fluctuating demand within a season.

It was an uncomplicated time and an uncomplicated landscape for hoteliers and consumers alike. For example, on the consumer side, corporate travel and group management budget planning was easier for travel managers as costs could be estimated based on the anticipated number of travelers and one or two rates per season. On the hotel side, deployment and tracking of revenue management strategies was easy because the rate structure was so simple. It was possible for revenue management to be implemented in a manual environment — no technology required.

### A Maturing Discipline

Once hoteliers started introducing more active ways of pricing, it became more complicated and time consuming to execute revenue management strategies. For instance, instead of one rate per room type per season, multiple rates per room type were set depending on demand. That meant manually opening and closing anywhere from two to twelve (or more) rates per room type across the channels used by the hotel (primarily reservation sales teams, the central reservation system [CRS], and

the GDSs). Imagine the amount of manual work for properties with many different room types!

At the same time, these multiple rates started being offered to different customer types. Where sales teams were once able to comfortably quote rates to a group and know how they compared to transient rates over the same dates, they found that it was no longer so simple. New systems and processes were required to keep all of a hotel's pricing, sales, and distribution teams on top of things. One enduring innovation is the revenue meeting (originally called the yield meeting). See Appendix A for today's revenue meeting best practices.

At this point of revenue management's development, the revenue leader, who was likely still the reservations director, had an overflowing plate of responsibilities. In addition to continuing to manage the reservations function, he or she was also responsible for strategically looking into the future, setting rates per day by room type, preparing for and running revenue meetings, managing questions on why or how rates were determined, and executing these changes. It was a lot of work for one person.

As the importance of this role became clear to the industry, owners, operators, and general managers began dedicating resources to it and creating stand-alone jobs focused solely on pricing and revenue management. The most common titles were yield manager, revenue manager, and in some cases, revenue director. For most hotels, this position reported directly to the director of sales and marketing, and in some cases to the general manager.

As hotels were adjusting to and absorbing the impact of these new pricing strategies, so too were consumers. Consumers were accustomed to paying the same price for the same room type and had a difficult time accepting the fact that hotel rates can and would change by day-of-week, or even daily. Even though they accepted that airlines employed this type of dynamic pricing strategy, it posed a significant, long-term communication and education challenge to hotels to help customers understand how it applied to and was being deployed in the hotel industry. Specifically on the corporate travel side, the new pricing approach disrupted corporate travel managers' planning and budgeting. They had to figure out how they would negotiate, set their annual budgets, and manage their travel programs when they did not know rates in advance.

Today, consumers — group, transient, and corporate — have become acclimated to the process and expect to see different rates. They even now know that they can pay one rate for the same room type while someone else is paying a different amount.

## Revenue Optimization Today

Today, the playing field is significantly more complex. Revenue management once meant opening and closing availability and rates. With the explosion of online distribution channels, transparent rates, user-generated reviews and social media, and a multitude of technologies, the revenue optimization discipline has become significantly more complex in order to meet the new demands it faces.

Automation made it possible for revenue optimization to keep up with the world around it. From automating reservation entry from one system to another, to automating the distribution of rates and availability from one system to another, more and more automation required less manual work from the revenue professional. But it presented a new challenge: the need for an entirely different skill set. Understanding and managing the data flow between various systems became critical, bringing a whole new set of responsibilities. Finding and developing talent to fill the role became, and remains, a challenge for the industry.

With the new demands on the discipline, including the increasing focus on revenue optimization for the entire hotel and all revenue streams, versus a singular focus on rooms, today it is nearly impossible to continue operating in a traditional manual environment. The complexities of the analytics involved, and the many variables that have entered the marketplace make it nearly impossible for anyone to keep up manually. Fortunately, technology has become the norm, the expectation, not the exception. Most owners and operators have invested in sophisticated tools to help manage and optimize revenue results.

While the fundamentals of revenue optimization remain the same, the approach to managing them has significantly changed as technology has become ingrained in the revenue optimization discipline:

- Automated systems use sophisticated algorithms to determine rates or rate hurdles.
- Rate shopping tools provide advanced insights into market pricing and positioning
- Business intelligence tools uncover booking patterns and rates within the market.

- Online digital initiatives drive traffic to brand.com sites.
- A variety of tools work together to help revenue professionals better understand profitability and costs, and so much more.

Hotel revenue optimization has become very complex. As the hospitality landscape, including owners, consumers, and hoteliers, becomes more sophisticated and demanding, so too do the tools and resources available from industry partners.

Changes in technology, customer behavior and expectations, owners' expectations, and more, have forced hotels and hotel companies to think and act differently when it comes to revenue optimization. Hoteliers who remain focused on "the way we have always done it" are falling behind, and quickly. Those that refuse to change and adapt to new technologies, new methods, or new talent requirements are restricting their hotels and companies from optimizing revenues to the fullest.

At the same time, outside of the hotel industry there is rapid adoption of revenue optimization, which is often accompanied by an increased focus on customer behavior. As more and more industries identify opportunities to increase revenue, they are learning more about their customers. These new insights allow them to enhance their revenue optimization strategies by personalizing offerings and more.

For example, Disney rolled out wristbands that track all of a guest's purchases (giving the company data on their likes), and make it easier for guests to spend money. Removing friction in the purchase process has led to an increase in spending in multiple areas. The company made a significant investment in this technology and is leveraging it to collect massive amounts of data to be used in targeted marketing and revenue optimization efforts.

Another example of an industry applying revenue optimization comes from the government sector. High Occupancy Toll (HOT) lanes are limited-access lanes reserved for buses and other high occupancy vehicles, but open to single occupant vehicles upon payment of a toll.

### *Revenue Strategy: The Future of Revenue Optimization*

Revenue optimization will continue to evolve and grow in sophistication as the practice matures, as the distribution landscape changes around it, and as new technologies emerge to support and disrupt hotels' strategies. It is highly likely that the discipline will become even more of a science than it is today with a heavy emphasis on data/science-driven pricing.

Today the hotel industry is increasingly focused on Revenue Strategy – an emerging discipline that takes revenue optimization to the next level. Revenue Strategy is a longer-term, comprehensive, holistic approach to driving profitability of the enterprise that is dependent on the collective and interdependent efforts of the equally important disciplines of revenue optimization, sales, marketing, distribution, and analytics. Revenue Strategy further breaks down these often-siloed disciplines so that they have access to the same data, are aligned on their goals, and are ultimately collaboratively focused on profitability.

Revenue optimization and its strategies are just one of the indispensable ingredients in Revenue Strategy. Overarching Revenue Strategy is the future of the hotel industry. HSMAI will continue to produce insights, research, and education around this topic. Find the latest information at www.hsmai.org.

## Questions for Review
- How has revenue optimization in hotels evolved?
- What were the most important influences on the discipline throughout its evolution?

# CHAPTER 2
## THE REVENUE PROFESSIONAL

### Learning Objectives
- To understand the role and responsibilities of the revenue professional
- To understand ways to qualify appropriate talent for your organization
- To understand the talent gap facing the industry, and identify opportunities to address it in your organization

The importance of revenue optimization has expanded, and the way hoteliers think about and manage their businesses has changed. It is no longer enough to manage demand to ensure an optimal mix, or just focus on optimizing top-line room revenues. Today, revenue optimization is broader in scope and much more strategic, with a focus on the bigger picture including top-line revenues and profitability, and revenue centers outside of rooms.

"The degree to which hotel operators rely on revenue management [and revenue optimization] to drive successful business operations has grown incrementally over the past 30 years. It has become high profile over the last decade to 15 years."[4] That means that now "[r]evenue growth is a fundamental driver of long-term hotel performance. A focus on revenue places the revenue management function, as the natural 'owner' of top line revenues, squarely at the forefront of driving a hotel company's success."[5]

As yield management has evolved into revenue optimization, the role and responsibilities of the professionals in the discipline have gone through significant change. And they continue to evolve and grow with the changing demands and needs of the industry. The discipline requires a more sophisticated leader, influencer, communicator, and collaborator — a strategist — versus the traditional "number cruncher" or manager needed in the past.

Modern revenue professionals are experts in driving sophisticated strategies for the hotel. They are strategic leaders with deep knowledge of forecasting, data analytics, and market intelligence. They must manage demand, customer segments, inventory, rates, booking windows, stay pattern controls, and the technologies that can support all of these functions. They typically report directly to the general manager or CEO, giving revenue optimization an equal voice with sales and marketing in decision making.

### The Role of the Revenue Professional
Anyone who has been around the hospitality industry for a while knows how much the role has evolved over the years — from reservations manager to yield manager to revenue manager to revenue strategist. Like the discipline itself, the professionals in these roles have dealt with significant and constant disruption since its inception.

The job description has shifted beyond "pushing buttons," generating reports, forecasting, and pricing. The revenue professional is no longer sitting in an office crunching numbers and reporting back. Today the revenue professional is focusing on driving total hotel profitability using, understanding, and communicating sophisticated data analytics, requiring them to lead, manage, and influence a whole new strategic level.

This work rests on a solid foundation of understanding of the profitability of channels, segments, and the costs of running the business. Only when the profit drivers and breakeven thresholds of the points of sales are understood will a revenue professional make the most profitable gains and articulate the right strategy with all internal stakeholders. They are driving the processes and determining the strategies for hospitality revenue optimization.

Revenue professionals are expected to interact with and influence colleagues at various levels and in key areas such as strategy, tactics, profitability, revenue-related processes, technology, and much more. At the same time, understanding of and involvement in revenue optimization by owners has significantly changed — and has become much more granular than ever before. Today, most owners and asset managers have a direct line to the revenue leaders in their hotel portfolio. That places revenue professionals in even more of a spotlight and places new requirements on them to be better leaders, communicators, and influencers as well as experts on the core revenue optimization fundamentals.

As the industry changes and disruption continues, the role of the revenue professional will surely evolve again. This book explores many of the changes happening today and those that are on the horizon — and the challenges that come along as a result.

## Setting Revenue Professionals Up for Success

From the corporate level, owners and operators would be well served to ensure the revenue optimization discipline is properly staffed and supported. This is a discipline that will easily pay for itself in the revenue and profit returns.

One of the bigger challenges accompanying continuous change is the industry's ability to adapt in order to preserve and grow profits. The disruptive distribution landscape impacts the revenue optimization world in a significant way. Managing revenue amid the constantly changing digital marketplace is one of a revenue professional's biggest challenges. Couple the impact of those big disciples with OTAs changing business practices, new entrants getting between hotels and the consumer, large companies — both hotel brands and third parties — consolidating their merchandising power, and more.

While all of this is happening around them, at the property level revenue professionals are inundated with the day-to-day needs and challenges of the hotel, and at the same time are expected to stay focused on future strategy. It would be difficult for anyone to remain focused on the important and urgent business of today while also understanding how to navigate and adjust to the day-to-day impact of fast-moving changes in the business around them. That is where it can be helpful to have corporate level revenue leaders who handle bigger-picture issues for the enterprise, identifying solutions and resolutions in support of property-level players.

## Tools to Assist in Revenue Optimization

If revenue professionals are working in a highly manual environment — extracting data, putting together spreadsheets, and updating inventory and rates in multiple systems and extranets — then it is nearly impossible for them to "get out of the weeds" and focus on strategy.

The more automation in place, the more productive a revenue professional has the potential to be. There is a plethora of tools today to help in the tasks that will allow the revenue professional to remain focused on strategy, and stay on top of and manage all the demands required of the revenue optimization discipline. This section provides some insight into the types of tools and the purpose of these tools. For information on specific tools and providers, see Appendix C.

Systems such as automated revenue management systems (RMS) can collect data, analyze the data, and make recommendations using sophisticated algorithms (e.g., rate recommendations, forecasting, displacement analysis, etc.).

Channel management tools are another important category of technology to consider. They allow for management of rates and inventory through one system versus having to manually update multiple systems. Another category of critical tools that more revenue professionals are using provides business intelligence.

When considering a tool, ensure that the integration between it and other revenue tools and systems in place is part of your evaluation. While not vital for every single tool, it is absolutely critical when considering an investment in an RMS. Ensure that all of your technology partners are willing to work together to ensure you get the automation efficiencies and/or data needed.

There are a variety of tools available to revenue professionals — and it can be difficult to understand which ones are most important, as well what is available. Consider the following.

| CATEGORY | TOOL TYPE |
|---|---|
| Technology | Revenue Management System (RMS) |
| | Central Reservations System (CRS) |
| | Property Management System (PMS) |
| | Channel Manager |
| | Group/Contract Pricing Analysis |
| | Spa Booking System |
| | Upsell Software |
| Data & Analytics | Competitor Rate Shopping Service |
| | Reputation Management System |
| | Booking Pace |
| | Demand Forecasts |
| | Operational Forecasts |
| | Aggregated Data Visualizations |
| | Market Intelligence |
| | F&B Analytics Tools |
| Reporting | Budgeting Templates/Tool |
| | 30-60-90-365 Day Forecasts |
| | Operational Forecast |
| | Pace Performance |
| | Pickup Performance |
| | Pricing Strategy |
| | Monthly/Regional Summaries |
| | Channel Costs/Profitability |

## Hard and Soft Skills Required

The overall role of the revenue professional is to be the champion of revenue optimization for the hotel. This includes big-picture thinking, continual analysis, decision making skills, expert presentation skills, the ability to translate data and analysis visually, the ability to manage relationships, and effective channel management.

The revenue professional must be able to consistently educate the hotel's management team on revenue optimization as a whole, and have the ability to convey the facts and convince the team to take the risk of changing strategies when it is appropriate. He or she must be comfortable standing strong to support a data-based decision even when others do not agree. This means working productively through disagreements with members of the sales team, front desk members, and even other executive committee members such as a director of sales, while maintaining a solid professional and positive working relationship.

The shift in the responsibilities of and expectations for the revenue professional position also requires a shift in the talent that hotels need. It is critical to look beyond the hard, or technical, skills such as specific system experience, forecasting accuracy, and pricing, to ensure a hotel has the right person leading revenue

optimization. Hard skills can be learned, but it is the "soft" skills, the personal attributes, that are much harder (some would say impossible) to teach.

Someone can learn a CRS, PMS, or RMS. But effective communication and the ability to influence while relating to others and being agile while doing it all is an absolute must today. A revenue professional who has the highest intelligence along with superior analytical skills, or the best knowledge of a system, will risk not being successful without these important soft skills.

If someone is hired for their soft skills, they can often learn the necessary technical skills. Conversely, if someone is hired for their technical knowledge and expertise, the hotel may miss out on having someone who has the ability to see the big picture or someone who is analytical. For example, if a hotel hires a candidate who is great with Excel or the hotel's PMS, then they have hired a person that can use that technology well but who may not have the attributes necessary to analyze the reports or explain the results from them.

Beyond looking for technical skills, it is important to identify the following soft skills in individuals who are being considered for a revenue optimization position.

| Competitive | Determined and committed with a strong drive to achieve goals |
|---|---|
| Verbal & Visual Communication | Ability to articulate revenue strategies and deployment to achieve strategies |
| Leadership | Ability to earn trust and directly or indirectly lead teams, at all levels throughout organization |
| Influence | Ability to influence decisions at all levels throughout organization; able to convince others to act based on data and information |
| Team Player | Collaborative and works effectively as a member of teams |
| Technically Savvy | Ability to understand, to a detailed degree, how technology can augment the revenue optimization function |
| Critical Observer | Good listener with strong observation skills; able to read situations, identify changes needed, understand environments, and respond accordingly |
| Interpersonal Skills | Ability to develop and maintain relationships with colleagues and third-party partners |
| Agile | Able to adapt quickly and efficiently according to business changes and needs; adept at navigating change |
| Priority Focused | Able to identify and prioritize a focus on highest revenue or profit generating needs compared to time-consuming tasks with low-yield impact |

The following skills are nice to have, but should not be requirements. For example, if a candidate has experience with the PMS specific to your hotel company, that is a huge benefit. However, it should not be a requirement. Most qualified candidates will have experience with one or several different PMSs. The basic concept of these systems is the same and a talented candidate will be able to apply their knowledge and experience to a variety of systems. Furthermore, they can be trained by an expert should there be a need. The following skills should not be the reasons for which a candidate is hired:

- Previous experience with a particular PMS, CRS, RMS, rate shopping tool, channel management tool, web booking engine, etc.
- Previous training or experience with digital marketing and/or finance/business
- Advanced Excel experience
- Strong forecasting experience
- Prospecting skills
- Sales skills

- Experience with reporting tools
- Online research skills
- Problem-solving skills
- Written & verbal communication

While not a skill, one additional point to be addressed is hiring someone for their ability to start immediately. Hiring someone just because they are able to start immediately may have a negative impact on the hotel if the employee winds up not having the right experience. A good revenue professional will most likely have commitments to honor with a current employer and may need time to complete those before moving to a different property or company. A bad hire is worse than no hire.

## Qualifying Candidates

Once the hotel has identified the required talent needed in its next revenue professional, the next step is to know how to qualify candidates. The following interview questions can be used for this purpose.

| INTERVIEW QUESTION | WHAT IT MAY TELL YOU |
|---|---|
| What is your biggest accomplishment and why? | May offer insight into how they measure success and work with others. Keep in mind at what point in their life or career the selected accomplishment occurred before making a judgment. |
| What has been one of your biggest challenges and why? How did you overcome this challenge? | May offer insight into what they see as a challenge, and how they handle and overcome challenges. May help to determine if this person is a problem-solution type person or if they offer problems only. It may also indicate whether the candidate is creative, based upon how they overcame the challenge. |
| How did you make an impact in your last revenue position? What was the goal? What was the approach? What were the results? | This can tell you if the person is goal oriented and focused on results. It will also tell a lot about their approach and if they are methodical by nature. |
| Should you be hired and accept this position, what would your approach be upon starting at our hotel? What would you do first? | This will tell you how the person prioritizes and how they approach new things. What would their priorities be? Again, a methodical nature is needed for this position. It will also tell you how much thought they have given to the position. |
| Provide some basic data about your hotel to a qualified candidate and ask them to prepare an analysis with some recommendations. | The results of their methodology, format, and actual analysis can tell you a lot about their skills. |

| | |
|---|---|
| What do you think your biggest challenge in this position would be? How would you overcome this challenge? | This will tell you what they see as a challenge and whether it lines up with your thoughts. Based on their answer, you can determine whether you believe they can overcome challenges. |
| Why do you like revenue optimization? | This may help you understand what they like best, and therefore, on what they focus their efforts. |
| What factors do you believe are most important about this role? | This should be in line with the hotel's philosophy. |
| If applicable: As a revenue professional during the last economic downturn, what was your response and approach? How did you handle revenue optimization at your hotel? | As you carefully listen to their response you will be able to tell whether they handled themselves in a reactive or proactive way. Were they a leader in the market or a follower? Was their approach a methodical, well-thought-out approach? |

Also consider:

- Overall, how are they able to articulate their responses and strategies? Based on your interaction and listening to their explanations, are they good communicators?
- Do they know their own hotels well? If they do not know their own hotels inside and out, they are not your next hire.
- Within the answers they provide, are they thinking big-picture or are they more focused on tactical items? Ideally, they should have an appropriate balance of the two — meaning more focused on the big-picture but able to do some tactical research before they turn to strategic or big-picture areas.
- If they quote a lot of meaningful statistics during the meeting, chances of their having a focus on goals and measurements are high.

If hotels are able to identify candidates with the right mix of hard and soft skills, they will find themselves in a much better position to elevate their approach to be more strategic and proactive. These are the hotels that will find they are able to lead in the revenue optimization arena. Hotels which have these competencies, when automation comes into play, will find they can embrace the technology much more easily and continue to elevate their level of sophistication.

### Job Description Example

As with every position, it is very important that each revenue professional has a job description. This ensures that everyone has the same understanding of what the responsibilities are as well as the evaluation metrics. See Appendix E for a sample revenue director job description.

## The Certified Revenue Management Executive (CRME)

Since 2006, HSMAI has offered the prestigious Certified Revenue Management Executive (CRME) certification, for which this book is the study guide.

A CRME certification denotes that the individual is:
- A professional in the field of revenue optimization and clearly conversant with its intricacies and importance;
- Competent to develop an infrastructure to support revenue optimization within the framework of an organization;
- Able to maximize revenue opportunities and optimize profits by managing revenue;
- Capable of making informed decisions to accept or reject pieces of business to meet overall organizational goals; and
- Proficient at the art and science of revenue optimization.

The hotel or company that supports their revenue professionals through the certification process will reap the benefits of having an employee with an enhanced level of understanding, knowledge, and capabilities in revenue optimization. Those who hire someone with the certification can be sure the individual is an expert in the area and will clearly bring significant benefit to the company.

For more information, see www.hsmai.org/crme.

## The Talent Gap

The increasing demands on revenue professionals have signaled a growing need for a deeper talent pool — more people and a higher caliber of talent — to support the revenue optimization discipline. At the same time, competition for this pool of talent is becoming fiercer: other industries (e.g., health care, law firms, and others) have recognized the value of the revenue optimization discipline and the success that hotels have experienced. As a result, they are looking to hospitality for talent and expertise and vying for the same recruits as hotels.

What can hotels do? To start, there is a need to streamline the transition of college graduates who have had revenue management courses (or are graduating with a revenue management degree) into professional revenue optimization roles in hotels. Working directly with hotel schools is an investment opportunity for hotels and hotel companies to capitalize on now. There is a lot of talent coming fresh out of hotel school ready to jump into the work force and make a difference. Additionally, there is an opportunity to start recruiting the next generation of revenue professionals from educational institutions focused on strategy, analytics, or data science.

Even before promising students get to college, there is an opportunity to influence the talent pipeline. Breffni Noone, Associate Professor, School of Hospitality at The Pennsylvania State University, said[6], "The starting point in developing a talent pipeline is to develop an understanding of those individuals who are most likely to fill the pipeline: hotel school students. [There are]…four key things that students are not clear on:

1. "What career progression looks like: Students know that they can 'go into' revenue management but do not have a clear idea of the potential career path in revenue management.
2. "What revenue management professional[s] do on the job: Closely related to career progression, students are not clear on what a job in revenue management actually comprises. They understand the fundamental elements of revenue management but do not have a full appreciation of the specific roles and responsibilities of revenue management professionals at different points along the revenue management career path.
3. "What opportunities exist while at school: Students are often unaware, or realize too late, that they can pursue an internship or externship in revenue management while at school. Two factors contribute to this. First, hotel companies tend to promote, and recruit most strongly for, operations positions rather than functions like revenue management during campus visits. Second, revenue management courses are frequently positioned on hotel schools' curriculums such that students don't take them until their third or fourth year in the program. Therefore, until the point at which they are taking these courses, students don't know to look for, or ask recruiters for, revenue management internship or externship opportunities.

"The importance of exposing students to revenue management through internships and externships cannot be underestimated. In my experience, without some exposure to revenue management in the field prior to graduation, students are less likely to 'risk' going into revenue management when they graduate. Equally, without some field experience before graduation, a company may be less inclined to hire a graduate to work in revenue management.

4. "How to 'sell' their skill set to potential employers: Students often struggle with determining how to communicate their revenue management training to potential employers. Compared to other disciplines like human resource management, accounting, and finance, revenue management is a relative newcomer to the hospitality school curriculum and consequently, the revenue management course content and rigor can vary significantly across hotel schools. In the absence of a standard revenue management certification that can provide a benchmark of a student's knowledge and skill set, students are challenged in terms of communicating the depth and breadth of their revenue management training."

Perhaps most startling among these student insights is that there appears to be a distinct lack of awareness among the next generation of hoteliers of the career opportunities that exist in revenue optimization. This sends a clear signal to industry and academia that we need to do a much better job of selling revenue optimization as a viable and sustainable career path.

HSMAI's revenue advisory boards globally are focused on developing broad stroke strategies to promote the revenue optimization profession across hotel schools, and provide revenue management educators with a toolkit of resources to leverage in the classroom. Think about what you can do at a company level to engage students and grow your own pipeline.

## The Certified Revenue Management Analyst (CRMA)

Created by hoteliers for those studying to join the industry, HSMAI's Certified Revenue Management Analyst (CRMA) Certification recognizes students for their understanding of the application of revenue optimization concepts.

Recruiters looking for candidates with a verified baseline of knowledge in the latest thinking and practices can use this certification to narrow their list to prequalified candidates. For students, the CRMA separates you from the pack, and demonstrates to current and potential employers that you have mastered the foundations of revenue optimization.

The CRMA designation is recognition that the certification holder understands the core facets of RM and can translate that understanding into making strategic and tactical RM related decisions.

Learn more at www.hsmai.org/crma.

## Career Development and Progression

Once talent is identified, it is critical to invest in them in order to retain them. Laying out a clear career path, or options for career paths, is critical. Hotel companies that offer a variety of career development options to revenue professionals will have more success in hiring top talent. While not a silver bullet for solving talent recruitment and retention challenges, offering options for career progression will most definitely help.

Once in the discipline, revenue professionals have more potential career paths available than ever before. Career progression within revenue optimization has opened to a wider variety of clearer paths over the last several years. Many brands and management companies today offer multi-property hotel revenue positions which allow for professional growth. Area revenue directors, responsible for two or three hotels, are recognized as a higher-level position typically offered to more seasoned individuals with proven results and solid experience. Remote-based revenue positions are also considered for more seasoned individuals with proven results.

There are other career path opportunities as well.

- Ownership and asset management now look at revenue optimization experience as one prerequisite for filling general manager positions. This is a pretty clear path moving forward for those who want to stay at the hotel level.
- Hotel companies that have a good infrastructure to support hotel-level revenue optimization often have regional revenue leadership positions. This would be a natural next step. And then of course, being the revenue leader for an entire company is a possibility.
- Paths into the development discipline have become of interest and proven successful for revenue professionals. Development for an ownership company or development within a hotel company are both possibilities.
- Real estate investment firms, and a variety of other asset management firms, are starting to employ revenue professionals with the sole purpose of working with that firm's portfolio of hotels to ensure optimization.
- Some hotel companies are moving toward a commercial approach where the revenue professional is more involved in, or has responsibility for, everything commercially focused, while driving revenue optimization through digital marketing, sales, and yielding.

At the same time that career paths are outlined and promoted, hotels must invest in training to build skills and expertise including exposure to other commercial disciplines like sales, marketing, branding, communications, public relations, and, most certainly, digital marketing.

## How will you know if you're doing it right?

There is a seemingly endless number of KPIs and formulas to help to measure the success of the revenue team's performance. In hotels, the most commonly used measure of the revenue team's success is revenue per available room (RevPAR).

Other metrics that are becoming more common include: Profit Per Available Room (ProPAR), because of increasingly profit-driven approaches where revenue optimization is the tool to get there; TRevPAR, which measures the total revenue per available room from all revenue centers; and, RevPAG, which helps hoteliers understand the total revenue per available guest.

See chapter 11 for more information and insight into performance analysis.

## Questions for Review

- What are some of the most important responsibilities of a revenue professional?
- Having access to which tools and resources can increase the productivity and effectiveness of revenue professionals?
- What are some of the most important skills for a revenue professional to have?
- What can hotels do to address and overcome the lack of experienced revenue optimization talent?

# CHAPTER 3

## DEPARTMENTAL INTEGRATION

### Learning Objectives
- To understand how to assemble and deploy an effective revenue team
- To understand commonly used organizational structures, and the benefits and challenges of each

Revenue optimization is not an independent business process or system. It is an approach to conducting business that delivers the most value if it is fully integrated throughout the organization, the business processes, and the mind-set of employees. Hotels and hotel companies must ensure they have a collaborative approach to revenue optimization and not practice it as a stand-alone discipline.

Key to integration and a collaborative approach is having a revenue optimization culture that is infused throughout every department and embraced by every team member. The importance of building this sort of corporate culture has become widely understood and recognized by CEOs, managing directors, and general managers today.

### Organizational Structure
There is no one organizational structure that will work in every hotel or company. The structure that works best depends on four key elements:
1. The company's overall organization
2. The company's culture
3. The talents in existing leadership
4. The company's goals

Common structures in hotels today include on-property revenue optimization, centralized revenue optimization, and outsourced (third-party) revenue optimization. These are not the only options, nor do they have to be exclusive within a hotel company. Learn more about the benefits and challenges of each in the final pages of this chapter.

### Leadership
Strong leadership at the top is often a place to start. Many owners and asset managers today seek general managers who have strong revenue optimization backgrounds to ensure their assets are led with a focus on revenue optimization. With a belief in and commitment to the contributions to results that revenue optimization can make, the buy-in from ownership and senior management ensures that the investments needed to implement and maintain a successful revenue strategy will always be a priority.

At the same time, hiring executives in all disciplines who understand the fundamentals of revenue optimization and keep it top of mind is essential.

### Goal Alignment
Contributing significantly to departmental integration is goal alignment. Too many companies create individual goals in a silo, which creates a culture of individuals focusing on what is best for them versus a revenue team that acts in the best interest of the enterprise. Instead, everyone should be incentivized to work toward the same objectives — by aligning individual and departmental goals with the overall revenue goals for the hotel or company.

The need for goal alignment extends beyond the individual property and into management companies and ownership groups that may have portfolios of competing brands. If owners are focused on their own revenue needs versus the overall portfolio or brand strategy, the company cannot achieve its maximum revenue potential.

### Communication and Teamwork
The responsibility of revenue optimization does not fall on one person alone. Every hotel needs a revenue team that contributes to and understands the decisions made and the strategies developed. Achieving optimal results requires not only strategies and their implementation, but also understanding and buy-in throughout all revenue impacting departments. For the revenue team to successfully leverage revenue optimization throughout the hotel, strong communication and teamwork among the appropriate departments is a must.

The composition of a hotel's revenue team, and titles, varies by property and company. However, common revenue team members, and their role on the team, are outlined here.

| POSITION/ DEPARTMENT | ROLE IN REVENUE TEAM MEETINGS |
|---|---|
| Revenue Professional | The revenue professional is the "chair" of the team and meetings. Depending on the hotel or company, their title might be revenue analyst, revenue manager, revenue director, or revenue strategist.<br><br>They will provide data such as pace, pick up, variances to budget for same time last year, forecasting, rates, promotions, and so on. They lead the meeting to ensure communication of all strategies, including what is working and what is not working, bring recommendations on rate changes and promotions, and solicit information needed from other departments. |
| General Manager | The general manager must have a solid understanding of the hotel's strategy including what is working, what is not working, and what may be needed from other departments to help boost revenues and ensure that everyone is on the same page and doing their part. The GM should also ensure that the revenue professional is receiving the proper support from all positions and departments. The GM is the "tie breaker" when the team is unable to agree and has the ultimate authority on the direction. |
| Director of Sales (or Director of Sales & Marketing) | The director of sales is responsible for group forecasting and providing detailed input to the revenue professional. This position has solid insight into what is happening in the group world that may impact pace and strategies. They also need to fully understand and be part of the strategic direction of the hotel. Inventory controls, rates, and revenue optimization strategies significantly impact the sales world. Support and communication of the strategy and direction to the entire sales team is needed. |
| Front Office Manager | This department needs a solid understanding of the revenue optimization strategies so that they buy into and support them. Front office team members have significant impact, on a daily basis, on a hotel's revenue success. They need to understand how they impact it from all customer contacts — upselling, closing the sale, and holistic customer experience and communication. The front office team also has tremendous input on the revenue optimization strategies from a tactical point of view. They have a lot to offer on what is working and what is not working when it comes to:<br><br>• Suite pricing and suite sales<br>• Price differentials between room types — they know if there is room to increase or need to decrease based on the customer feedback<br>• Challenges customers may have with the overall booking experience<br>• Customer feedback direct from customers daily in such areas as hotel amenities, hotel product, and competitive set experiences including service, amenities, and product<br>• Local offerings that may be an opportunity for partnerships to drive more business |
| Director of Operations | The director of operations needs to understand the strategies as they need to support the surrounding decisions that impact them or may be impacted by them. This team member will have solid input on the strategies as they interact directly with the guests, as well as all the surrounding departments. |
| Business Transient Sales Manager<br><br>Wholesale Sales Manager<br><br>Group Sales Manager<br><br>(depends on the hotel and positions) | This position must understand the need to yield out corporate negotiated accounts during specific demand periods and/or specific days of the week. They will have good input into feedback from the clients, as well as a solid understanding of what may or may not be needed for the following year's negotiations. |
| Reservations Manager | It is important for the reservations department to understand the revenue optimization strategies for all the same reasons as the front desk. Reservations will also have important information to share during team meetings. |
| Director of Finance | The director of finance often sees the end result, so including them in regular discussions can ensure they understand the "whys" behind all the decisions. They will have important input on how the strategies may impact cash flow. |
| Director of Catering/ Convention Services/ Banquets/Events | This department needs to know how the hotel's strategies, and high- and low-demand periods, may impact their events and the needs of the events. |
| Ecommerce Manager | The ecommerce discipline has critical information to share about online trends and customer data. Understanding the strategies, need periods, special offers, and so on, will help them optimize online strategies to support the overall revenue needs. |

### Revenue Team Meetings

Revenue meetings are the forum in which the revenue professional provides updates to the team on booking pace, unexpected changes in the market, current strategies, and recommended strategy changes. The team reviews the hotel's strategies, reviews everything impacting those strategies, and discusses the plan for moving forward.

To ensure good communication, buy-in, and consistency, revenue team meetings must be held on a regular basis on a schedule that works for the hotel — typically from multiple times a week to once every other week. The key to success is consistent scheduling and participation.

A standard agenda should include standing items that are covered in every meeting, and additional items that need to be added when applicable and appropriate. These one-off discussion items allow for delving deeply into specific areas, for additional brainstorming sessions, and/or for proactive and creative idea generation.

See Appendix A for a sample revenue meeting agenda. It is important to note that this is a sample agenda. Each hotel or company should customize the agenda items to meet its specific needs.

## On-Property Revenue Optimization

Traditionally, especially for full-service hotels, revenue optimization has resided at each property. Since revenue optimization is an integral part of the executive committee at a hotel, this approach has been very logical for many hotels. Since the intent today is to drive total hotel revenue rather than focus only on rooms revenue, the exposure to conversations in all areas of the hotel is critical for the revenue professional. Successful revenue optimization requires a collaborative approach.

On-property revenue optimization structures vary from property to property. In the past, some hotels have organized revenue optimization under sales and marketing. Today, however, many hotel companies see the benefits of having revenue optimization at the same level as sales and marketing, reporting directly to the general manager and part of the executive committee. Additionally, some have a corporate structure that includes a dotted reporting line to a regional director of revenue for accountability and mentoring.

On-property revenue optimization produces the best results when the revenue professional is part of the executive committee of the hotel and can balance both operations and sales with a revenue-driven approach.

### Benefits

Having a revenue professional onsite offers many benefits, chief among them is the daily interaction with different departments within the hotel and with daily operations. For example, an on-property revenue manager can have regular conversations with the sales team when they face difficult decisions about group pricing, inclusions, and total group value. This results in trust built through regular face-to-face communication.

Another benefit is the ability to consistently communicate with on-site departments that may otherwise be overlooked. A good example is front desk personnel. It is important to both educate them on revenue optimization strategies and provide support for execution at the front desk, and solicit their feedback and insights that can help in revenue strategy decision making. Having a champion on property also positions revenue optimization at the forefront of the strategy development as opposed to potentially being "out of sight, out of mind."

Finally, this structure allows for a dedicated focus on the hotel's specific and potentially unique needs and circumstances. Many general managers see this as the most beneficial result because they still feel that they have control in this type of environment.

All that being said, talent trumps location. More and more hotels are willing to support offsite or remote offices for revenue professionals in order to secure the right talent.

### Challenges

Having a dedicated on-site revenue optimization leader is not without challenges. One of the biggest is the need to hire an extraordinarily talented individual who can negotiate with the team, stand their ground when necessary, and make the right decisions at the right time to maximize revenue. Many hotels struggle to find the best revenue talent and are in constant competition for them. As the distribution landscape continues to evolve along with consumer buying behaviors, more and more key stakeholders (e.g., owners and asset managers) recognize the importance of this role and have their own opinions on who the "right" person is.

Added to that is the challenge that many seasoned revenue professionals are looking to broaden their portfolio of expertise by managing multiple hotels versus a single property.

From a hotel company perspective, when there are many revenue professionals located at different properties, all having varying skill levels and expertise, it can be difficult to provide consistency in deploying a systemwide revenue optimization strategy. For some, ensuring that all revenue professionals in the field have proper and consistent training, education, support, and tools is a big challenge.

On the other hand, some companies provide very structured brand training, education, support, tools, how tos, and step-by-step instructions. While this ensures that all hotels are operating under the same guidelines, the challenge is that the revenue professionals act very tactically and do not necessarily learn how to be strategic leaders.

Finally, the most obvious challenge to the on-site structure is the cost associated with a full-time dedicated revenue professional. Despite the clear return on investment (ROI), it is not possible for every hotel to support this from a cost standpoint.

## Centralized Revenue Optimization

Centralizing revenue optimization for a company basically restructures its resources. This approach typically has revenue coordinators or managers who work in a team and report to a regional or corporate revenue professional or vice president. This experienced executive needs to have superior revenue optimization skills and is often called upon to deploy a strategy quickly, successfully, and consistently across large groups of hotels.

There are varying approaches for implementing a centralized structure. Some companies prefer to segment their resources by brand, by type of market, by type of hotel, or even by geographic location. How a hotel company structures its centralized revenue optimization will depend upon many factors.

■ Number of Hotels: Knowing that the ideal solution is to have one revenue optimization professional dedicated to each hotel, it is important to understand that with every additional hotel for which one person is responsible, their ability to have a micro-focus decreases significantly. Therefore, the level of responsibility must be adjusted accordingly, and on-property support (for data gathering, implementation, etc.) allocated.

■ Geographic Location of the Hotels: It is not realistic to expect one person to be an expert on multiple and varied markets. Therefore, depending on the number of hotels in a portfolio, and their locations, the person responsible for understanding and communicating local market trends and challenges may need to be located on-site.

■ Type of Hotel: Hotels differ in many ways: full versus limited service and everything in between, business traveler versus convention focus and everything in between, different customer segmentation, different products and services such as golf, spas, and casinos, and more. Knowing the mix of hotels for which a revenue professional is responsible is important when determining their level of responsibility.

It is critically important to ensure that the revenue professional's responsibilities are reasonable and allow for proper focus. It may necessary to add or reassign resources on-property and/or at the corporate level to support this structure.

| PORTFOLIO TYPE | POSSIBLE SCENARIOS | CLUSTER OR AREA | CORPORATE OR REGIONAL | BY BRAND OR BY LOCATION | BY LOCATION OR TYPE OF HOTEL |
|---|---|---|---|---|---|
| | Hotels in one geographic location, such as in the same city or on the same coast | X | | | |
| | Multiple brands in various locations | | X | X | |
| | Different types of hotels, such as transient- or group-focused | | X | | X |
| | Hotels in different locations but all with a similar target market | | X | | X |

## Benefits

One benefit of a centralized approach is the ability to recruit talent with a higher level of expertise. These people are often at a higher pay scale which makes it easier to attract talented individuals. A hotel company can have a "brain trust" of regional people who can take the entire company to the next level of profitability.

A centralized approach also allows for a greater level of consistency and ease of standards adoption across multiple properties. It is much easier and more effective to standardize 10 regional revenue offices than 100 individual hotels.

In most scenarios, there is typically a cost savings in a centralized approach as well, without sacrificing the quality of the end product.

## Challenges

Though there are many benefits to centralization, there are also inherent challenges that must be addressed. Often in a centralized environment, there can be a greater lack of camaraderie, trust, and teamwork. The revenue executive does not see the staff at the property level as often and therefore does not typically build as strong a working relationship with them as an on-site revenue professional does. However, this can be overcome if all team members are committed to making it work. Regularly scheduled visits and regular calls (especially video calls) will go a long way toward advancing the relationship.

If the goals are not aligned so that the revenue professional and hotel executives are all working toward the same objectives, friction is created and ultimately the centralized approach will not work. Everyone must be working toward the same goals and end result. Determining and understanding accountability is also important. It must be clearly understood with whom the final responsibility resides, and that person must be held accountable for the final results and decisions.

There can also be conflict among the various hotels in a revenue executive's portfolio as they compete for time and attention and disagree over revenue and pricing decisions. If one hotel is especially demanding, the hotel that is not as vocal may feel ignored.

Each hotel falling within the centralized environment of one revenue professional's responsibility will most certainly not reap the benefits they would if they had a dedicated resource. This may not apply to hotels that are smaller and have limited services as they may not require a full-time resource. However, it most definitely applies to those large properties that offer more services and require more overall attention.

If the regional center is not located in the city in which a hotel is, there can also be nuances of the market that a regional director could miss simply by being isolated from the daily activity.

## Outsourced (Third-Party) Revenue Optimization

From a structural perspective, outsourcing revenue optimization is similar to centralizing or regionalizing revenue optimization. The difference is that outsourced revenue optimization means a hotel engages a third-party who provides a fee-based, consultancy type approach to revenue optimization.

Why would a hotel outsource revenue optimization? Outsourced revenue optimization allows hotels to tap into expert resources without having to make significant investments in human resources. If you are asking yourself, "Why is it difficult for my hotel to attract or keep revenue talent," then outsourced revenue optimization may be a solution. The outsourced revenue professional operates virtually and visits the hotel on a predetermined schedule. This allows each hotel to pay for the type and amount of revenue services they require.

## Benefits

One of the most obvious benefits is the potential to reduce costs. It may be less expensive to outsource the revenue optimization function than employ a dedicated, onsite revenue professional. This allows a hotel that might not otherwise have any type of revenue optimization expertise to leverage a revenue professional to provide recommendations and strategies without incurring the expense of hiring someone full time.

Outsourcing also makes it possible to:

- Engage a dedicated expert who can be focused solely on revenue strategy without any other distractions.
- Get beyond geographic restrictions. Hotels that are intent upon hiring someone who lives in a specific geographic location shrink their pool of potential talent. Sometimes looking for the best talent versus the best talent within a specific location is the hotel's best option.
- Reduce disruptions in the event of turnover. Turnover of personnel is the responsibility of the third-party company which will find a suitable replacement should the need arise. They likely have experts on their existing team from whom to choose.

## Challenges

As with every other approach, the outsourced structure comes with some challenges. Not all hotels will want to share resources with others. Some may not trust that they are actually getting the time investment for which they are paying. Some may fear their strategies will be shared with competitors. Some owners and operators worry about the potential for losing control of the revenue optimization strategies when a third-party is involved.

Other challenges include not being able to effectively build camaraderie with the on-site team members. When a resource works off-site and less than full time it can be challenging to build trust and alignment with the rest of the hotel team. A focus on communication is essential to mitigate this issue.

These are very real challenges but nothing that cannot be overcome with the right guidelines, rules, and checks and balances. For instance, it is important to ensure that the shared resource is not being shared with a direct competitor.

## Questions for Review

- Which organizational structure is said to bring the most value to an organization?
- Who are the common members of a revenue team?
- What is the difference between centralized and outsourced revenue optimization?

# CHAPTER 4
## ECONOMICS AND ITS ROLE IN REVENUE OPTIMIZATION

### Learning Objectives
- To understand the relationship economics has with the practice of revenue optimization
- To comprehend how supply and demand impact a hotel's revenue optimization strategy
- To understand the difference between macro and micro economics and how each can impact a hotel's performance

Understanding the basics of economics and how it applies to revenue optimization in the hotel industry is a prerequisite to learning about the market and how it impacts a hotel's revenue optimization strategy.

The economic environment has a direct relationship with, and impact on, hotel pricing and revenue optimization strategies. Therefore, understanding the fundamental components of economics, including supply and demand and price elasticity of demand, is essential for all involved in developing a hotel's revenue optimization strategies.

### Economics 101
The main premise of economics is simple enough: you cannot have everything you want. But who gets what? Why? And is it the best we can do? And on a larger scale, how does our global economy work?

Virtually everyone agrees on the importance of economics, but there is far less agreement on just what economics is. Among the many misconceptions is that economics is something that tells you how to make money or run a business or predict the ups and downs of the stock market. Economics is not personal finance or business administration. Predicting the ups and downs of the stock market has yet to be reduced to a set of dependable principles.

There is no one universally accepted answer to the question "What is economics?"

Definitions range from a more technical explanation:

### Economics is the study of the production, distribution and consumption of wealth in human society.

To a simpler definition:

### Economics is the study of making choices.

Economics may appear to be the study of complicated tables and charts, statistics and numbers, but it really is the study of rational human behavior in the endeavor to fulfill wants and needs.

As an individual, you face the problem of having limited resources with which to fulfill your wants and needs. As a result, you must make certain choices with your money. You will most likely spend part of your money on rent or mortgage, electricity, and food. Then you might use the rest to go to the movies and/or buy a new pair of jeans.

Economics as a discipline includes some basic principles[7]:
- **Scarcity** can be defined as the situation when needs or wants exceed means. Economists study the choices people make in these situations.
- **Rationality** is when people systematically gauge the pros (benefit or "utility") and cons ("cost") of all alternatives or options they are facing when deciding. It is assumed that rationality guides people's choices or decisions.
- **Preferences:** People are equipped with fixed and given preferences that allow them to assign a utility value to each option they have, and to choose the option that maximizes net utility.
- **Restrictions:** People face constraints that they cannot change themselves, and thus have to take as given (such as budgets, input cost, etc.). Maximization is always constrained by restrictions.

So, what does all of this mean as it relates to revenue optimization and the hotel industry?

Revenue optimization is what we do to optimize the revenue earned from a fixed, perishable resource. Scarcity, rationality, preferences, and restrictions are all evident in the options and issues faced by a revenue professional. Remember, the revenue professional's challenge is to sell the right resources to the right customer at the right time and for the right amount to maximize revenue for the hotel.

### Macroeconomics
Macroeconomics examines the economy as a whole and answers questions such as:
- What causes the economy to grow over time?
- What causes short-run fluctuations in the economy?
- What influences the values of various economic indicators and how do those influences affect economic performance?

The following sections review on a macro level the factors that influence the economics of the hotel industry.

## GDP and its Relationship to Hotel Performance

What is Gross Domestic Product (GDP) and how does it impact hotel performance? GDP is simply the sum of all goods and services produced in an economy. It measures the market value of all final goods and services produced by a nation, and it is a fundamental indicator of an economy's performance. It is highly correlated with personal income and standard of living. GDP can be viewed as a true measure of the value of an economy.

The calculation of GDP boils down to the sum of the following four items:

Personal consumption
+
Public or government spending
+
Total personal and business investments
+
Net exports (exports — imports)
=
GDP

Thus, GDP is a measure of what is consumed today (consumption) plus what is put aside for tomorrow (investment) plus our net sales to others around the world. That combined figure roughly represents the income a nation produces from all of those activities.

GDP is the broadest measure of a country's overall economic health, and it defines the economic "pie" from which everyone ultimately enjoys a slice. If it is healthy and growing, times are good. If it is stagnant or declining, it will most likely sooner or later affect your standard of living.

When it comes to GDP and the hotel industry, you can see from the following chart that, since 1989, the correlation between U.S. hotel demand growth and real GDP (seasonally adjusted) growth has been .73.

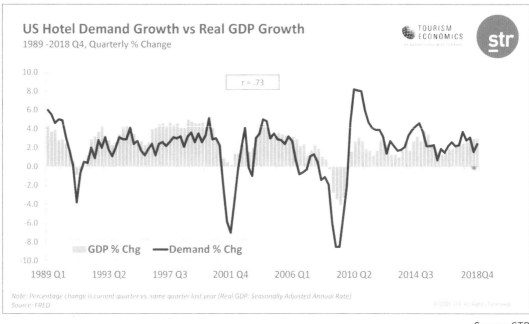

Source: STR

A related measure of consumption and investment is the GPDI, Gross Private Domestic Investment, which is the amount of GDP generated by business investment, excluding government investments. As illustrated by the following chart, since 1989, the correlation between U.S. hotel demand growth and GPDI growth has been .81, indicating that GPDI is a stronger economic indicator for the hotel industry to watch.

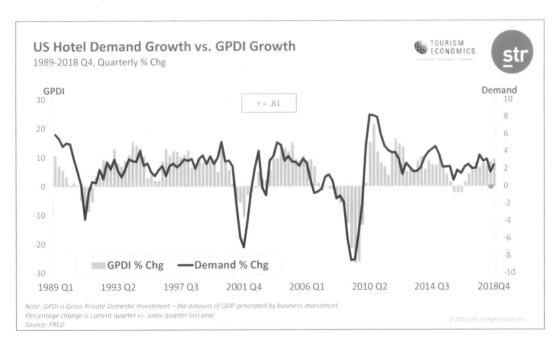

## Market Performance Resources

Understanding how a hotel is performing within a market is an important piece of information for all hoteliers. Several measurements, explored in more detail in the following chapters, have traditionally been leveraged to track and compare a hotel's performance:

- Revenue Per Available Room (RevPAR): The primary measurement, RevPAR is the daily revenue of a hotel divided by the total number of available rooms at that hotel. Daily hotel revenue / Total # of available rooms in hotel.

- Occupancy: The percentage of available rooms that were sold during a specified period of time. Occupancy is calculated by dividing the number of rooms sold by rooms available. Occupancy = Rooms Sold / Rooms Available.[8]

- Average Daily Rate (ADR): Metric derived by dividing actual daily room revenue by the total number of rooms sold. Actual Daily Room Revenue / Total # of Rooms Sold.

- Market Share: The percentage of the market for a product or service that a company supplies. Total number of rooms in a hotel as a percentage of total rooms within a competitive set: (Total # of rooms in hotel / Total # of rooms in competitive set) x 100 [results in a percentage].

- Market Penetration: The ratio in comparing total occupied rooms with the total occupied rooms within a competitive set: Total occupied rooms in hotel / Total occupied rooms in competitive set.

## Microeconomics

Microeconomics is the study of economic decisions made at a low, or micro, level. It examines the decision making and resource allocation of individual consumers, households, and firms and analyzes the factors that affect those decisions, and how those decisions affect others.

For example, if wages increase, an individual may have an increased desire or willingness to work more hours. Or, if the price of gasoline decreases, an individual may have increased propensity to drive on vacation rather than fly.

### Supply and Demand

Supply and demand is one of the most fundamental concepts of economics. It is the backbone of a market economy.

Demand refers to how much (quantity) of a product or service is desired by buyers. The quantity demanded is the amount of a product or service people are willing to buy at a certain price. The relationship between price and quantity demanded is known as the demand relationship.

Supply represents how much the market can offer. The quantity supplied is the amount of a certain good or service that producers are willing to provide when receiving a certain price. The correlation between price and how much of a good or service is supplied to the market is known as the supply relationship.

Since price is in the definition of both the demand relationship and the supply relationship, it is fair to say that price is a reflection of supply and demand. Revenue optimization implements the basic principles of supply and demand in a tactical way to generate incremental

revenues. There are three essential conditions for revenue optimization to be applicable.

1.  There must be a fixed amount of resources available for sale.
2.  The resources sold must be perishable. This means there is a time limit to selling the resources, after which they cease to be of value.
3.  There must be different customers who are willing to pay different prices for the same amount of resources.

The fortunes of the hotel industry are driven by basic supply and demand. When the industry has created an oversupply of hotels, the result has often been a drop in hotel occupancy. Accompanying price wars have depressed ADR on the already reduced number of occupied rooms.

The increased supply is only part of the story, however. Demand plays just as big a role. A large enough increase in demand for hotel rooms can offset the increased supply, and a decrease in demand can aggravate the problems caused by oversupply.

The following chart illustrates what has been happening with hotel supply and demand over the past three decades in the United States.

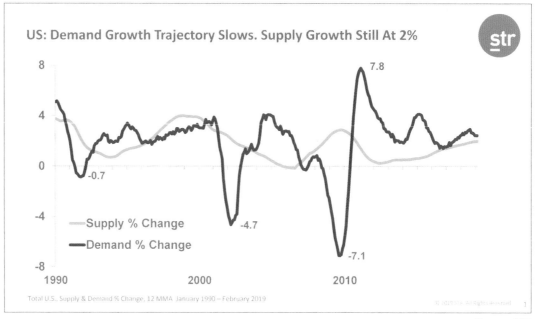

Source: STR

In contrast, the next chart illustrates the relationship between hotel supply and demand in the United Kingdom where supply remains relatively steady.

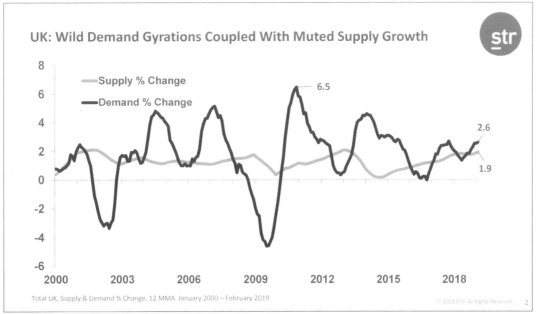

Source: STR

The third chart also illustrates the hotel supply and demand relationship — this time in China where supply growth is steady at a high level, and growth has softened.

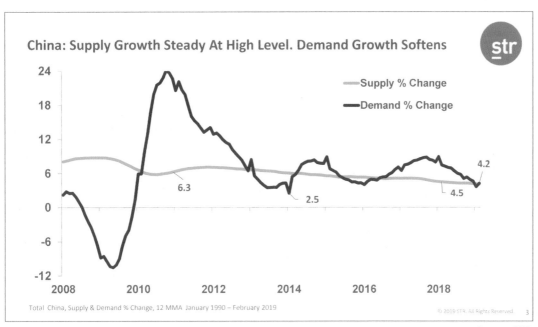

Source: STR

No matter where in the world a hotel is, a sound revenue strategy will aim to achieve the right balance between maximum occupancy and the highest possible room rate.

### Unconstrained Demand

Supply and demand cannot be addressed without reviewing constrained and unconstrained demand.

A very important part of revenue strategy is to determine how much demand a hotel would enjoy in the absence of any pricing and inventory constraints. One of the most critical elements to the success of hotel revenue optimization is the ability to accurately forecast future unconstrained demand based on historical and current booking activity.

True unconstrained demand for a hotel is determined by tracking the true demand for the hotel regardless of any space capacity limitations. In other words, if one room could be built for each additional request for a room, the total would be the unconstrained demand for that hotel.

In the following simple example, the hotel's capacity is 100 rooms. The unconstrained demand — demand minus any constraints — is clearly more than the hotel's capacity on several dates.

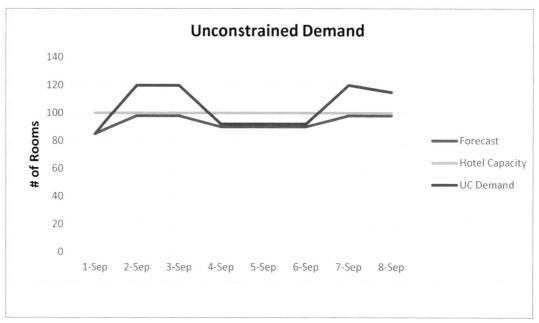

The purple line represents the unconstrained demand and shows that if the hotel did not have any type of constraints, such as number of rooms, rate restrictions, or length of stay restrictions, it could sell 120 rooms on September 2, 3, and 7 and 115 rooms on September 8.

The hotel can't change its total number of rooms, which in this example is 100. The hotel can, however, manage other restrictions like rates, length of stay, and inventory controls. The forecast line represents what the hotel's revenue team believes will actualize after its pricing and control decisions are applied.

The use and application of unconstrained demand for hotels will be explored in the demand forecasting section in chapter 7.

### Price Elasticity of Demand (A Customer's Willingness to Pay)

Many businesses charge different prices to different groups of consumers for more or less the same products or services. This is called price discrimination and it has become widespread in nearly every market and industry. When the amount demanded changes based on the price charged, the product or service is considered to be price elastic.

Prices are not simply numbers plucked out of the air. While hoteliers may put whatever price they wish on an available room, that price will become an economic reality only if customers are willing to pay it. This depends not on whatever price the hotelier has chosen but on what prices the competition is charging for the same type of room with the same type of services, and what customers are willing to pay. Because hotel room prices are essentially transparent, meaning that all customers can see all rates, hotels need to not simply match their competitor's prices but consider customer price elasticity when pricing their rooms.

Hotels do charge different prices to different customers. For example, the customer who is price sensitive and time conscious (books far in advance) generally pays a lower price for the same type of room that was booked by another customer who booked the room only one or two days prior to their stay and is willing to pay a higher price. In this way, we can see that price elasticity varies by customer segment.

Thomas Sowell in Basic Economics: A Common Sense Guide to the Economy provides illustrations which allow for better understanding of this concept.[9]

The following chart shows an example of inelastic demand — a one unit increase in price has a small decrease effect on quantity sold.

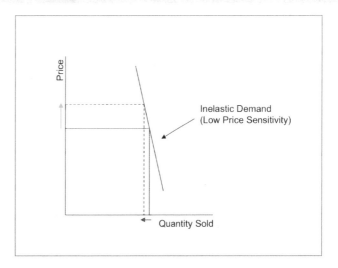

The second chart illustrates elastic demand — a one unit increase on price has a large decrease effect on quantity sold.

### A Few Words About Costs Factors

Hoteliers have various costs associated with every occupied room, and different types of costs impact a hotel's profitability potential in different ways.

A fixed cost for an occupied room is the cost the hotel incurs regardless of the total number of rooms occupied. Hotels incur costs regardless of how many rooms are occupied on a given night. For instance, a certain level of front desk staffing is always required. These costs are incurred when the hotel opens its doors and operates regardless of the number of rooms occupied.

Variable costs are incurred when additional rooms, or services, are sold. A variable cost will change, and is dependent on the total number of additional sales. An example of a variable cost is an additional housekeeper that will be scheduled to work only after a certain number of rooms are sold.

Identifying and understanding the expenses per occupied room allows revenue professionals to both control expenses and identify trends that may be impacting business. In any effort to increase occupancy, the costs associated with those additional occupied rooms need to be weighed against the additional revenue that can be generated by selling those rooms. That give you a clear picture of the profit from an occupied room.

## Questions for Review
- How can economics impact a hotel's revenue optimization decisions?
- How does supply and demand impact a hotel's overall revenue optimization strategy?
- How is a hotel's pricing impacted by market conditions?
- What is unconstrained demand and why is it important?

# CHAPTER 5
## UNDERSTANDING THE MARKET

### Learning Objectives
- To understand how external and internal influencers, market trends, product positioning, demand indicators, and competition influence revenue optimization strategies
- To appreciate various types of benchmarks and why they are important
- To know how to create a useful competitive set(s)
- To understand how a hotel's market position relates to pricing

Understanding the market is the basic starting point for any revenue strategy and is always a very important part of a hotel's business plan. It requires insights into:
1. The economics of the market, and how external and internal influences impact it and the hotel's position within it.
2. The hotel's competitive set, market share, and position in the market.
3. The difference between the desired position for the hotel in the market and its actual position.

Research into and analysis of these factors will prepare the revenue team to conduct proper and accurate competitive benchmarking, and to determine the most appropriate pricing for their hotel.

### External and Internal Influencers
Every hotel should undertake both an external and an internal analysis on an annual basis.

An external analysis provides hoteliers with a view of what is happening within the market. This includes consumer trends (demand) and competitors (supply). By understanding the behaviors of both consumers and competitors, a hotel or hotel company can better position themselves to be prepared to meet the needs of, and overcome the challenges specific to, their market.

Some useful resources to help with this include CBRE Hotels forecasts, STR trend reports, Forrester Research, and local destination marketing organizations and convention and visitors bureaus for city specific information such as pace and events. Local realtors are also a great resource to gain insight from their experiences and information on hand such as relocation packets. Commercial business intelligence tools are also available (see Appendix C for specifics).

Questions to ask during an external analysis include:
1. Is there any new product that has entered the market since the last analysis that can be considered competition?
2. What type of new inventory is entering your market?
3. Has any inventory left the market? If so, why? Was it permanently closed? Is it closed for renovations intending to reopen?
4. When was each competitor's most recent renovation?
5. Is there construction nearby any of my competitors?
6. Have any of my competitors switched flags or management companies since the last analysis?
7. What benefits have been added or lost with this change such as distribution partners, group sales resources, and central reservation contribution?
8. Have any of my competitors implemented revenue management systems or changed distribution partners since the last analysis?
9. What are the reviews my competitors are receiving on social media sites?
10. Are there any significant citywide events that are driving demand? If so, what is the volume of this demand and what dates may be impacted?
11. Are there any citywide events that are no longer returning?
12. Have any large corporations moved into or out of our market during the past year? For example, what office sites may now be vacant or are newly occupied? What future economic developments or redevelopments are planned? What is their timing?
13. Have any large companies in the market been acquired recently?
14. Have any of your primary accounts changed their travel procurement procedures?
15. Is there any significant change to how consumers are traveling to the market this year such as driving versus flying?
16. How is the booking process on the competitor sites?
17. What are the market's booking policies including cancellation periods? What is the market's cancellation percentages?
18. Does the market offer channel-specific booking or cancellation policies?
19. What is the landscape of the airlift coming into your destination?
20. Have you or your competitors added new fees such as a resort fee, facility fee, energy surcharge, parking, etc.? If any fees are already in place in your market, have there been any major changes?

An internal analysis provides hoteliers with an understanding of what is happening within their own hotel or company that can influence their position within the market. This means taking a close realistic look at what is happening within the hotel such as understanding service standards and the quality of the product.

Questions to ask on an internal analysis include:
1. When was the hotel's most recent renovation?
2. Is the product in need of improvement? If so, in what areas?
3. Is our service in need of improvement? If so, in what areas?
4. Are any significant closures occurring this year, e.g., pool, restaurant, etc.?
5. Is there construction nearby?
6. Do we have adequate meeting space to attract the right groups?
7. Do we have enough sleeping rooms to accompany our meeting space?

## Market Trends

After completing an analysis of both external and internal influencers, the revenue professional should turn to identifying the market trends for the specific market. This requires looking at consumer behaviors, booking trends, competitive trends, pricing trends, segmentation trends, and distribution trends not only within their specific market but also throughout the industry in general and in other markets.

For example, if the economy is struggling, corporations often tend to stay closer to home for conferences and meetings. Therefore, a hotel may have to make a shift in their sales efforts to focus on different organizations than they have in the past in order to achieve their group and transient corporate sales goals. Additionally, other markets may become competition because they have recently added a new attraction, convention center, or high-tech conference center.

Understanding the segmentation strategies among the competitors is critical to knowing how the hotel will compete in the market for the same or similar customers. Knowing if the competitive set sells to corporate customers based on LRA (Last Room Availability) and if they offer static or dynamic pricing will help to determine the appetite for the contracts.

What is the market experiencing with consumer booking trends? How is the market driving or impacting these trends? Knowing what the competitors are doing with their same-day pricing through mobile sites can have a big impact on a hotel's pricing and channel strategy. Has the customer been trained to wait for the same-day discount to be offered through a mobile app? (More about pricing factors will be explored in the chapter specific to pricing.)

New entrants in the distribution space (e.g., Airbnb) can impact both consumer behavior and the market. Identifying and understanding new entrants, as well as changing models, is a key factor for staying in tune with the market.

For example, Airbnb has changed some of the rules for the hotel industry. While Airbnb's financial effects on hotels can be argued, the point is that hoteliers must understand the impact to the market and consumers in order to properly position themselves to compete where it makes sense. Otherwise, they will lose out on future opportunities.

There are many companies that offer business intelligence reports that assist hoteliers in understanding what is happening in the market. For a listing of companies that provide such information and reports see Appendix C.

## Demand Indicators

Once market trends have been identified, demand indicators need to be considered. Demand indicators are factors such as behaviors or events that will have a direct impact — both positive and negative — on the demand for a market and/or for a hotel. Understanding demand indicators, such as consumer confidence, will greatly impact a hotel's revenue optimization success. Every market has unique demand generators as well as common ones that are applicable to many or all markets. It is important to understand both types.

An example is date-specific demand generators which create demand only for specific dates. A citywide convention is an example of a date-specific demand generator in a unique market. Along these lines, it is necessary to know the generators that may depress demand such as cultural, regional, or religious holidays which can impact normal business patterns and are applicable to all markets. Holidays often change dates from year to year and can have a negative impact on demand. Thus, each year the hotel must be aware of the dates of these events and must adjust the demand forecast accordingly.

Another market-specific example is an ongoing attraction that drives business to one hotel, such as a state-of-the-art luxury spa at a four-star property, or a large convention center located next door to a hotel. A demand generator that is applicable to multiple markets is the work of national marketing organizations, such as Brand USA in the United States or the German National Tourist Board in Germany. These organizations execute global marketing efforts to promote their country as a travel destination to worldwide travelers. Their campaigns and initiatives can impact multiple markets simultaneously.

Another influencer on demand is the use of flash sales — private and public, and through a third party or on a hotel's own brand.com site. Hotelier opinions about flash sales vary greatly depending on the hotel, the market, and the way they are used. If leveraged appropriately they can alleviate depressed demand or even create artificial demand for a specific time period, filling rooms that would otherwise sit empty. Some also argue that they help to create awareness about a hotel.

Conversely, flash sales can be very challenging as they typically require a deep discount of the room product plus a hefty commission. This has led to debates in the hotel industry regarding the long-term impact these discounts may have on rates and overall hotel performance. Specifically, this could impact the hotel's bottom line, rate of return, brand equity and value, ability to attract the right customer mix, rate recovery efforts, and pricing strategies. More will be explored on its impact on pricing in chapter 8.

Regardless of whether a demand generator is negative or positive, it is important for hotel revenue executives to know and understand the potential impact of demand generators on their market, their specific hotel, and their competition.

## Competition

Identifying the appropriate competition is important for all companies throughout all industries. For some it is easier to identify who their competitors are, and for others it can be a bit more complicated.

Identifying the right competitive set is an important part of the overall hotel revenue optimization process. It is also integral to identifying the hotel's market position. Hoteliers are challenged with identifying the most appropriate competition based on multiple traditional criteria including location, brand, product, amenities, experiences, and so much more — they all play a role in establishing the right set. At the same time, digital marketing and distribution technologies have expanded our capacity to understand and reach travelers especially in the leisure segment, which means hotels need to consider as competition the hotels that are innovative and relevant in deploying local and curated digital marketing initiatives.

Those who misalign themselves will encounter ongoing challenges — especially when it comes to the price-value relationship in the eyes of the consumer, as well as the results achieved in comparison to the competitive set selected. This will be apparent in benchmarking data such as the Revenue Generation Index (RGI).

A hotel's competitive set is typically defined by its ownership and/or management company. Competitive set selections should be reviewed on a regular schedule to ensure their relevance, as markets are continuously in flux due to many factors, some of which include changes in the market supply, changes in brand affiliations, and changes in demand generators. Fundamentally, a competitive set with the most accurate depiction of a subject hotel's competitiveness can drive and impact actual results.

### Advice from the Trenches

"I have a hotel that has established three comp sets. We have found this to be extremely valuable in our market to best analyze our performance. In our situation, we have our 'true' comp set which focuses on the traditional criteria of location, brand, and product. The second one is an 'aspirational' comp set where we have positioned ourselves against a group of resorts one tier higher. The third comp set is a 'conference' set where we compare against the larger group houses, which has been very helpful during times of group compression.

–Eric Gravelle, CRME,
Vice President of Revenue Management, North America,
Diamond Resorts International

# Benchmarking

Proper benchmarking is necessary to define the competitive landscape.

Competitive benchmarking is an objective comparison of one hotel to others. It helps hoteliers identify potential strategies to implement in order to improve or maintain their competitive positioning.

Hotels should consider three types of benchmarking. Complete them in the following order for maximum impact and insight:

1. Product Benchmarking — Results in a thorough product analysis of the subject hotel and its competitors
2. Process Benchmarking — Results in an understanding of the processes and channels of both the subject hotel and its competitors
3. Rate-Value Benchmarking — Results in an analysis of rate structure for the subject hotel and its competitors, and is dependent upon the results of Product Benchmarking

## Product Benchmarking

The first type of benchmarking is a competitor-to-competitor comparison focused on the hotel itself. It ideally results in an unbiased view about your product and identifies areas of needed improvement and opportunity.

A useful methodology for product benchmarking is a SWOT analysis, a tool used to evaluate a hotel's Strengths, Weaknesses, Opportunities, and Threats. In a SWOT analysis the strengths and weaknesses of a hotel are compared to those of its competitive set. Opportunities and threats are the external factors that may influence the hotel's business.

There are several ways to organize a SWOT analysis, but one of the easiest is to use a simple comparison chart. The chart can assign columns for the subject hotel and for each hotel to which you want to compare it.

Rows on the chart organize specific information. The initial information to collect is factual: the year the hotel was built, the number of rooms and suites, the number and type of restaurants, the total number and size of meeting rooms, additional amenities like exercise facilities or a business, and the shops on premises. The next sections address the hotels' strengths, weaknesses, opportunities, and threats.

Use the example in Appendix B as a guide to create a product benchmark for the subject hotel.
- Fill in the hotel's name in the first column (i.e., replace "Hotel A") and then do the same for each of its competitors.
- Add and delete columns and rows as needed.
- Adjust each of the attributes according to what is relevant for the area and the hotel.

First, complete the general information for all hotels. This information should be readily available online (via the hotel's website, TripAdvisor, Cvent, Yelp, etc.).

Next, compile a list of strengths and weaknesses of the subject hotel. Leverage all resources at hand including consumer reviews and hotel employees. Employees of the hotel at all levels and from all departments are valuable sources of insight on the hotel's strengths and weaknesses. Any employee who receives input from guests about their likes and dislikes of the hotel can make a valuable contribution to this brainstorming activity. The resulting list will likely be long, and contain some vague items. Avoiding any gray areas, condense it into a short list of the most specific and realistic strengths and weaknesses, and put those on the comparison chart.

Then complete the chart with the competitors' strengths and weaknesses. Start by comparing the strengths and weaknesses of the competitor hotels. Always analyze competitive hotels in relation to one another. For example, if one of a competitor's strengths is a new guest room product due to a recent complete room renovation, make sure the year and scope of the most recent renovation at competitive hotels are listed as well. If poor visibility of the subject hotel from street level is one of its weaknesses, ensure that the visibility of the other hotels is evaluated as well.

With strengths and weakness identified, turn your attention to opportunities and threats which are mostly external factors that will affect business at the subject hotel. They can be local, regional, national, or global factors. Often, they will affect all hotels in the same way. For instance, if a city raises the tax rate on hotel stays, all hotels in the city may lose some competitive edge to hotels in other cities. Sometimes opportunities and threats will affect hotels differently. If the subject hotel gets a much larger share of visitors from one specific geographic region than its competitors do, any positive economic development in that region could be a better opportunity for that hotel than for its competitive set.

Examples of opportunities include:

- New market entrants such as geographical additions or a new type of industry (e.g., pharmaceutical)
- New alliances or mergers
- Markets lost by weak hotels, hotels that closed, or hotels converted to another use
- Shifting market share from a less to a more profitable segment
- New business or industry trends

Examples of threats are:

- A new hotel opening or one that greatly improved its product
- Price wars with competing hotels
- A competitor offering a new or greatly superior service or product
- A competitor gaining better access to a distribution channel through a new alliance or brand affiliation
- Technological innovation by a competitor
- Access by consumers to a supply of condo hotels, time shares, and home rentals
- Alternatives for leisure dollar spending, such as cruises and adventure vacations
- Competitor providing more state-of-the-art meeting space

Depending on the strengths and weaknesses identified, any change in external business conditions has the potential to turn into an opportunity or a threat.

See Appendix B for an example of a SWOT analysis for a hotel.

## Process Benchmarking

Another very important component of competitive benchmarking and knowing the competition is understanding their processes and the channels they leverage. Keep in mind that this information can change over time. Therefore, collecting process benchmarks should be regular and ongoing. Be sure that as new information is identified, all revenue team members are kept informed.

Answer the following questions for each of the properties within your competitive set. As with the SWOT analysis, this information can be compiled through a variety of sources including calling the hotel directly, using a company with expertise in business intelligence (see Appendix C for a list of providers), reviewing competitive websites, online searches, and so on.

1. With which third party sites does the competitor work?
2. What is the competitor's cancellation policy(s) for various rate types?
3. Do they have reservations on property or is it centralized?
4. Are their reservations agents able to effectively and comfortably convey product knowledge?
5. How many different room types does the competitor have?
6. What are the room types?
7. Do they display the lowest priced room types on their site first?
8. Do they have a revenue professional on property? To whom does he/she/they report?
9. What kind of a strategic focus does the revenue professional have?
10. How sophisticated is the revenue professional?
11. Do they use an automated revenue management system?
12. Do they differentiate between weekdays and weekends with respect to rates?
13. List the hotels in the order from highest rates to lowest rates. Where do you want to position your hotel's rates on this list, and why?
14. Does the competitor identify you as part of their competitive set on their intelligence reports?

## Rate-Value Benchmarking

Rate-value benchmarking allows the hotelier to rank their hotel against the competition. This provides an opportunity to perform a qualitative comparison by identifying specific attributes that are relative and ranking each of them. It is especially useful in understanding a hotel's market position.

The goal of this exercise is to ensure the competitors identified by the revenue team are competitive with the subject hotel and to identify the areas in which they are competitive. This is done by seeing if all are within a reasonable ranking compared to the subject hotel.

This is important because it allows the revenue team to ensure it has identified the specific attributes a competitor has that make it a competitor. Some competitors may have attributes that the subject hotel does not. In those cases, that attribute may keep the hotel from competing with them in a certain market segment. However, it is important to determine whether this should keep the team from identifying them as a competitor all together. For example, a hotel that has 35,000 square feet of banquet space compared to the subject hotel's 15,000 square feet may not be a competitor in some parts of the convention segment, but still would be a competitor in the leisure segment.

Start by completing a chart similar to the following example which includes a "weight" assigned to each factor. In this example, quality of service has a weight of "5" and curb appeal has a "2." This means that, for the hotel completing the analysis, quality of service is extremely important (or weighted heavily) but curb appeal is not as important (or weighted as heavily). If you use weights in your rate-value benchmarking, set them so that they relate to the importance of that variable to the consumer.

The next step in rate-value benchmarking is to compare the rates and market share of the subject hotel and its competitors. Use the various business intelligence reports available to collect this information (see Appendix C for a list of providers).

Start by reviewing the intelligence report(s) and identifying the competitors' rates. Your goal is to identify significant variances between the subject hotel's rates and those of its competitors, incorporate that intelligence with the comparison chart, and look for interesting and valuable insights. For example, if a competitor that ranked significantly higher than the subject hotel on the comparison chart is offering significantly lower rates in a specific market segment, such as corporate or qualified rate, that hotel may be implementing a revenue strategy focused on trying to steal market share. Watch carefully!

## Chart Example

| | SUBJECT HOTEL | | COMPETITOR #1 | | COMPETITOR #2 | |
|---|---|---|---|---|---|---|
| | Hotel Score | Weighted Score | Hotel Score | Weighted Score | Hotel Score | Weighted Score |
| Location weight: 5 | 5 | 25 | 3 | 15 | 1 | 5 |
| Curb Appeal weight: 2 | 3 | 6 | 5 | 10 | 1 | 2 |
| Quality of Service weight: 5 | 5 | 25 | 3 | 25 | 5 | 25 |
| Quality of F&B weight: 3 | 3 | 9 | 5 | 15 | 3 | 9 |
| On-site Restaurant weight: 3 | 3 | 9 | 3 | 9 | 1 | 3 |
| On-site Room Service weight: 4 | 1 | 4 | 3 | 12 | 1 | 4 |
| Bell Service weight: 3 | 1 | 3 | 3 | 9 | 1 | 3 |
| Meeting Space weight: 2 | 5 | 10 | 3 | 6 | 5 | 10 |
| Total Score | 26 | 91 | 28 | 101 | 18 | 61 |

Key: 5=excellent, 3=good, 1=poor/does not exist

Conversely, if the subject hotel's rates are significantly lower than the competitor's, but it ranks higher on the comparison chart, the hotel's rate structure may need to be reviewed. However, it is important that the revenue team does further research before taking action. Speak with all hotel staff who can give their perspectives on the variances, and collect information that the hotel receives directly from guests. For example, get input from the front desk and reservations staff. Collect as much information as possible, involve all revenue team members, and make a collective decision as to whether a change in rate structure is needed.

Use market intelligence reports on a regular basis to ensure you are optimizing revenues and positioning the hotel properly. Some of these reports provide hotels with trend statistics including market share, ADR Index, Revenue Generation Index (RGI), and Occupancy Index. The index balance is an indicator of whether the hotel has played the market conditions optimally. In general, a good point of reference when reading these reports is to aim to keep the occupancy and rate indexes within 10 points of one another.

## Maximizing Market Position

Once the benchmarking exercises have been completed, hoteliers then can show the unique differences of their products and services compared to the market's offerings. This differentiation allows hotels to position themselves favorably in comparison to competitors.

There are occasions when a hotel must be repositioned in its market. This includes when the product has been upgraded and when the product is getting tired but there are not capital funds available for a renovation. It is important that a hotel is repositioned at the appropriate time or the result could be lost revenue and opportunity.

When a hotel has a solid and realistic understanding of its positioning in terms of products and services compared to its competitive set, it can then properly position pricing. Getting the price-value position of the hotel correct is fundamental to optimal market positioning. Those that can find the price that works for the hotel, and is a good perceived value for the customer, will find success.

Once a hotel is sure that the appropriate competitive sets have been determined and that the hotel is appropriately aligned within the sets, the next step is to ensure the hotel maximizes its market position to allow for optimal and appropriate pricing. Consider the following:

- When adjusting rates, the market position must be considered. Rates should never fluctuate above or below a hotel's market position.
- Suitable inventory controls should be utilized to ensure the appropriate product is available at the right price at the right time in the current market.
- Hotels can provide value-added pricing to incentivize consumers to book their product rather than the lowest priced product in their competitive set.
- Rate parity and integrity are fundamental to maximizing a hotel's market position.

## Questions for Review

- What are the factors that influence market conditions?
- What are some questions to be asked during an external analysis?
- What are some questions to be asked during an internal analysis?
- What types of competitive benchmarking that should be done for each hotel? In what order should they be completed?
- How does a hotel ensure that it is appropriately positioned within a market?

# CHAPTER 6

## SEGMENTATION AND SOURCES OF BUSINESS

### Learning Objectives
- To understand the how views on segmentation have evolved
- To understand the influence of USALI on segmentation

Segmentation has always been a very important part of a hotel's revenue optimization strategy. By defining segments, you can understand a hotel's different customer types including their purpose for travel, price sensitivity, booking lead times, and so on. This insight allows a hotel to price and apply inventory controls in order to maximize revenue from various sources of business, and tailor its sales and marketing efforts. Therefore, defining a hotel's segmentation mix is part of building a solid foundational strategy for a hotel. Once the mix is defined, strategies can be created to support it.

As with other areas, the fundamental need for segmentation remains.

It is important to note that segmentation for sales and marketing purposes may be different from segmentation for financial and forecasting purposes. The intent for segmentation in revenue optimization is to help determine and group similar behaviors so as to improve forecasting, pricing, and inventory management.

### Traditional Definition: Focus on the Purpose of Travel
The general market is divided into distinct groups to direct sales and marketing efforts for which a hotel specifically targets budgeted sales and marketing dollars. Typically, each segment identified by a hotel will have a unique strategy for pricing, promotion, policies, distribution, and sales.

Traditionally, segmentation has included having a clear understanding of customer segments that apply to the hotel and to the corporate level, and an understanding of the source of business. At the most basic level, two segments used throughout the industry are group and transient (individual travelers).

Market segments were initially defined as the purpose of the customer's visit to a hotel, such as someone traveling on business staying at a corporate negotiated rate. Prior to the inception of the Internet and the use of the Internet as a channel through which to receive hotel reservations, it was relatively easy and sufficient to define market segments as each customer's reason for travel.

If the reservation was made via the telephone directly with the hotel, the reservation associate would simply ask the direct question, "What is the purpose of your visit to the hotel?" If the reservation was booked via a Global Distribution System (GDS), the confirmed rate or rate code would typically provide the reservation associate with the reason for travel. For example, someone traveling on corporate business but not with a preferred company would typically book the public corporate rate. (This was obviously long before hotels offered more complicated rate structures.) In other words, it was clear and typically very easy to understand the customer's purpose of travel, making it easy to track and measure. But today, we operate in a very different environment, and the purpose of our current market segments has become less clear.

### The Blurred Lines of Segmentation
Today's consumer is often traveling for dual purposes, adding leisure time to their business trips, making their purpose of travel "bleisure." At the same time, travelers have the option to book through the channel of their choice — from opaque channels (where they don't know the specific hotel or hotel brand until the booking is complete) to the hotel's website and almost every conceivable variation in between.

Today's business traveler no longer automatically books his or her negotiated rate. And they rarely book through the traditional channels that allowed an easy understanding of the purpose of their travel. If they do book through a traditional channel, the caller may not share that he or she is traveling with company XYZ with the hope of getting a better rate as an individual traveler.

All of this means that the purpose or reason for traveling is no longer apparent to the hotelier based on the type of rate confirmed. As a result, hoteliers have found themselves adding channels to their market segments. This allows hoteliers to track the reservations that arrive via specific channels, but they cannot identify the purpose of the guest's stay.

Hoteliers are finding that market segments as currently defined are less and less meaningful due to these blurring lines of segmentation.

## Evolved Thinking: Focus on the Channel

Today, the traditional approach to market segmentation has become much more difficult to apply and accurately track. This is due to the great variety of channels through which hotels can receive reservations, and to the more advanced/complicated rate structures created by hoteliers.

The new way of thinking about segmentation is looking at the sources of business or the channels through which a booking arrives to the hotel. Examples of sources or channels include:

- Brand.com (the hotel's own website)
- Voice (phone) or call center/800 number
- Online Travel Agency (OTA)
- Group rooming list or call-in
- Global Distribution System (GDS)

A development to watch involves model shifts which may blur this focus on sources of business. For example, take the integration between a major OTA and American Express. Historically, American Express bookings were made through a GDS; soon they will be using one of the major OTA platforms for their booking needs. Unless the OTA can provide a secondary source code to the booking details, carving out the American Express bookings from the traditional OTA bookings will likely be challenging for all involved. OTA business will look artificially inflated. How will hoteliers accurately identify commission payments due? How will this impact the cost per booking?

After channel, the secondary level of categorization usually separates rooms booked by the purpose of the guest's travel, such as business or leisure. Sub-segments are then further developed and customized to unique demand drivers in a market. These are commonly referred to as market segments.

## The Next Stage: Focus on the Customer

A new and interesting trend to watch is the consideration of how customer segments may, in part, shift toward being more customer-specific centric. As more hotels embrace customer relationship management (CRM), personalization, and the concept of the lifetime value of a guest, it will likely become common practice to have a one-to-one relationship with the customer. As a result, targeted marketing initiatives, pricing, and inventory dynamics may be tailored specifically to the individual customer versus groups or segments.

## What Does USALI Have to Do with It?

USALI is the Uniform System of Accounts for the Lodging Industry and is the guide for hotel owners, managers, and other parties for reporting and presenting hotel financial statements. The resulting standardization established by the USALI permits internal and external users of financial statements to compare the financial position and operational performance of a specific hotel with similar types of hotels in the lodging industry.

Due to the standardization provided by USALI, most loan agreements and hotel management contracts contain specific provisions that require hotel owners and operators to prepare their financial statements in conformity with the Uniform System. Changes required by the Uniform System may also affect the basis for management incentive compensation amounts which are based on departmental results. Therefore, it is important that hoteliers remain knowledgeable of the standards and any changes made to these standards.

The Uniform System impacts the way hoteliers track and report revenues. Therefore, it is important that the person in charge of revenue optimization for a hotel or organization understands the impact and sets up tracking and reporting accordingly.

Some of the most recent updates to the USALI that are impacting revenue optimization, and specifically how hoteliers track segmentation, are outlined in the following chart.

The key to understanding what all this means for revenue optimization is to ensure that the teams are completely aligned in their reporting. By ensuring proper reporting within the organization, a hotel will be better able to compare equal information in relation to the competitive set; but even more importantly, it will allow the hotel to be aligned in all revenue streams. Ultimately, hoteliers want to ensure that this alignment provides the ability to drill down to profit contribution.

| MARKET SEGMENT | USALI 11TH EDITION CLASSIFICATION | DEFINITION |
|---|---|---|
| Airline | Contract | Contract airline crews or transient airline travel |
| Association | Group Association / Convention | Rates negotiated with an association/convention for the purpose of group travel (10 or more rooms on peak night) |
| Consortia | Transient Qualified | Travel booked by mega agencies or consortia |
| Contract | Contract | Rates which have been negotiated with a particular organization for the purpose of individual business travel (less than 10 rooms on peak night) requiring a contractual obligation for performance from the client; a consistent block of rooms for a contracted time period of more than 30 days (e.g., airline crews, railroad crews, etc.) |
| Corporate Group | Corporate Group | Rates negotiated with a corporate organization for the purpose of group travel (10 or more rooms on peak night) |
| Government Group & Active Military | Group Government & Active Military | Rates negotiated with a government body for the purpose of group travel (10 or more rooms on peak night); may include federal, state, or local government bodies as well as active military groups |
| Government Transient | Transient Retail | Local, state or federal government individual travel; bookings for government agencies, foreign or domestic, including consulates, embassies, government agencies, etc. |
| Incentive Travel | Group | Travel purchased usually by an incentive agency or company as an employee incentive or reward |
| Internet Opaque | Transient Discount | Rates sold via third-party opaque partners where the hotel is not revealed to the customer until after the reservation has been booked (e.g., Priceline, Hotwire) |
| Leisure Individual | Transient | Individual leisure travel for vacation or getaways, not business related |
| Negotiated | Transient Negotiated | Rates which have been negotiated with a particular organization (e.g., Johnson & Johnson, IBM, Deloitte, etc.) for the purpose of individual business travel (less than 10 rooms on peak night) without a contractual obligation for performance from the client |
| Non-Qualified Discount | Transient Discount | A rate open to the general public (non-qualified) under which the guest pays less than the retail rate; identification is not required upon check-in (e.g., loyalty redemptions or offers, advance purchase, timed sales, length-of-stay promotions, seasonal sales, mobile offers, pay-per-click offers, repeat rates, walk-in rates, walk rates, vendor rates, etc.) |
| Packages | Transient Discount | Any transient rate bundled with package components for convenience or perceived value (e.g., bed & breakfast, adventure, dining, parking/transportation, pet, shopping, sports, etc.) |
| Qualified Discount | Transient Retail | A rate that requires the customer to be associated with a particular organization or to have a specific affiliation in order to book; identification is required upon check-in (e.g., AAA, AARP, employee rate, resident rate, university/alumni rate, etc.) |
| Retail | Transient Retail | All publicly available rates for which guests do not have to qualify and may or may not pay a commission to an agency or company; includes BAR bookings via an OTA with a commission attached; excludes merchant model bookings |
| SMERFE | Group SMERFE | Rates negotiated with a social, non-active duty military, educational, religious, fraternal, or entertainment group for the purpose of group travel (10 or more rooms on peak night) |
| Third Party Net Retail | Transient Retail | Net-rated retail rates through OTAs |
| Tour Group | Group Tour / Wholesalers | Rates negotiated with a tour operator or wholesaler for the purpose of group travel (10 or more rooms on peak night) |
| Wholesaler | Transient Wholesale | Rates sold via a third-party receptive or traditional wholesaler where the room is bundled with additional travel components such as airfare, ground transportation, etc. (e.g., Bonotel, Crystal Holidays, Despegar, Hotel Beds, Tourico, Ski.com, etc.) |

Brad Garner, Senior Vice President of Client Relations at STR, and Robert Mandelbaum, Director of Research Information Services at PKF Hospitality Research, reviewed the key changes having an impact on revenue optimization practices.[10]

### Rooms Department Changes

- The 11th edition of the USALI includes changes in definitions of the segments of business listed in the rooms department charges. The 11th edition separates rooms revenue into three classes — transient, group, and contract — but it includes fewer sub-segments under each class than were included in the previous edition. Transient covers retail, discount, negotiated, qualified, and wholesale; while group includes corporate, association/convention, government, tour group/wholesale, and SMERFE (social, military, educational, religious, fraternal, entertainment). No changes were made to the contract segment.
- "These changes line up more with the nomenclature of online travel agencies and the segments we track," Garner said.

### Resort Fees and Surcharges:

- Under Other Revenues in the rooms department, Resort Fees and Surcharges was changed to Surcharges and Service Charges. Garner said service charges are standard in hotels in some global markets and are recognized in the new edition.
- Resort fees were moved out of the rooms department ledger and will be credited as miscellaneous income and not included as a component of average-daily-rate or revenue-per-available-room metrics.
- Service charges are defined in the new edition as a mandatory amount billed to a guest for which the guest has no discretion as to the payment or its distribution to employees. From an accounting standpoint, service charges are treated as revenue, and payment to employees is considered a wage expense.

## Questions for Review

- What is the purpose of market segmentation?
- How has the industry's approach to segmentation evolved over time?
- How does the Uniform System of Accounts impact revenue optimization practices?

# CHAPTER 7
## *FORECASTING*

## Learning Objectives
- To understand the different types of forecasts and why they are necessary for optimal performance
- To increase the ability and confidence in developing and creating an accurate forecast
- To know what information is needed to create different types of forecasts
- To understand who needs which forecast and how frequently they are needed

Challenging as it may be, forecasting a hotel's future revenue, including occupancy and average rate, is an extremely important and foundational factor in the hotel's ability to design successful revenue optimization strategies.

It all begins with accurate forecasting of the hotel's top-line room revenues. An accurate rooms forecast is an indispensable planning tool for other departments throughout the hotel. It helps each department accurately forecast its departmental revenues, as well as control expenses and labor as appropriate.

From there, hoteliers must understand the demand forecast, strategic revenue forecast, and operational forecast in order to achieve maximum potential in the market. Each type of forecast has a different objective and approach, and each is critical to optimizing a hotel's results.

Today's owners have heightened expectations that high-performing operators will provide accurate forecasts for both top-line revenues as well as bottom-line profits. These expectations include the ability of operators to manage operational expenses and labor costs against the top-line forecast to ensure proper flow-through.

The good news is that, more than ever before, automated tools are available to aid in forecasting. A key benefit of automation is the increased level of granularity when it comes to data and analytics, which ultimately improves the forecast. While every tool is not perfect, they have made forecasting much less manual and allow for more accuracy if used appropriately.

## Forecasting is the Foundation
Sound forecasting is an essential part of any revenue optimization process. As a matter of fact, the forecast is so important that it is considered the foundation of a hotel's revenue optimization program. Without an accurate

forecast and the right types of forecasting, even the best revenue optimization strategies cannot be realized.

Ironically, forecasting is one of the biggest challenges for many hoteliers. One reason for this is that many revenue professionals are not confident in their forecasting abilities. There are a variety of reasons for this lack of confidence. Perhaps they are unsure where to begin, or how to collect the information, or even what information should be tracked. Perhaps they are not confident in taking the steps that should be taken to put together a forecast.

The second reason that forecasting can be so challenging is that many hoteliers are not aware of the importance and purpose of the different types of forecasts that should be created and managed. Most revenue professionals put together one or two different types of forecasts — one to satisfy the operational needs of the hotel and one to satisfy stakeholder needs.

There are, however, different forecasts that allow hoteliers to satisfy different objectives. Each forecast may require a different approach and information may be specific to individual forecasts.

The third reason that forecasting can be such a challenge is that much of forecasting includes a certain amount of intuition or "gut" feeling that must be taken into consideration. Many hoteliers find this to be intimidating. Common questions surrounding this are, "How do I know exactly how much business I can anticipate?" and "Is there a formula I can use to come up with the forecast?"

Some would argue that there is a fourth reason why forecasting is difficult: revenue professionals are often pushed to back into a number in order to appease an owner or asset manager. See chapter 14 for best practices for optimizing expectations, communications, and collaboration, which may help overcome this forecasting challenge.

The good news is that there are specific steps that can be learned to improve the methodology and accuracy in forecasting procedures, as well as the comfort level in putting all of this information together.

This chapter will help develop a better understanding of forecasting and its importance, and will answer the following questions:

- What are the different types of forecasts?
- What are the objectives for each of the types of forecasts?
- What information do I need to put each forecast together?
- How do I find this information?
- What questions should I ask when putting together each of the forecasts?
- How often should I be putting together each of the forecasts?
- What are the steps that I need to follow to put each forecast together?

One thing that is important to remember is that forecasting is an art. Therefore, it can and will take practice, and over time if you follow the proper procedures and apply the level of detail that forecasting requires and deserves, the comfort level and accuracy will improve. The ideal solution is having a fully automated revenue optimization system that provides the appropriate information and detail to support the forecasting process.

Automation allows hotels to monitor not only the historical aspect of channel business but also the future trends much more quickly than a manual environment. This allows hoteliers to quickly identify shortcomings as well as opportunities well in advance while there is still time to influence the outcome.

One important point to note about this section is that it is focused purely on rooms forecasting. But the same principles can be applied or expanded to other revenue streams throughout the organization or hotel. Refer to chapter 10 for more ideas on additional revenue streams.

## Different Forecasts for Different Objectives

There are different forecasts that should be put together for every hotel, and each forecast has a different objective.

The following table introduces the types of forecasts along with their supporting objectives. They are listed in the order in which they should be completed. Each forecast, including its supporting methodology, is explored in more detail in this chapter.

| FORECAST TYPE | OBJECTIVE | WHEN/FREQUENCY |
|---|---|---|
| 1. Demand Forecast | To determine the anticipated demand for the hotel absent any constraints. | Long term based on booking window / quarterly and/or monthly |
| 2. Strategic Forecast | To support strategic objectives such as understanding the impact of the unconstrained demand and its effect on occupied rooms. | Medium term / monthly |
| 3. Revenue Forecast | To have a realistic picture of probable future occupied rooms and rates to use to compare to budget and identify variances. | Short term / weekly |
| 4. Operational Forecast | To use for operational necessities such as scheduling. | Short term / weekly |

## Demand Forecasting

Of all the different types of forecasts that are critical to a hotel, demand forecasting is the most crucial. Ironically, this is the forecast that is most often not utilized and sometimes not even understood.

### Purpose

A demand forecast is determined by the amount of demand a hotel would have for its rooms on a given night in the absence of any constraints. This is referred to as unconstrained demand.

A hotel's unconstrained demand or demand forecast is the forecast on which all revenue optimization decisions including rates, availability, and restrictions are based. Important note: This is NOT the forecast that is to be shared with ownership or senior management for the purpose of explaining the forecasted end result. The revenue forecast is the forecast that will be shared with them for that purpose. Instead, the demand forecast is to be used by revenue professionals and shared with the revenue team to ensure proper strategies are discussed and implemented to support the projected demand. Provided ownership and senior management understand the purpose and definition of demand forecast, they absolutely should review it as well.

In an effort to provide hoteliers with a guideline and to help understand the concept of demand forecasting, a general calculation is provided. It is vital to understand however, there is no one scientific calculation that can be followed for the purposes of calculating a demand forecast. This calculation is shown to illustrate the concept of how to arrive at the demand forecast. Each hotel must derive its own specific forecast.

> "On the Books" Transient Bookings
> +
> Anticipated Unconstrained
> Transient Bookings
> +
> "On the Books" Group Bookings
> +
> Anticipated Group Bookings
> =
> Demand Forecast

One final point to understand is that a hotel's unconstrained information will only be as good as the hotel's tracking of historical and future activity. Without solid tracking methods in place, the demand forecast will not be accurate.

### Important Things to Know

Demand forecasting requires the use of historical patterns and current trends to forecast future demand. Therefore, there is specific information that must be tracked and reviewed for the purpose of putting together the demand forecast.

The following items must be available and accurately tracked in order to create a demand forecast.

- Room Nights
- RevPAR
- Revenue
- Cancellations
- Lead Time / Booking Pace by Segment
- Transient Rooms
- No Shows (both guaranteed and non-guaranteed)
- Arrivals
- Group Rooms
- Walk-ins
- Departures
- Early Departures
- Extended Stays
- Length of Stay Pattern
- Denials / Regrets
- Transient and Group Mix
- Demand Generators
- "On the books" Bookings
- Rate Changes
- Group Wash
- Comp Set Availability
- Supply Changes
- Sell-out Frequency (of your hotel and the competitors)
- Tracking of past marketing demand drivers (e.g., flash sales)
- Tracking of significant weather events in your major source markets or in your own destination
- Tracking of special in-market events (e.g., Super Bowl, volcano eruption, major conference)

It is ideal to have this information tracked day-by-day for one full year or more as it will assist hoteliers in understanding the patterns and trends for the hotel. Be sure to shift the data to show alignment of the days of the week from year to year (so you are comparing Monday to Monday for example). This data will be used to determine the hotel's historical pattern and will assist with anticipating future demand patterns.

While a solid understanding of the historical pattern is very beneficial, understanding current trends should be weighted more heavily. Historical information is helpful to use as a base so hoteliers have a place to begin, but current booking information should supersede historical trends. This is because booking trends change, and hoteliers must adapt their forecasts to incorporate the current trends and weigh these more heavily.

Tracking this information is not always easy and of course some information may be easier to track than other information. Ease of tracking depends on the technology available and the processes that each hotel follows. For those using technology that limits the ability to track or retrieve any of the previously listed information, a business process needs to be put into place allowing it to be tracked from this point forward. For those using an automated revenue management system, this information is most likely being tracked and can be easily accessed.

The following are key points for each hotel to address before a demand forecast can be created:

- Identify the current technology that is being used such as the CRS, PMS, SCS, and RMS. It is important to review each and understand what information is able to be retrieved and/or tracked;
- Identify reports that are available and that can provide the necessary information;
- Identify all gaps in tracking ability. In other words, what information are you not able to retrieve from existing technology? What is missing?
- Where possible, implement manual business processes to track the missing information to close the gaps.

For those who lack sophisticated technology to help track much of this information, it is vital that you capture as much as humanly possible. It may not be possible to gather and track everything but the more you are able to track, the more accurate your demand forecast will be. It may require something as simple as using Excel spreadsheets to enter the data and possibly even cross reference the information so it can be sliced and diced according to the needs of the hotel.

## The Process

Putting together a demand forecast can be quite overwhelming as there are multiple steps and requirements. As mentioned earlier the methodology to create a demand forecast can be broken down into steps that are technical in nature and easy to learn. But it also includes a level of intuition or "gut" feeling which is not easy to learn. A certain comfort level with it will develop over time. It comes easier to some than to others.

This section will outline a step-by-step process for putting together a demand forecast. However, depending on the sophistication of each hotelier's forecasting tool some steps outlined may or may not apply. Therefore, each hotelier must identify the steps that apply to the specific tool customized for their corresponding hotel or organization.

The flow chart below outlines the process. The explanation supporting the flow chart is provided immediately following.

The first step in putting together a demand forecast is identifying the right forecasting tool. There are probably as many versions of forecasting tools as there are hotels. Some hotel companies have a corporate standard while others do not. The key is finding the right forecasting tool that works for each hotel. It is also important to realize that a hotel will gain only as much benefit from the demand forecast as the amount of time and information put into it.

Once the tool is identified and agreed upon within the organization, it is time to set it up to reflect the constants of each hotel — for example, the customized market segments, the total number of rooms in the hotel, and any type of special parameters that may be specific to each hotel's forecasting philosophy, such as whether to include out-of-order rooms in the availability count. Some companies opt to include out-of-order rooms in their availability count and some consider they are not available for sale and therefore they do not include them. If they are not included, they do not impact the hotel's RevPAR.

The next step is to determine how far out the demand forecast should be completed. It is recommended that the demand forecast be completed for as far out as the hotel receives bookings. For example, for a hotel that receives group inquiries five years in advance, the demand forecast should be put together five years out.

Now it is time to collect all of the information that is required and available to you in support of creating the forecast. (see prior "Important Things to Know" section)

Now the data entry begins — by market segment.
1. Enter special parameters such as out-of-order rooms on specific days, as well as special events or demand generators.
2. Enter all of the "on the books" information including number of rooms, revenue, and ADR. This should be done day-by-day for as far out as there are bookings — including group bookings (blocks).
3. Enter the projected (gain or loss) demand for each market segment day-by-day. This should be done as far out as bookings are accepted.

Entering the projected demand for each market segment for every day into the future is obviously the most challenging part of demand forecasting. And remember, the projected demand means that it should reflect the total amount of demand a hotel would enjoy absent any constraints — the unconstrained demand. What this means for this forecast is that you must ignore length of stay restrictions, overselling, price restrictions, and any other types of restrictions. The projected demand number needs to reflect the total number of rooms the hotel could sell without restrictions or limits.

Use the information that is available to assist with identifying the demand for each day. Reference some or all of the following information as it is applicable:

■ Historical information by market segment for the same day in the previous year.
■ Demand generators that may be different from year to year.
■ Current booking pace; compare it with the previous year's booking pace if it is available. Identify differences to assist with adjusting the historical information and apply to demand information.

■ Identify patterns such as every Tuesday in the month of March historically looks the same. Apply these patterns (if they still make sense based on the current booking trends).
■ Refer to the internal analysis — what may be different within the organization compared to previous years? Are there new products or services that may impact the demand? Are there new targeted segments?
■ Refer to the external analysis — what may be different within the market compared to previous years? Is there a new product? Are competitors targeting new segments compared to previous years?

Once you are confident in the demand by market segment, by day, enter the information into the forecast. This includes rooms, revenue, and ADR information. Congratulations! The most difficult part of the forecasting process is now complete.

## Strategic Forecasting
The strategic forecast is used to support strategic objectives such as understanding the impact of the demand forecast and its effect on occupied rooms. The strategic forecast is the place where hoteliers will assign their rate strategies based upon the demand forecast.

### Important Things to Know
The two major requirements to complete this forecast are:
1. Demand forecast
2. Pricing strategy

As mentioned, the demand forecast will be used for the creation of strategies such as which rates will be offered for specific time periods based on the unconstrained demand.

The pricing strategy is important because it will be required when creating rate strategies based on the forecast. The rates that will be assigned to the demand forecast will be based on the hotel's pricing strategy and will be in line with its philosophy.

### The Process
As mentioned earlier, the demand forecast is the most challenging forecasts. But the strategic forecast has the potential to be a more streamlined process provided the hotelier sets up the hotel's rates according to the demand forecast.

Depending on the hotel's location around the globe, common pricing strategies may include a length-of-stay approach, a dynamic pricing approach, or the more traditional method of static pricing. Regardless of the approach used, the hotelier can set up a process that defines a "base" rate from which rate adjustments can be made in accordance with the demand forecast.

Using a dynamic pricing approach as an example, the Best Available Rate (BAR) tends to be used as the base rate. That is the lowest standard rate that the hotel is prepared to offer to guests. Generally, all other rates will be defined from this rate, often as a percentage. For example, a 10% discount may be applied to all consortia rates off of BAR or an additional 20% might be added to BAR for a package offer. Any time the BAR rate is changed, the other rates are adjusted accordingly.

The strategic forecast is much easier if you have built in pre-defined thresholds and aligned BAR rates according to various levels of the demand forecast. In another example, if the demand forecast for a given day is predicted to be 90% occupancy or higher, the BAR, consortia, and LRTA could all be open and available for booking while all non-LRTA, government rates, and discount packages are closed and not available for booking on corresponding days.

Setting up these rules will vary depending on the technology in place at the hotel. For example, a hotel with a revenue management system (RMS) can set up these parameters within the RMS, making the process fairly seamless. Those working in a manual environment can accomplish the same results by taking the time to lay out a framework for rate availability based on specific parameters outlined in the demand forecast. It is an investment of time but will make it much easier to manage in the long term.

The strategic forecast should be completed for the same timeframe as the demand forecast. It should also be updated and reviewed each time the demand forecast is updated.

## Revenue Forecasting

Once the strategic forecast is complete the next step is to complete the revenue forecast.

### *Purpose*

The purpose of the revenue forecast is to provide hoteliers with a realistic picture of probable future occupied rooms that they can use for budget comparison purposes and to identify variances.

This is the forecast that is appropriate to share with stakeholders to communicate the realistic forecast for the hotel. It is not, however, to be confused with the budget. Instead, it should be used as a comparison to the budget in order to understand the variances (both positive and negative).

### *Important Things to Know*

In terms of the information that will be needed, the revenue forecast is similar to the demand forecast. It requires the use of historical patterns and current trends to forecast future realistic occupied rooms, revenue, and ADR. Therefore, the information that was reviewed for the purpose of creating the demand forecast will also be used for the revenue forecast. However, this time the focus will be on what hoteliers believe will actualize for the hotel.

The following items should be referenced in the development of the revenue forecast.

- Arrivals
- Cancellations
- Demand Generators
- Denials / Regrets
- Departures
- Early Departures
- Extended stays
- Group Rooms
- Group Pick Up
- Group Wash
- Lead time / Booking Pace by Segment
- Length of Stay Pattern
- No Shows (both guaranteed and non-guaranteed)
- "On the books" Bookings
- Rate Changes
- Revenue
- RevPAR
- Segmentation Mix
- Transient Rooms
- Walk-ins

### *The Process*

The process of creating the revenue forecast is essentially the same as the process for the demand forecast. The only difference may be in the forecast totals. The same information should be included, and the same patterns should be applied. This time, however, the total forecasts by market segment may (or may not) be lower than the unconstrained information.

1.  Review special parameters such as out of order rooms on specific days, as well as special events or demand generators to ensure they are complete and up to date. Because they should be the same as the demand forecast, they can be carried over from that tool.

2.  Ensure all of the "on the books" information including number of rooms, revenue, and ADR is accurate and up-to-date. This should be done day-by-day for as far out as there are bookings and should include group bookings (blocks).

3.  Now it is time to enter in the projected (gain or loss) forecast for each market segment day-by-day.

Remember, the projection should reflect only the totals you believe will actualize for the hotel. The timeframe for how far into the future this should be completed will vary by hotelier. Most will need to complete one year into the future, but some may need to go farther out.

Information is available to assist with identifying the demand for each day. Reference some or all of the following information as it is applicable for each respective hotel:

- Historical information by market segment for the same day in the previous year.
- Identified demand generators that are different from year to year.
- Compare the current booking pace with the previous year's booking pace if it is available. Identify differences to assist with adjusting the historical information and to apply to demand information.
- Identify and apply patterns (e.g., "every Tuesday in the month of March historically looks the same").
- Refer to the internal analysis — what may be different within your hotel or organization compared to previous years? Are there new products or services that may impact the demand? Are there new targeted segments?

- Refer to the external analysis — what may be different within the market compared to previous years? Are there new products? Are competitors targeting new segments as compared to previous years?

Once you are confident in the demand by market segment, by day, enter the information into the forecast. This includes rooms, revenue and ADR.

4.  The final step for the revenue forecast is to determine how often it should be completed. This is another area that will vary by hotel based on specific requirements and needs. There are a couple of factors that need to be considered when deciding how often to complete the revenue forecast:
    - The most obvious factor is the requirements of each hotel or company's management. Some companies require weekly updates for one to three months into the future while others require monthly updates for one full year out;
    - The other factor is how busy the hotel is and what type of activity it has. Hotels located in a downtown city center that cater to business travelers will most likely have a very busy booking window 30 days out but find that outside 30 days the activity significantly slows down. In this case the hotelier may opt to revisit the revenue forecast two to three times per week for the next 30 days and less often for 30+ days.

## Operational Forecasting
The operational forecast is the final forecast created.

### Purpose
The purpose of the operational forecast is exactly what the name implies — it is for operations. It provides the operational departments with the information they need to know in order to properly prepare their areas of responsibility.

### Important Things to Know
The operational forecast is relatively easy to put together and, in most cases, requires only basic information that is easily extracted from the revenue forecast. Some hotels will simply distribute the revenue forecast to the appropriate departments while others prefer to extract

the specific information required for each department and distribute that.

In order to complete an operational forecast:
- Identify each of the departments that will rely on this forecast.
- Understand the specific information each department requires and for what purpose. For example, front desk and housekeeping will most likely need to know the arrivals, departures, and expected stay-overs and early departures for each day in order to staff their departments appropriately.
- Identify how often and when each department requires updates.

### The Process
The process for the operational forecast is relatively simple once you have identified the appropriate information.

1. Identify a format that works best for the hotel. The required information can either be extracted directly from the revenue forecast with some supporting formulas to calculate certain information (e.g., total occupied rooms / Average Length of Stay [ALOS] will result in arrivals) or be entered by hand into a spreadsheet. Some hotels find it helpful to include arrivals and departures so front desk and housekeeping can track business volumes for staffing. This information is often readily available in the hotel's PMS.
2. Determine a schedule for distribution, communicate this schedule, and stick to it.
3. Upon completion, distribute the report to the appropriate departments.

## Questions for Review
- What are the four primary types of forecasts?
- What are the objectives for each of the primary forecasts?
- What information is needed in order to properly complete each forecast?
- How often should reach forecast type be completed?
- What is the most important goal of forecasting?

# CHAPTER 8
## PRICING

### Learning Objectives
- To understand the impact of pricing on the bottom line
- To comprehend the differences between strategic and tactical pricing, and how to leverage each
- To understand the pitfalls of discounting, and alternatives to it

There is a science to implementing correct pricing for perishable room inventory, and there is an art to applying the appropriate principles to price the right product for the right customer at exactly the right time. When a pricing opportunity is missed, the result is often lost revenue, both on rooms and the hotel's other outlets. Pricing is also a key factor in driving the "right" customer to the hotel. This is why the revenue optimization discipline is critical and powerful for hotels.

When revenue optimization principles are not applied appropriately, downturns in business can cause a panic reaction that sends prices spiraling. The recovery from this type of knee-jerk reaction can take months or even years. A good example of this is the "Great Recession" of 2008 and the impact it had on hotel ADRs. Hotels dropped prices during the downturn and struggled to recover as quickly as demand was driving occupancies.

It is critical for hotels to remain true to revenue optimization best practices even when they find they are on course to miss budgeted revenues. Employing congruent, sensible, and practical revenue optimization practices is essential to successful long-term revenue optimization.

While pricing is a key factor in driving the "right" customer to the hotel, it is no longer the biggest factor. Today many consumers value other elements more than the actual price itself. Consumers are focused on consumer reviews along with the price as part of the decision making. Hotels with negative reviews are often quickly disregarded from the selection process.

As Dr. Kelly McGuire states in Hotel Pricing in a Social World: Driving Value in the Digital Economy, "Driving revenue and stealing market share is no longer mainly about just competing on price. Consumers are clearly turning to user-generated content to aid in the purchasing decisions, in particular, reviews. This means that hoteliers must not only keep an eye on how they are priced relative to the market, but also on how they are positioned in terms of reputation."[11]

Industry experts agree that when a hotel realizes revenue growth through rate, 95% flows to the bottom line, and if the growth comes through occupancy, approximately 50% flows to the bottom line.

This drives home the importance of pricing and the impact of appropriately developing a hotel's pricing strategy and managing the tactical execution of the strategy. In the past, revenue optimization practices had a strong focus on the management of stay controls, such as length of stay requirements in an effort to maximize revenues, and pricing was secondary. Today, the focus has grown to place more of a priority on the importance of pricing strategies.

Pricing strategies allow hotels to charge different room rates for the same or similar rooms according to customers' characteristics and needs. For example, a senior citizen traveler looking for a AAA discount has different needs, different characteristics, and a different willingness to pay than a corporate traveler has. As a result, they may book the exact same room but pay a much different price. Along with the different price may be certain booking requirements or unique restrictions.

Once the market segments are defined for a hotel, it is up to the revenue professional, along with the director of sales, to ensure a healthy mix of the segmentation. This is a key component to optimizing a hotel's pricing strategy and approach.

Since hoteliers offer multiple rates for essentially the same room type it is critical to understand the importance of pricing and all it encompasses.

### Strategic Pricing
Developing a long-term pricing strategy is a very important part of a hotel's overall revenue optimization process. Proper creation of a pricing strategy and proper deployment of that strategy will ultimately provide the hotel with an opportunity to identify and capture the optimal revenue opportunities in both good and bad economic times.

Too many hoteliers take a tactical approach as opposed to starting with a strategic approach. Developing a long-term strategy allows hotels to look out into the future and do a proper analysis of the realistic needs and opportunities and determine the most appropriate pricing for their hotel in the current market. This is the best approach and is a good start to ensuring the hotel has an eye out to the future and is focused on long-term benefits.

A strategic pricing strategy allows hotels to be proactive and provide guidelines and plans for the entire hotel sales team to effectively sell the products.

Pricing guidelines will allow the sales department to effectively and confidently quote rates for the future because they will know the price points for specific demand periods and specific dates. With pricing guidelines, the sales team will have the opportunity to analyze the potential business themselves and work quickly with the customer without having to take the time to discuss pricing with the revenue professional unless there is an unusual circumstance. Ultimately, this allows for more empowerment and confidence in the sales department as they will have a solid understanding of the hotel's future outlook, peak demand times, and times of need. In addition, if the sales department's incentive is tied to profitability as discussed earlier, having pricing guidelines will help them reach their personal goals.

Strategic pricing done right:
- Reflects overall corporate or hotel strategies such as maximum growth, maximum revenue, or new market growth objectives.
- Communicates positioning, image, and branding for targeted segments.

- Communicates expectations of product quality, status, and value to prospective customers.
- Determines long-run revenue flows and ROI.
- Can be used as part of the process for building long-term customer relationships.

### Creating a Pricing Strategy

Creating the pricing strategy must include all of the revenue team members. This is something that must be done as a team and not by one person alone. Each revenue team member will have a unique perspective and important input. Additionally, this will ensure that buy-in to the final strategy is positive across the board with everyone who must support the strategy moving in the same direction.

Creating a proper pricing strategy requires an understanding of customers' willingness to pay, customer segmentation, consumer psychology, competitive value analysis, market research, value creation, and, of course, revenue optimization.

Every pricing strategy must address the elements outlined in the following chart.

| ELEMENT | PURPOSE / CONSIDERATIONS |
|---|---|
| Mix of Business | The most effective way to increase ADR is to change the mix of business. Be careful not to overinflate pricing in one segment as the effect can potentially decrease ADR. Focus on how to replace discount segments with higher-rated segments such as BAR, consortia, or corporate negotiated. |
| SWOT Analysis | This tool helps develop a solid understanding of the hotel's unique attributes, and the strengths and weaknesses for both services and product. Learn more and see an example in Appendix B. |
| Market Position | Every hotel must carefully evaluate itself compared to its competitors. It is important to understand the market position of the hotel within the competitive set. This is an essential part of determining the pricing for the hotel. See chapter 8 for more information. |
| Seasonal Demand | One of the fundamentals for a pricing strategy is to understand market demand for the various seasons in the market. Flexibility for seasonal rates must be taken into consideration. |
| Day-of-Week Demand | In addition to considering seasonal demand, it is also important to take day-of-week flexibility into consideration. What are the hotel's peak days throughout the week? What are they for each season? |
| Length of Stay (LOS) | Offering pricing based on various lengths of stay can lead to increases in revenue simply by pricing according to the length-of-stay demand. It can, however, be a challenge to manage without automation such as a sophisticated revenue management system. |
| Customer Segmentation | Understanding the customer segmentation specific to the market and to your hotel is critical. Every hotel must identify the target customer segments appropriate for the hotel and accordingly create price points to satisfy each segment. |

Chart continues next page

| | |
|---|---|
| Special Need Periods | Identify the hotel's need periods and areas of opportunity for promotional offers. This may include holidays, special events in the market, or low demand times. Identify these times and create promotional offers as part of the hotel's overall strategy. This will ensure the team will not need to create something at the last minute and potentially miss an opportunity. |
| Room Type or Product Demand | Understanding the product needs within a market and how the hotel can optimize the opportunities is critical. It is also important to know the demand by room type. For example, is the hotel targeting families for vacations? At the most basic level, this will indicate a need for family suites, rooms with two beds, and/or connecting rooms. Think about: <br>• When can the hotel sell each room type at full rate versus needing to set oversell strategies and upgrade for free? Different demand periods (e.g., seasonal, day-of-week) will dictate these strategies. <br>• Hotels can work to transform lower room types into higher room types. For example, identify opportunities to combine room categories so that lower rated rooms are eliminated or limited. This will help lift the hotel's revenue and ADR. <br>• For group or business travel markets, identify opportunities to create a higher-level room type offered at a higher rate. <br>• Managing room type availability for contracted rates can be another part of a hotel's strategy. Close out availability or set restrictions on lower room types for the contracted rates, and only sell the higher rated room types. |
| Channel Strategies | Defining multi-channel pricing strategies is a must in today's distribution landscape. Identify all of the appropriate channels — offline and online — in which the hotel participates or should participate. Address both pricing, and the influence of consumer reviews visible through various channels. |
| Customer Loyalty | Every hotel has specific customers or customer types that must be considered in their pricing. Ensure that loyalty program customers are addressed in the pricing strategy. |
| Education | Education on the pricing strategy process and approach is especially important for sales and reservations. Educate reservations about how they are expected to sell the product. How should rates be quoted? Top down or bottom up? Should they offer the rate up front followed by the description, or should they offer the description and benefits followed by the rate? There are many different approaches that can be taken by reservations and sales. It is critical to establish in the sales strategy how to sell the value of the products and rates. |
| Room Costs | Knowing the direct, indirect, and incremental costs associated with rooms puts a spotlight on profits and ensures they are incorporated into the pricing strategy. |
| Rate Fencing Rules | Ensure that the revenue team strategizes about the various fencing rules that can be applied to specific rates. This will allow hotels to define booking conditions or parameters that need to be met in order to book a room rate. This will ensure that the hotel strategically considers and protects specific segments from being diluted from lower or discounted rates. |
| Distribution Strategy | In the past, revenue teams had to have a strategy to address price parity. That is, did they offer the same rates on all channels, or did they have a best rate guarantee? Today, with metasearch sites like Kayak, TripAdvisor, Google Hotel Finder, and so on, it is extremely easy for consumers to find the "lowest rate." This reinforces the need to ensure that a sound channel management/distribution strategy is in place. For most, this requires more sophisticated connectivity to allow for easier rate management. |
| Channel Costs | Understand the cost by channel and its impact on ADR. See chapter 9 on Inventory Control for more information. |
| Cost of Acquisition | It is critical that hoteliers understand the impact on profits of all costs of all distribution channels. |
| Consumer Reviews | Consumer reviews and feedback will impact a hotel's ability to properly define its pricing strategy. Therefore, it is critical that hoteliers understand the consumer's perception of the hotel. What are they saying about the hotel online? What are they saying about the competition online? |
| Booking Policies | Since customers shop around it is important to remain competitive and ensure that booking policies do not conflict with each other. Clearly define the booking policies (e.g., cancellations, prepaid bookings) for each rate type and each distribution channel, and thoroughly understand the booking policies in the market. <br><br>Do not fall victim to customers who book early and then find a better deal on a last-minute site. They will cancel their original higher-priced reservation and book through the last-minute channel. |

In addition to understanding the elements that must be considered for the pricing strategy, it is important to understand the timeframe for which the pricing strategy should be created.

Like the demand forecast, a pricing strategy must be created for the same timeframe for which the hotel receives booking requests. If the hotel receives group inquiries five years out, then the pricing strategy must support this timeframe. Hoteliers must also understand the booking windows in detail, and deploy pricing based on the customers' propensity to book specific rates at specific times.

### Pricing Strategy Best Practices

1. Share the results of any pricing research and the overall pricing strategy with the sales team. It will help build confidence in the pricing strategy.
2. If booking pace is slow, do not assume rate is the problem. It may be something else, in which case a price cut is not the answer.
3. Include the sales team in the pricing strategy development process. It will enhance buy-in and reduce roadblocks.
4. Be sure the sales team, including reservations, is asking good questions about customer needs. Qualifying the customer helps reduce the necessity to discount.
5. Make the connection between the product offering and what the customer wants.
6. Ensure the offer is focused on the value, not the price. Educate the reservations team on making the offer, asking for the sale, and overcoming objections.
7. Negotiate later in the process. Giving discounts in the early stages of discussions does not make the customer feel they received as high a value as they do if the discount is given at the end.
8. Price objections are often a disguise for deeper concerns.
9. Establish the hotel's value early or the hotel will always be defending price.
10. Include the pricing strategy as part of the annual business plan. The more specific the direction the better.
11. When determining costs to support a pricing analysis, consider how the costs change as the volume changes. What are the incremental costs?
12. Put a process in place that requires reviewing the number of price adjustments made over time.

If there are too many adjustments, identify the concerns and address them.
13. Measure the margin performance of the sales team and reward high performers. Provide incentives to book business during low-demand periods.
14. Implementing a price increase can be done in several different ways. For example, consider reducing discounts to less profitable customer segments.
15. Be sure to communicate the value being delivered after the sale is made. This will reduce price resistance the next time they buy.
16. Be sure to measure the won/lost ratio for all inquiries. It will help to identify trends and reduce the perceived need to be reactive.
17. Consider the costs of retention versus those of acquisition when determining the discounting policy.
18. Watch for "system beaters," those who complain every time they inquire about a room or service just to get a discount.

### Keeping the Focus

If it has not already been stressed enough throughout this section, and even throughout this book, it is important to review it again: it is absolutely vital that hoteliers ensure pricing is driven by an overall strategic focus and plan. This should apply to every aspect of revenue optimization.

High-value product and service providers must base their pricing decisions on the changing needs of their customers, not on the pricing moves made by their lowest-cost competitors.

In weak economies, hoteliers employing smart pricing outperform their nervous rivals by confidently honing their strategic focus and deeply understanding changes in customer demand.

### Pitfalls of Losing Focus

It is very easy to fall into a trap and believe that the best thing to do is abandon the pricing strategy and go rogue. When unexpected or even expected changes begin to occur — one of the most common expected changes is a competitor significantly dropping their rate — do not panic. First, it is important to do research to identify the reasoning for the change. The fact that a competitor decreases their rate or seemingly changes their strategy completely does not automatically require the same activity at your hotel. Perhaps the competitor received a last-minute group cancellation and they are desperately trying to fill the void. Perhaps they are panicking because they are finding they are not bringing in the level of business they had originally set out to get. Perhaps they have a general manager who forces changes without sound reasoning. Perhaps they have a revenue professional who is making poor revenue decisions. Their poor choice in tactics does not require other hotels to follow and make the same poor choices.

This is where developing and maintaining a strong SWOT analysis is critical. Having the right information on the hotels within the competitive set will help the revenue team better understand when hotels react and even understand the reasoning when the unexpected does occur.

Drastically modifying a pricing strategy — while in the short term it may drive short-term results — in the long term it may negatively impact customer confidence and can ultimately damage long-term pricing goals, specifically in relationship to improved market mix and market position. This damage can have long-term effects on the performance of the hotel that can last years. If you do not trust your pricing, how will others? Hotels that easily divert from their market position will struggle with revenue growth in the long term as they have degraded their value in the market.

If booking pace is slower than anticipated do not assume price is the problem. Do the research to identify the issue. If it is not pricing, then cutting prices is not the answer. That could mean immediate and unnecessary lost revenue.

Go back to the original strategy, how it was arrived at, and why. Are the foundational principles still the same? It is important for owners and asset managers to understand the long-term negative impacts on asset profitability as a result of focusing on short-term decisions such as covering cash flow. Those that continually tweak strategy are not allowing the overall strategy sufficient time to impact change.

During good times hoteliers are more apt to pay attention to their own needs and price as a benchmark of what the market will bear. During downturns, hoteliers tend to follow the herd to the bottom. There are always opportunities to maintain or grow rate even in a down economy.

## Getting Tactical

As mentioned earlier, strategy setting is an ongoing process. However, there are times when it may be necessary to adjust the strategy due to unforeseen circumstances and make some tactical changes.

Tactical pricing is the process of reviewing and changing the existing long-term strategy in order to have a shorter term, more immediate impact. It can be very beneficial if considered and applied only when the overall long-term strategy needs to be adjusted due to unforeseen circumstances. However, it is important to fully understand that tactics should never ignore the overall hotel revenue optimization strategy.

Tactical pricing, when done correctly, allows hoteliers to:
- Manipulate last-minute or late-booking demand through price incentives.
- Achieve short-term cash flow.
- Determine daily revenue yield.
- If appropriate, match competition by the quickest available method and send warning signals to the competition of aggressive action.
- Promote brand or product trial for first-time customers.
- Provide a vital, short-run tool for crisis management.

Tactical pricing can be an opportunity to drive performance from targeted markets and achieve short-term cash flow as long as it is supported by the hotel's overall long-term strategy. It is important that the tactical strategy supports the market position of the hotel. Tactical strategies that are deployed on their own can be costly and less impactful. Tactical solutions utilized in conjunction with long-term strategies can often help jump start a long-term revenue strategy as long as they are used sparingly.

The key point to tactical pricing is to use caution in applying tactical solutions. Tactical pricing should be considered carefully and applied in a way that does not go against the hotel's overall strategy.

## Discounting

Most hoteliers agree that discounting is necessary during difficult economic times. It is also necessary during up times. Discounting is typically done to achieve additional revenues by enticing guests into booking hotel rooms by lowering rates in order to increase occupancy in the short term.

Research conducted by Cornell University's Center for Hospitality Research on the topic of discounting was released in two articles: "Why Discounting Doesn't Work;"[12] and, "Why Discounting Doesn't Work: A Hotel Pricing Update." [13]

According to the research, "Overall, for hotels that held their price below that of their competitive set, average percentage differences in occupancy was higher, but average percentage differences in RevPAR were lower as compared to the competition. For hotels that held their price high relative to their competitive set, on the other hand, average percentage differences in occupancy were smaller, but average percentage differences in RevPAR were greater."

Additionally, hotels with ADRs 12% to 15% lower than those of their competitive set had 10.38% higher occupancies but recorded a 4.44% lower RevPAR. However, hotels that priced 6% to 8% above their competitive set obtained a lower occupancy by 1.84% but a higher RevPAR by 5.02%. The research also included information about the different hotel market levels. The results show that the relationship holds true across all different hotel levels, from luxury to limited service.

In addition to the two cited above, many other research studies have proven that discounting is not the best course of action just because a hotel needs to achieve its budget or to generally increase revenues. Key findings over the years have shown that:

■ Hotels have not learned that dropping rates will not recover enough revenues to cover the discounting.
■ Discounting can cause price wars! And, it can cause "rates versus perceived services" issues. Too low of a price may damage a brand's perceived image.

According to Jessica Comaskey, CRME, Area Director of Revenue for Two Roads Hospitality's Chicago Athletic Association Hotel, "Discounting is not a demand generator unless the discounting is tied with a strong marketing plan. Discounting as it is practiced by most hotels allows for customers to buy up but does not necessarily drive demand. Instead discounting has a cascading effect that will impact the overall competitive landscape."

### Why Do Hotels Discount?
The basic principle and foundation of discounting is to try to fill rooms that would otherwise remain empty.

Discounting is an attempt to increase occupancy. This is achieved by potentially stealing market share from the competitive set by enticing leisure customers or price-sensitive customers who may respond to the perception of a better value.

Additionally, by increasing occupancy it provides the hotels with opportunities to generate revenues throughout the other revenue generating departments at the hotel. It also provides the hotel with more cash flow during difficult economic times. While there are some potential benefits to discounting it is of the utmost importance that hoteliers understand the complexity and dangers that discounting may potentially bring.

The following charts illustrate the complexities of discounting and how important it is to understand the impact discounting has on a hotel. They illustrate the occupancy needed in order to make up for the discounts that are applied to the rates.

Using this example, if a hotel running a 60% occupancy drops its rate by 10% it will now have to obtain a 66.7% occupancy in order to reach the same overall forecasted revenue. This increase in occupancy is necessary just to break even. In order to increase revenue, the hotel would have to achieve an occupancy greater than 66.7%.

A hotel that drops its rates by 20% and previously ran a 60% occupancy would need to obtain a 75% occupancy to make up for the lost revenue.

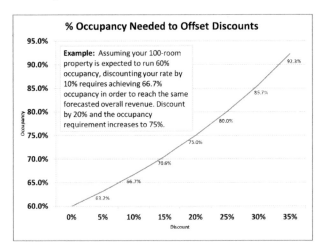

| Discount | Occupancy % | * | ADR | = | RevPAR | Revenue |
|----------|-------------|---|------|---|--------|---------|
| 0% | 60.0% | | $100 | | $60 | $6,000 |
| 5% | 63.2% | | $95 | | $60 | $6,000 |
| 10% | 66.7% | | $90 | | $60 | $6,000 |
| 15% | 70.6% | | $85 | | $60 | $6,000 |
| 20% | 75.0% | | $80 | | $60 | $6,000 |
| 25% | 80.0% | | $75 | | $60 | $6,000 |
| 30% | 85.7% | | $70 | | $60 | $6,000 |
| 35% | 92.3% | | $65 | | $60 | $6,000 |

*This scenario assumes your property has 100 rooms available to sell.*

The following simple model can be used by every hotel. Prior to offering any discount, determine the break-even point and how feasible it is that the discount can make up the lost revenue that it creates (by driving additional bookings).

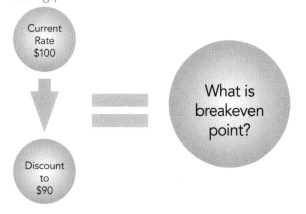

The break-even point is the number of additional reservations needed at the discounted rate in order to break even with the original potential revenue. That means that if a hotel is to apply a certain discount, there needs to be a high level of certainty that it can capture additional reservations over and above the break-even point.

| REVENUE GOAL | | $10,000 | |
|--------------|------|------|------|
| Price Points | $100 | $90 | $80 |
| Number of reservations needed to achieve the goal | 100 | 112 | 125 |

At a 10% discount ($90), the hotel will need to be certain it can capture an additional 12 reservations to achieve the same revenue goal. At a 20% discount ($80), the hotel will need to be certain it can capture an additional 25 reservations to achieve the same revenue goal.

A vital part of this exercise is to test it. Draw a line in the sand, record the probable outcome prior to discounting, and compare the actual results. Did the hotel achieve the desired gain? Continue to test over and over again. This will truly give you an idea of whether or not the discount will achieve the end goal.

It is important to note that during times of low demand in a market, the number of rooms needed to recoup the revenue lost as a result of discounting can be extremely challenging. Since discounting itself will not increase demand — instead it may help to shift share — the market impact of discounting must be considered.

If one hotel discounts to try to shift share, the next competitor may do the same in order to be competitive. This then turns into a price war and can easily become a vicious cycle where the hotels drive their own prices down. More about the pitfalls of discounting are explored in the following section.

It goes without saying that the break-even point is just one piece of the decision-making process. There are several other points that must be considered before the decision to discount a rate is made.

- Marketing Plan — "Discounting will ONLY create demand when it is tied directly with some type of marketing initiatives," offered Warren Jahn of IHG. What type of marketing plan will the hotel put into place to target the right segments and capture the right amount of additional reservations?
- Long-Term Impact — By offering this discount, what long-term impact will it have on the hotel?
- Ancillary Revenues — Can the hotel capture the segments which are likely to have solid spend in other areas of the hotel?
- Existing Business — By offering the discount will the hotel risk diluting existing business which may cancel reservations on hold and rebook at the newly offered discounted rate?
- Target Segment — By discounting the rate, are you targeting the appropriate customer? What type of customer will you be attracting?
- Hotel Staff Perception — Ask the customer-facing staff at the hotel what their perception is regarding rates. They are the ones talking directly with the customers and gaining feedback daily. What do they hear? What are their recommendations?
- Customer Perception — What is the customer's perception of your hotel? What other hotels do they

consider when booking? Who do they consider to be your competitors? Are they comparing pricing with the same competitive set you are? Many times, customers that are searching for that discount will be the most vocal on consumer review sites and most critical.

- Tracking — Are you tracking regrets and denials and reviewing the information? What does this data show you? Is it really price resistance that is the reason for the lack of bookings? Are you training your loyal customers to wait for discount offers? Have you changed their behavior and booking channel?
- Competitive Set — Why is the competitive set decreasing its rate? Following their lead without understanding the reason behind it is not a good strategy.

Before hotels even consider decreasing pricing, appropriate research must be done. Perhaps pricing is not the issue at all. Use caution before automatically jumping to discounting prices.

## Discounting Pitfalls

Deciding to discount rates without understanding the long-term impact is a mistake that is made by many hoteliers. Too many hoteliers automatically jump to offering discounts in an attempt to capture more of the demand. This may or may not be the right short-term approach and it may also create long-term challenges. Discounting rates does have a long-term impact which is often not understood by hoteliers. Often, rates are discounted to capture short-term demand, competitors follow, and then the consumer expects these same levels of rates to be available again.

According to Ypartnership, research shows that consumers will only accept up to a 5% increase in rate year-over-year. So, for hotels that discount their rates by 25% for short-term gain, this means it can take them five years to successfully bring their rate back up to its original starting place.

Hoteliers must also consider what discounting does to the demographics. It is important to anticipate change in the demographics. Good examples of this are hotels in Las Vegas as they rely heavily on ancillary revenues for their mainstream of income. When hotels in Las Vegas offer discounts, they find the customers enticed by the lower rates are those who go out or order pizza instead of those who eat in-house.

As mentioned, regardless of the reason, when hoteliers decide to discount their rates, experience shows that in all markets the majority, if not all, of the competitors will follow.

Hoteliers have many tools available to them today that allow competitors to see rate drops almost immediately. It goes without saying that if the competition then drops their rates, the first hotel to start the price drop will lower their price again…and so the cycle begins. This is a vicious cycle, often referred to as a "price war," that leads to devastating negative consequences.

Hoteliers attempt to lower their pricing in an attempt to maintain or increase their market share. But it often has a devastating, long-term impact on the hotel's performance and profitability.

Offering discounts in an attempt to steal market share also has its challenges. As stated in the previous section, discounting may allow one hotel to steal price sensitive customers away from another hotel, but what is to say this customer will remain loyal for their next booking? This customer will most likely book the hotel that is the least expensive and the price war continues.

Customers who are driven by discounting may fulfill short-term needs of the hotel but could be displacing potentially long-term loyal guests and higher yield segments. Discounting tends to drive performance from the costliest channels and can impact a hotel's long-term market mix needs. Hotels that rely on discounting to drive performance tend to struggle with performance from higher yield segments as those segments find value in BAR positioning. Consistent discounting will degrade the value of BAR and will impact a property's performance from higher yield, less costly channels.

The final pitfall of discounting remains that hoteliers continue to discount without the full understanding of the long-term negative impacts, the negative impact on RevPAR, and the vicious cycle of price wars.

Discounting, especially in the shape of qualified discounts, definitely has a place in the industry. But it must be approached and executed smartly and cautiously. This is where maintaining a long-term calendar of high-demand and low-demand dates are key. Understanding those dates will ensure minimal reliance on discounting to drive performance. Hoteliers need to ensure that strategy and rates are guarded and valued. If everyone can get on board with this philosophy, the industry as a whole will prevail.

### Qualified Discounts

Qualified discounts is a common market segment for which pricing is developed. It typically is a percentage discount off of BAR. A customer has to qualify for the discount hence the name. Rates such as Government, Senior Citizen, and AAA are all examples of this segment. These segments are often not made available unless the customer has a specific booking code for use online or requests the discount directly. Hotels control the discounts for these channels so should monitor and adjust based on demand, target customer, and day of week.

## Impact of Discounting

- Budgets and forecasts are impossible to manage.
- Risk of cannibalizing existing business and damage to brand.
- In an upward market, everyone follows the best practices of the market leader. In a downturn everyone follows the first person to panic.
- Smaller properties cannot make up in volume what they lose in rate.
- Decisions are based on competitors' action rather than the hotel's strategic initiatives and revenue needs.
- The ability to manipulate behavior using price is severely limited in a falling market.
- Discounting often 'doubles up' the loss of occupancy and rate.
- Profitability is often overlooked and can be adversely affected by reductions.
- Markets take years to recover.

## Pricing Methods

There are a variety of different pricing methods in use in hotels today. There is no "one size fits all" approach for pricing. The method a hotel uses will vary based on many different factors including market conditions, the hotel type, and the technology available to support pricing methods.

The following table outlines common pricing methods in the hotel industry along with the benefits and challenges of each.

| PRICING METHOD | DEFINITION | BENEFITs | CHALLENGES |
|---|---|---|---|
| Daily BAR Pricing | Price is determined by day and can change daily throughout a guest's stay | Allows the hotel to focus on the optimal rate for each individual day<br><br>Relatively easy to set up and manage | Rates can change throughout a guest's stay which can be frustrating and confusing to the customer<br><br>Opens the door for potential adjustments due to complaints and lack of understanding on the part of the consumer<br><br>Some systems do not support different rates by day<br><br>Some systems do not support a "pull" of different rates by day into a confirmation letter |
| Arrival Based Pricing | Pricing is determined for the guest's entire length of stay based on the day of arrival | Allows for optimization of rate for the entire stay based on when the guest is arriving | Requires significant technology for set up and ongoing management<br><br>Very challenging to manage without an automated revenue management system<br><br>Some OTAs do not support this pricing method; therefore, the hotel will always be out of parity |
| Full Pattern Length of Stay Pricing | Pricing is determined for the guest's entire length of stay based on the value of the entire length of stay | Allows for optimization of rate for the entire stay based on the length of stay | Extremely challenging to set up and manage without an automated revenue management system<br><br>Some OTAs do not support this pricing method; therefore, the hotel will always be out of parity |
| Slash Through Pricing | Strikes through the original price and offers a discount, with both the original and the slash-through price displayed | Gives the customer the impression that they are getting a deal<br><br>Helps hotel gain higher placement, and potential for more bookings, on the OTAs | Hotel may always appear to be "on sale" in the eyes of the consumer |
| Value Add Pricing | Allows hoteliers to add value to an existing rate (e.g., breakfast, executive level access, wifi, etc.) | Places emphasis on value versus discount<br><br>Gives the customer the impression that they are getting a deal<br><br>Helps hotel gain higher placement on the OTAs, and potential for more bookings | Value-adds can dilute the hotel's profit margins if not carefully designed<br><br>Need to ensure that the value-adds are not giving away what customers would have paid for anyway |
| Dynamic Packaging | Allows customers to customize their own packages based on their unique needs | Can be attractive to customers | Some systems do not support this approach<br><br>OTAs and GDSs do not support this functionality<br><br>Hotel may not realize efficiencies of scale due to multiple package elements needed |
| Dynamic Pricing | Selling the same products at different prices to different customers | Allows hotel to optimize rates by changing them as often as needed based on conditions of market and hotel | Can be confusing in the eyes of the consumer<br><br>If not done right, hotel can lose opportunity<br><br>Requires flexible technology and highly integrated systems to manage |

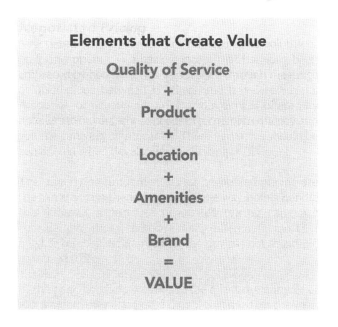

**Elements that Create Value**

**Quality of Service**

+

**Product**

+

**Location**

+

**Amenities**

+

**Brand**

=

**VALUE**

### Pricing Premiums

In addition to the pricing methodology and segmentation, there is another critical element that needs to be taken into consideration in order to maximize a hotel's pricing strategy.

Pricing by room type means determining the price premiums or price differences between each of the room types. The price differences between the room types is an opportunity to push a hotel's ADR during all demand times. Pricing premiums need to be evaluated on a regular basis. Factors to consider during each evaluation include:

- Time of year — Seasons or time of year will definitely impact how you price rooms. Peak demand times can yield higher premiums.
- Offers — Have a clear strategy of the premiums between the various offers to ensure that the differences make sense to the consumer from a demand and value perspective.
- Market — Understanding what the entire market has to offer for products will be key in some of the premium pricing. If the market lacks a product that your hotel has, then a higher premium can be charged (assuming there is the demand for it in the market).
- Competitive Set — Knowing the competitive set's pricing premiums will help guide some of the premiums to be set. For example, if your competitive set is charging an additional $200 for suites over their base room type and

you are charging $80, then there may be an opportunity to increase your premium. Of course, understanding the products and doing a product comparison is critical to support the decisions.

- Today's Usage — Be sure that the hotel is set up to track paid bookings by room type. This will help determine if there is strong demand for a product. If so, opportunity may exist to increase the pricing. Conversely, lack of demand or paid bookings may indicate premiums that are too aggressive.
- Conversion — It is essential to evaluate conversion of room types to understand if the premiums are helping to drive ADR. If a premium is overpriced, the conversion will be low, and those room types will be used as complimentary upgrades. If the conversion is high, there is a possibility to increase the premium. It is important to evaluate regularly as overpriced premiums can negatively impact a property's ability to drive ADR as they are relying on the base category room type to drive performance.

### Price Points

For pricing methods to succeed, appropriate price points must be established. In the simplest terms, price points are multiple levels of rates that are offered based on the demand for the product. The price at which the hotel decides to offer its product (based on the customer's willingness to pay) is a price point.

Each customer segment has a varying level of willingness to pay. For example, the customer who is price sensitive and time conscious generally pays less by reserving in advance. The customer who is willing to pay more books the room one or two days prior to their stay and often does pay more. This demonstrates the need for a hotel to create appropriate price points according to the demand from each segment while considering the local market and the hotel's position within it.

Creating price points can be challenging as it is important to ensure the right number of price points that allow the hotel to manage according to demand. If there are too few price points, a hotel risks losing customers who may have been willing to book at other rates. If there are too many, the hotel risks the ability to manage rates appropriately and effectively. There is no one recipe or formula for creating a hotel's price points. However, there are best practices and guidelines for the revenue team to consider.

| | |
|---|---|
| Booking Windows | Understanding the booking windows by segment can help determine various price points to be offered based on time of booking. |
| Value-Based Pricing | Price the products based on the value created for the consumer. |
| Consumer Reviews | Similar to Value-Based Pricing, hoteliers should consider feedback and reviews from the consumers. Compare the hotel's reviews against its competitors' reviews and pricing for helpful insights. |
| Cost | Know the fixed and variable costs associated with the products. Be sure these costs are calculated into pricing to understand their implications on profit. |
| Demand Curve | Consider how the pricing will impact the demand. |
| External Factors | Know what external factors may impact pricing. Are there local restrictions, such as government per diem rates? Will the hotel's pricing impact competitors' pricing and trigger price wars? |
| Perception | There are certain price points at which consumers become more willing to book a room. For example, instead of offering a rate at $200, a better perceived rate may be $199 or $195. |
| Positioning | Know your position in the market. Is pricing a key factor in your positioning? Are you positioning the hotel on value? For a hotel that positions itself as an exclusive luxury hotel, a low price can hurt its image. Price does need to be consistent with the positioning. Consumers hold true to the idea that you get what you pay for. |

## Customer Segment Pricing

The power in pricing clearly sits with the consumer. The consumer decides the price and the conditions they are willing to accept. And the definition of what is acceptable will vary tremendously for any product, depending on the consumer's circumstances at any particular point in time.

Consumer behavior, however, is not easy to predict. The factors that drive the purchasing decision and the price the consumer is willing to pay are not necessarily linked to demographics or psychographics. The same individual can exhibit different behavior when purchasing the same product.

One example of this is the consumer who regularly stays at the same hotel and books the same type of room and

the purpose of the stay is generally for business. This person generally makes the reservation a few days prior to the arrival date, confirms a business rate, and can expense the cost of the hotel stay back to the company for which he or she is traveling. However, the same person can book the same type of room when traveling for pleasure and the characteristics of their needs will be different. In this case, they may book further in advance and want a value-based price as this expense will come directly out of their own pocket.

Hotels must identify the types of customers they have and the prices the customers are willing to pay for utilizing the hotel's products and services. The following table is a guideline and some parameters to use in understanding what this means for a hotel. It is one example and must be customized for each market and hotel specifically.

| PHYSICAL CHARACTER-ISTICS | HIGH PRICE | LOW PRICE |
|---|---|---|
| View | Pool view, ocean view, hill view, city view | Non-scenic view |
| Size | Larger rooms offering more facilities | Smaller rooms with fewer facilities |
| Temporal | Weekday bookings | Weekend bookings |
| Length of Stay | Shorter stay — one or two days | Longer stay — several days or weeks |
| Flexibility | Cancellations and rebooking allowed with little or no penalty | High penalty for cancellation and schedule changes |
| Time of Purchase | Bookings made close to arrival date | Bookings made far in advance |
| Privileges | Awarded loyalty privileges | No loyalty privileges |
| Size of Business Provided | Corporate business customers book and stay frequently | Self-funding vacationers booking infrequently |
| Point of Sale | Physical delivery of confirmations | Confirmations sent by e-mail or phone |

## Negotiated Pricing

Negotiated pricing, sometimes referred to as volume or preferred pricing, is a basic concept that has long been embraced by hoteliers. It is established through meetings or discussions between hoteliers and travelers/buyers. A special, or negotiated, price or discount is offered by hoteliers to buyers whose needs in terms of frequency and volume can vary significantly. These variances should be considered when developing the pricing or discount.

The underlying fundamentals for negotiated pricing are the same across the industry, but the way hotels handle the different aspects of negotiated pricing can vary considerably. Today, there are many different factors that need to be considered, making the process not as simple as it used to be.

In the past, hoteliers would ask the client the number of room nights they estimated they would need for the year.

Based on those production estimates, hoteliers would look up the rate they should quote based on where the total volume fell in a predetermined chart of volume ranges and rates. The focus was mainly on the estimated production for the year. It did not take into consideration profits, actual production, time of year, and so on. Today, most hoteliers understand the importance of focusing on more than just the production in determining the best pricing structure for negotiated rates.

Depending on the resources, experience, and technology that is available, hotels will have varying levels of sophistication in their approach. However, it is extremely important that all hotels embrace modern industry best practices for negotiated pricing structure. The following are factors that must be considered when creating the pricing structure for negotiated accounts. The goal is to understand which accounts bring the most value versus those with just the most production.

| ESTIMATED VOLUME | IDENTIFY THE TOTAL VOLUME |
|---|---|
| Seasonal Usage Pattern and Day of Week | The ideal negotiated accounts are those that have people who travel during the times when your hotel needs the business, during your slower months and/or slower days of the week for example. |
| | Identify the estimated stay pattern and include the time of year the guests are traveling. For example, determine the typical travel months and the day of week for travel. |
| | This information is a key factor in deciding the appropriate value of this company to your hotel. Therefore, this will impact the most appropriate rate and room type to offer. |
| | For example, if a company typically travels during your hotel's peak week days and/or peak months only, then the rate offer needs to reflect this. If you wish to still negotiate an offer with this company, offer a higher rate or room type that typically has lower demand. |
| Ancillary Revenues | Understand any additional revenues that may be applicable from this account. Ancillary revenues will definitely bring additional value to the account and will therefore have an impact on the rate that can be offered. |
| Booking Method | What is their method of booking? This will impact the profit to the hotel and, therefore, the value of the account. The rate offered should reflect this. |
| Fixed or Dynamic Pricing | Is the hotel prepared to work with a fixed or a dynamic pricing structure? Is the client prepared to work with a fixed or a dynamic pricing structure? |
| Expectations of Value Adds/Inclusions | Consider what inclusions the competitive is offering and ensure that the hotel's reservations and operations staff understand the expectations for any inclusions in the rate such as free wifi, parking, breakfast, etc. |

Determining the best pricing structure for negotiated accounts is one of the first steps to ensuring a focus on profit for each hotel. The second step is to include the factors used to evaluate an account's value to the hotel, as well as a review clause in the contract. If performance expectations are clearly defined for the account and the performance metrics are regularly reviewed with them, the hotel can more easily adjust the rate as necessary throughout the year based upon performance.

Including performance expectations, parameters, and goals in the contract communicates that the hotel has a clear expectation of the performance required from the account in order for the client to receive the rate offered in the agreement. The client then clearly understands that, should the performance expectations not be realized, the hotel has a legal right to change the rate and even potentially collect money due to the hotel to make up for lost profit based on missed performance goals.

Including a review clause allows the hotel and the client to review the actual production and true value of the account based on what has been realized. By doing this, it allows both parties to identify and understand any discrepancies, as well as identify where production or profit may be lacking and make immediate adjustments instead of having to wait until the following year's negotiations.

It is highly recommended that every hotel implements a tracking method that ensures each account's production can be easily reviewed. This tracking method needs to include the total production and have the serviceability to be viewed by day of week and time of year.

The review clause must also state the frequency of the reviews. It is highly recommended that the reviews be conducted quarterly. However, these should be reviewed internally within the hotel each month so that issues are identified as they occur. Hotel sales managers should always know the current performance of their accounts and should be prepared to discuss any performance issues as they happen.

One final point is to be sure that these reviews with the client actually take place each quarter. It is one thing to put the review clause in the contract, but it is quite another to prepare for and conduct them, and then take action based on the key performance metrics. The following is a guideline of areas that should be included in every negotiation process. It is broken out to include contract terms and items to include in the review clause.

| FACTOR | CONTRACT | REVIEW CLAUSE |
|---|---|---|
| Estimated Production | Include the estimated production in the contract. | Is the actual production in line with the estimated production? Ensure it is stated that this will be reviewed every month or quarter (whatever is deemed most appropriate and realistic by the hotel). |
| Stay Pattern | Include the estimated stay pattern that was provided by the client and used in the analysis in the contract. Ensure that it is outlined in as much detail as possible as this information is critical to the hotel's profitability. | Is the actual stay pattern production in line with the estimated stay pattern production? Ensure that it is stated in the review clause that this will be reviewed every month or quarter (whatever is deemed most appropriate and realistic by the hotel). |
| Room Types | All accounts should have more than one room type and rate negotiated in the terms of the agreement. A general guideline is to negotiate two to three room types. This allows for more booking options in general and more availability options when one room type is sold out. | |
| Last Room Availability (LRA) | This means that if any room is available—regardless of the specific room type available at the time of booking—the hotel must allow the company to book the available room type at the lowest negotiated rate. This should be reserved for only the highest value clients and offered in the contract/rate agreement only when necessary. A hotel should not have more than a few accounts with this included in their contract. This limits any opportunity to revenue manage this account. | |

## Opaque Pricing

Quite the opposite of negotiated pricing, opaque pricing is a practice that is used for selling hotel inventory at a price without revealing the specific hotel or hotel brand until after the completion of the booking transaction. It is targeted at transient, price-sensitive consumers who are not brand loyal.

Opaque pricing is most commonly used through sites such as priceline.com and hotwire.com. The primary target consumer who uses these sites is price sensitive, and flexible in their travel needs. Consumers see this as a way of being able to book a higher value hotel room at a much cheaper price. The hotelier's main goal in participating in this type of program is to fill rooms that would otherwise go unfilled.

However, not all hotels participate and offer their brands through these sites. Some hotels, especially those that are considered to be luxury brands, view these sites as potentially diluting their brand perception because the view of the customer is that these sites offer low rates. Hoteliers, however, need to understand that extremely low rates are not a requirement for participation in these programs. Discounting rates from the hotel's normal rates is required but going below what the hotel identifies as an appropriate rate for their market position is not required. The difference is in how the hotel creates and manages its pricing structure.

## Rate Fences

Discounted rates should be offered only to select market segments. Building effective rate rules or "fences" that limit the discounts to specific customer segments is key to an effective discounting strategy. By setting appropriate requirements that must be met to qualify for a particular rate, hotels can encourage purchases by some market segments, while preventing other, less price-sensitive customers from booking the lower rate. If used properly, rate fencing can be very successful. If not used properly it can be disastrous, resulting in huge trade-downs from one segment to another. In the end, the result is based on how well the offer is designed.

To develop good rate fences, a hotel must know its customers well and understand what types of rates and rules will be effective in attracting particular market segments. In addition, fairness and rate parity issues must be considered. There are four categories of commonly used rate fences.

1. Product: Limiting the offer to one or a set of products such as a specific room type or types
2. Transaction: Apply restrictions to the process of booking or ability to book such as restricting the booking window period and requiring advance booking of a specific number of days or weeks
3. Customer: Target a specific customer type
4. Availability: Apply restrictions to the availability such as requiring a specific number of nights in the stay

The following chart outlines examples of rate fences and their associated categories.

| RATE FENCES | | EXAMPLES |
|---|---|---|
| Room Related | Basic product | Room type |
| | | Room location or view |
| | | Room furnishings such as linens, bed, iPod player |
| | Amenities | Free breakfast, airport pick up, etc. |
| | | Toiletries |
| | | Valet parking |
| | Service level | Priority check in |
| | | Dedicated service hotlines |
| | | Personal butler |
| Transactional Characteristics | Time of booking or reservations | Discounts for advance purchase |
| | Location of booking or reservation | Guests booking rooms from different countries are charged different prices |
| | | Customers making their reservation online are charged a lower price than those making a reservation by phone |
| | Flexibility of reservation | Fees or penalties for canceling or changing a reservation |
| | | Non-refundable reservation fees |
| Consumption Related | Time or duration of use | Minimum length of stay |
| | | Saturday night stay |
| | Location of consumption | Price depends on departure location, especially in international travel |
| | | Prices vary by location (between cities, city center versus edges of the city) |
| Guest Related | Frequency or volume of consumption | Members of a certain loyalty-tier (e.g., platinum members) get priority pricing, discounts, or benefits |
| | Group membership | Child, student, senior citizen discounts |
| | | Affiliation with certain groups |
| | | Corporate rates |
| | Size of customer group | Group discounts based on size of group |
| | Geographic location | Local customers are charged lower rates than tourists |
| | | Customers from certain countries are charged higher prices than those from other countries |

## One-to-One Revenue Optimization

While rate fencing is an effective tool, increasing the level of one-to-one revenue optimization could have an even more significant impact on a hotel's profitability in the future. Revenue optimization has traditionally analyzed and predicted customer behaviors by segment. Hotel companies now realize the importance of understanding each individual customer's behaviors and patterns whether it is someone who stays frequently with a hotel or at multiple hotels within the same hotel company, or if it is someone who stays once or twice.

Hotel companies that can afford to utilize loyalty program databases or customer relationship management (CRM) databases can easily capture information about each individual customer. Most of these databases track the customer's purchase patterns in great detail. The more sophisticated systems can capture, store, and analyze additional information about each customer, including demographic profiles, booking source profiles, sales data, requests, complaints, and even survey responses.

There is a disconnect with revenue optimization, however. The majority of these systems are not linked to revenue management systems and many times are not even easily accessible to revenue professionals. In fact, this level of detail is not typically included in the revenue team discussions.

At some point, this information needs to be tapped to identify and better understand the most valuable customers and to examine customer profitability and lifetime value. By understanding more about each customer and their individual needs, behaviors, and buying patterns, hoteliers can enhance the relationship with that customer. The objective is to capture a greater share of the customer's spending by understanding their full and unique needs.

For the purpose of generating future demand, customer-centric revenue optimization will mean reaching out to past customers in a personalized way with targeted packages that optimize their response. This capability could include promotions to fill off-peak periods or advertising campaigns with a more targeted message sent to narrow customer sets with known behavioral responses. Based on an understanding of customers' responses to those offers, hotels will target and optimize promotions. Moreover, they will integrate promotions into their revenue management systems. New insights about customer behavior patterns can be used not only to grow and develop the customer base, but also to afford loyal customers differential treatment using revenue optimization processes.

Casino hotels typically do a good job in this area. They understand which guests are the top spenders. The hotels understand their customers' behaviors, focus offers around them, and continue to nurture these relationships.

For those hotels that cannot afford large, expensive databases to collect and access all of this information, other more affordable options are now available to help. While they may not provide the same level of sophisticated data that a full-blown CRM database may provide about specific customers, these tools will be helpful in understanding more about a customer. By putting the work into the set up and reporting, hoteliers can gain a lot of insight about who, what, where, and why customers are searching for their hotels.

Tools such as Google Analytics track the guest behavior on the brand websites. It measures where traffic comes from, what the traffic does when it lands on the brand website, and when the traffic converts. Again, it is not specific to unique customers, but it does provide insight into customer shopping trends and interests. Reports such as future dates and lengths of stay for which customers are shopping the hotel can be extracted.

**AFFINITY CATEGORY (REACH)**
64.13% of total sessions

| | |
|---|---|
| 5.52% | Movie Lovers |
| 4.94% | Cooking Enthusiasts / Aspiring Chefs |
| 4.55% | TV Lovers |
| 4.46% | Technophiles |
| 4.43% | Travel Buffs |
| 4.35% | Shoppers / Shopaholics |
| 4.33% | News Junkies & Avid Readers / Entertainment & Celebrity News Junkies |
| 3.43% | Home Decor Enthusiasts |
| 3.15% | Foodies |
| 2.87% | News Junkies & Avid Readers |

TripAdvisor also provides useful insights into a hotel's customers. Through its TripAdvisor Business Advantage Analytics Suite, the hotel can better understand its online visitors. Marry this information with the Google Analytics Affinity Category data to better understand how a value add, like a cooking class weekend, is received by the target customer.

## Overbooking by Room Type

Hoteliers are notorious for overbooking the base or standard room types and then upgrading guests to a higher room type for free upon arrival. This practice needs to be understood and managed very carefully, ensuring that room types are sold and paid for based on their availability. A well-planned overbooking strategy can produce a lift in revenues and ADR.

When developing an overbooking strategy, it is important to understand the demand drivers of the market at least one year out. Overbooking strategies are most effective when deployed in conjunction with long-term pricing strategies. By understanding the wash factor of the hotel it will minimize the free upgrades and help push ADR performance.

It is also key to ensure that the overbooking strategy supports the hotel's ideal mix of business, room type product demand, and length-of-stay needs. Overbooking strategies when used effectively can help improve shoulder dates within a week, and can help drive conversion with premium room types. In order to deploy a successful overbooking strategy, it is important to evaluate room type conversion, turn-aways by room type, and length-of-stay opportunities. Too often hotels deploy length-of-stay restrictions too late, losing out on opportunity to build out shoulder dates during compression periods.

Often hotels utilize overbooking strategies on base-level room types when pricing strategies are not effective. When deploying overbooking strategies on base-category room types it is important to ensure that the overbooking is being utilized to maximize performance and not to drive performance. If higher tiered room types are not converting over key periods it is important to evaluate the pricing strategy as a whole. Overbooking cannot compensate for a pricing strategy that does not align the property properly within the market.

Groups also play a large role in overbooking strategies for some hotels. Hotels that have solid group business must take care to ensure that the room types confirmed for the groups are strategically approached. Too many hotels just use the base or standard room types as the "go to" room types to confirm. This can cause many problems in optimizing the room type demand, as it may skew the true demand for that room type. It also displaces other potential room type demand that may be willing to pay higher rates. It is important that hoteliers have a strategic plan in pricing the groups by room type. This will also help avoid those random upgrades of the group customers by the front desk on day of arrival as they are trying to balance out the house.

## Questions for Review

- What are some of the benefits to creating a strategic pricing plan?
- What are some of the elements every pricing strategy should include?
- What are some of the pitfalls of losing focus on a hotel's overall pricing strategy? How can these be avoided?
- Why do hotels discount?
- What are the benefits to discounting?
- What are some of the negative results that discounting can bring to a hotel?

# CHAPTER 9
## INVENTORY CONTROL

## Learning Objectives
- To understand the importance of inventory controls and how they impact a hotel's revenue performance both positively and negatively
- To learn how to complete a channel cost analysis that directs a hotel to apply the appropriate inventory controls to garner the most profitability
- To understand how to apply appropriate stay patterns and channel management to maximize revenue potential

In addition to pricing, inventory decisions can significantly impact a hotel's revenue maximization. Having the "right product available to the right person at the right price at the right time" is integral to success.

Inventory control will both strategically and tactically provide hoteliers with the ability to determine how much total capacity is available and how much of each product will be sold. Using inventory controls allows hoteliers to leverage high demand periods by closing shorter stay patterns and lower rates in order to deliver greater revenues and profits to the hotel.

This chapter provides an overview of the most commonly used inventory controls, and it reviews items that must be considered prior to determining the use of inventory control strategies at a hotel.

## Inventory Control Strategies
Stay, or inventory, controls have been around since the beginning of revenue management. As a matter of fact, this is how hotels yielded inventory prior to pricing by segmentation and dynamic pricing. Stay controls still exist and are still commonly used but not as often as in the past. Pricing is a more effective lever to use in yielding and optimizing. However, stay controls do still have a place.

The following is an overview of the most commonly used inventory controls.

| STAY CONTROL | HOW STAY CONTROL IS USED |
|---|---|
| Open | Free sell. No restriction on availability. |
| Closed | No availability is for sale. |
| No Arrival or Closed To Arrival (CTA) | No reservations are accepted that arrive on a particular day/date. This is used to extend bookings into the surrounding dates or only accept lengths of stay that will include one or more of the "shoulder" dates. |
| No Departure / Closed To Departure | No reservations are accepted that depart on a particular day/date. |
| Maximum Length Of Stay (MaxLOS) | Restricts stays to a maximum time period. This may be applied when the goal is to restrict a discounted rate or package availability. |
| Minimum Length Of Stay (MinLOS) | Requires stays for a specific time period. This is applied during periods when occupancy of one or more nights surrounding a high demand night is low. (Note: some systems read this stay control differently and it only impacts arrival dates that touch the restricted dates.) |
| Full Pattern Length of Stay (FPLOS) | Allows a hotel to accept discount rate up to a peak period, for example 2 and 3 length of stay, not allowing stays at a discount rate for the peak, but then again open up the discount for longer lengths of stay, thus improving occupancy on the shoulder nights and increasing overall revenues. |
| Allocations | Specific numbers of rooms are allotted to be sold. The total allocated does not have to equal hotel capacity. |

## Channel Costs
In implementing inventory controls, hoteliers must consider the cost of distribution so the appropriate controls can be established in order to focus on the most profitable channels. Hoteliers receive bookings through a multitude of different distribution channels and each of these channels has different costs associated with it. The various costs associated with each channel are not commonly understood nor are they taken into consideration by many hoteliers.

Today many hoteliers are lacking a cost analysis model to assist with understanding the cost for each channel. This section will review the purpose and importance of understanding the cost for each channel, as well as elements to consider when performing a channel cost analysis.

## Creating a Channel Cost Structure

The following is an excerpt from HSMAI's Distribution Channel Analysis report. This explores the varying costs and net values for each channel, and considerations for how this plays into a hotel's strategy.

## Variable Marketing and Reservation Fees by Channel

The sample shown in Exhibit 2 represents a composite of many hotel types; it illustrates typical costs for a $100 rate at a one-night length of stay. The costs to acquire and deliver a $100 room night for a one-night stay range from $14 to $46. Offline advertising such as television or magazine costs have not been included in these calculations since they may influence all channels.

A more detailed analysis is documented in the Flow-through Analysis section of this chapter, taking into account differences by channel and chain scale in terms of room rate, length of stay, ancillary spend, and all marketing, reservation, and transaction costs.

### Exhibit 2 Variable Marketing and Reservation Fees by Channel

| $100 BAR Length of Stay: 1 | Voice-direct | Voice-third party | Voice-travel agent | GDS | Hotel's own website (brand.com) | OTA merchant | OTA opaque via GDS |
|---|---|---|---|---|---|---|---|
| Labor | $10 | n/a | $10 | n/a | $2 | n/a | n/a |
| Direct marketing | n/a | n/a | n/a | $1 | $3 | Included in commission | Incicluded in commission |
| Discount or commission | n/a | Sometimes 10% | $10 | $10 | n/a | $25 | $40 |
| Loyalty program (on portion only) | $2 | $1.50 | $1.50 | $1 | $3 | n/a* | n/a* |
| Transaction channel fee | n/a | $25 | n/a | $6 | $5 | $5 | $6 |
| Credit card fee (on portion only) | $2 | $2 | $2 | $2 | $2 | n/a** | n/a** |
| Total Cost | $14 | $28.50 | $23.50 | $20 | $15 | $30 | $46 |
| Cost % | 14% | 28.5% | 23.5% | 20% | 15% | 30% | 46% |
| NET | $86 | $71.50 | $76.50 | $80 | $85 | $70 | $54 |

*Many hotels accept a loyalty card from OTA purchasers when requested and incur corporate costs for them.

Given these costs, if a hotel decides to "sweeten the pot" by offering something else in addition to a room rate, it would be counted as an additional marketing cost to trigger additional business. For example, if a $50 gas card is included to add to the benefits of booking in a given channel, that fee has to be added to the direct marketing category to determine its impact. This value-add may be a marketing expense that is shared between the hotel offering it and the vendor who puts it on the market.

Exhibit 3 shows the differences between the rates a hotel receives net of channel-specific costs. The fees a brand charges for website or call center reservations may be partially embedded in a marketing and/or reservation fee. There are third party reservation providers that support independents, small chains, and those who need representation in feeder markets where a hotel has no other partner. Pricing between chain central reservation system (CRS) and third-party CRS, if applicable, will also vary based on a chain's allocation formulas. Many brands absorb the individual components of distribution delivery and marketing costs and charge flat amounts or flat percentages per channel. Some costs may be additional, such as a performance marketing fee that is used for search engine marketing and can have a quantifiable benefit that can be assessed relative to the spend.

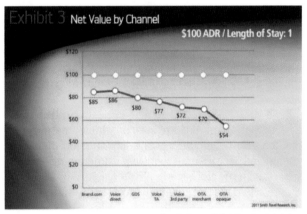

### Exhibit 3 Net Value by Channel

$100 ADR / Length of Stay: 1

*Scenarios shown are for illustration only and actual prices vary based on negotiated arrangements with vendors and internal staffing and cost levels.*

Based on these scenarios, a marketer would automatically assume it is best to choose channels in order of cost, but there are other variables to consider.

It is rare that a hotel can sell all room demand volume at top price. Hotels have to layer in their business to try to find the highest-rated demand at any given time. Think of it like a line of faucets filling an ice cube tray. Each faucet represents a channel and the ice cube tray represents all the rooms and rate types of the hotel for a day. Hotel management needs to put the tray under the faucets that are running and to turn them on and off as needed to fill up the tray as fully as possible. The hotel needs to consider all of its room and rate types and match them with the types of business flowing from the different faucets at any given time.

There are lean times when it is only possible to fill a hotel with business that may be lower profit than a hotel would usually like to take. Therefore, in spite of higher acquisition costs, if the room is being sold at a profit, even a small profit, and there is no business flowing through higher value channels, then it may be worth using the costlier distribution channel. If there is no profit, then in most cases, this practice may not be worthwhile. It is management's role to decide how many rooms should be available through each channel based on daily demand forecasting for each part of the week and each season of the year. If a hotel is obliged to sell through marginal channels during high demand times, in order to gain access to those channels during need periods, a cost/benefit analysis would be in order to assure management that there is a net benefit overall.

There are other times when a low-margin source of business can be worthwhile.

1.  Create a base for compression. If low margin room nights can be laid in early enough to add to a base that creates a higher level of compression in the comp set of the hotel, then it can serve as a springboard to yield higher rates from other channels during the peak booking time. For example, if there is a way to stimulate low-rate paying customers to book in the 21-40 day lead time window, then it can prove valuable to a hotel by pushing up rates for business booked within two weeks of the arrival date. Many hotels can make the mistake of using low-profit channels without regard for lead time and end up filling in with low rates closer to arrival; this contributes to the impression by consumers in the marketplace that you can get a better rate if you wait until the last minute. This behavior has been reinforced by media messaging where waiting for a lower last-minute rate is the explicit theme (see Online Marketing and Consumer Behavior chapter for examples).

    Traditionally, hotels would be best served by booking their lower rated business further out so they can push rates up closer to arrival when demand is likely to be highest. If a hotel takes lower rated business earlier for fear it won't fill, and then offers last-minute low rates in the last week or two before arrival there can be two outcomes, both of which may contribute

to sluggish ADR growth: (1) the percentage of higher rated business will decline overall and (2) travelers learn that waiting can guarantee lower rates so the consumer is less inclined to book early even when lower rates are available.

2.  Bring business you cannot bring yourself. Assuming the rates yield a contribution to profit, low-margin business is worthwhile if the hotel benefits from a valuable market it is not capable of tapping itself, either due to technical issues or access. If it diverts business that would come otherwise through a hotel's own website or call center, then it may not be worth incurring a higher cost. However, as an example, for those hotels in a market that is attractive to international feeder markets, or to fly-in markets in which air/hotel packaging is a major source of demand, then those channels specializing in packaging, such as OTAs, can be a valuable channels of choice, provided there is no feasible alternative to getting that business through a higher margin channel.

3.  When ancillary spend is high. For hotels with strong potential for ancillary spending beyond the room rate, (i.e., revenue centers such as parking, premium internet services, golf), and that ancillary spend carries a high profit margin, the full benefit of that booking should be considered when evaluating the business. Even if the contribution to profit from the room rate is small, if the ancillary spend yields a substantial profit contribution, then low margin business can be an attractive option for a hotel. However, it should be compared to alternatives to determine if it is still more beneficial than other demand streams available in the same time period.

4.  Hit the threshold. Some hotel brands set threshold occupancy levels that trip a premium in reimbursement to hotels for loyalty point redemption. When a hotel is near that threshold (e.g., 95% occupancy), it chooses to top off and hit that mark by taking the lower rated and marginally profitable business, often through the OTA channel, in order to qualify for the much higher reimbursement from the brand loyalty program. Feeling like a game of "whack-a-mole," where a wide range of demand may pop up in a few channels given a busy period in a particular market, this short-term quick fill may sometimes

be a diversion of bookings that would have come through brand. com. But, being a quick fix and a reliable way to siphon off any last-minute demand coming into a market by the hotel that wants to hit the threshold, it works.

5. Fill a hole. When a large group cancels or a citywide event does not fill a hotel as expected, the mass marketing benefit of the OTA can be highly effective at plugging those holes for a given hotel, especially when they are unexpected and/ or offer little lead time to launch other marketing initiatives to a large audience. The third-party sites are adept at share shifting and one needy hotel may turn on the spigot that will direct much of the demand for a comp set to it during these need periods.

6. Cover cash flow. If a hotel is in such a desperate situation that it cannot reach its threshold of daily operating expenses, then lower margin business can still serve as "fast cash" to cover cash flow needs. This is not often a sustainable situation, but it is a method that a hotel can utilize when no other option exists, either because it does not have the internal skills to stimulate other demand sources, or because the market is so economically depressed that there is no other option to shift the limited existing demand. However, it is often a case where one hotel in a comp set gains volume, but due to limited demand, all of them rarely do. The tendency is for the hotel taking the lead in the market to lower rates, followed by the others in the comp set who feel they have to drop rates to avoid loss of market share. In the worst case, when all hotels have lowered rates, the only method to gain the limited demand in the comp set requires continual rate reductions and all hotels have to operate at lower margins; some call this a "race to the bottom."

## Implementing a Demand-Driven Inventory Control Strategy

Once a hotel knows the cost of each channel, then a demand-driven inventory control strategy, taking into consideration the channel costs, needs to be executed. Applying stay controls can be a very complex issue and many hoteliers underestimate the impact the controls have on revenues — both positively and negatively. If used without a complete understanding of the full impact on all stay patterns, stay controls can ultimately be devastating to a hotel's revenue (domino effect). If applied properly

and carefully, the hotel can truly capture the optimal business. However, if applied without an understanding of the impact, the hotel can miss opportunities and turn away significant amounts of business.

Prior to applying inventory controls there are some items that must be understood and considered. The first is the general rule of thumb that in order to apply any stay control(s) there must be periods of excess demand. Otherwise, the hotel will be turning away business unnecessarily. More about this and its impact will be addressed in the stay pattern management section.

Before any inventory control strategies are implemented it is also important to know the impact of overselling, walk costs, channel management, and managing group wash. Each of these areas has a direct impact on inventory control.

### Overselling

Management wants to ensure the hotel reaches its maximum potential capacity for any given stay pattern in order to maximize revenue. Sometimes that means selling out the hotel to 100% capacity. It is often necessary to oversell the hotel in order to achieve this goal.

Overselling is the practice of accepting more reservations for a particular day than there actually are rooms in the hotel. This is in order to compensate for the estimated wash factor. The wash factor is the hotel's estimate of no-shows plus cancellations and early departures.

Knowing how much to calculate as a wash factor can be quite challenging. The wash factor is determined by taking the historical no-show and cancellation information that is being tracked by the hotel and comparing it to the current booking pace activity. Additionally, it is important to look at the number and breakdown of arrivals. For example, the number of guaranteed reservations versus non-guaranteed reservations will be a factor in estimating potential wash.

When considering an oversell strategy it is important to include all costs associated with this — both tangible and intangible.

"Walking" is the result of what needs to happen when a hotel is oversold and the no-show plus cancellation estimate is too high. This means that a guest has a guaranteed booking at a hotel but the hotel will not be able to accommodate the guest for that night. Therefore, the guest is "walked" to an alternative lodging facility.

The process of "walking" can be handled in two different ways. The first is probably the most common practice. The guest arrives at the hotel to find that the room reserved is not available and they will be staying at an alternate location — ideally already selected and reserved by the "walking" hotel. The second and less common practice is when a hotel contacts the guest prior to their arrival to inform them of the alternative lodging arrangements. This latter practice typically happens in a situation of extreme oversell.

The costs associated with "walking" are both tangible and intangible as stated above.

Some of the tangible costs are obvious such as the payout to the receiving hotel to which the guests are being sent, and any corresponding transportation costs such as taxis. These are normally absorbed by the hotel needing to "walk" their guests.

The intangible costs are a little bit more difficult to identify and many times are not weighted as heavily as they should be. Some intangible costs associated with overselling thus resulting in a "walk" are:

- "Ill will" or potential loss of a customer to the competition. This guest may not return again regardless of the efforts made by the hotel to make the situation as comfortable as possible.
- Reputation of the hotel due to the need to walk the guest. Unfortunately, viral marketing can work in reverse in this type of situation. Customers who have had a bad experience with one hotel can verbally spread the word and the hotel may develop a poor reputation.

A dollar value should be put against both of these items so it can be included in future displacement analysis. One other point that needs to be considered is a cross between the tangible and intangible costs and that is distance between the original hotel and the location to which the guest is walked. This can vary based on the time of year. For example, during fall foliage time in New England, a hotel in Boston will have a very difficult time finding an available hotel within a reasonable distance. Therefore, the dollar value that is placed on a "walk" during fall foliage in Boston should be much higher than it is at other lower-demand times of the year.

The following is an example of how to arrive at a "walk" cost.

## Walk Cost Example

| | |
|---|---|
| Room & Tax | $100 |
| Taxi | $15 |
| Breakfast | $15 |
| Customer "Ill Will" | $175 |
| **Total "Walk" Value** | **$305** |

The "walk" cost is important to take into consideration when implementing inventory management. If the controls are not appropriately applied, and the hotel has to "walk" customers, it is important to understand the complete impact for the hotel.

That being said, it is important to understand that the practice of overbooking which results in "walking" is a cost of doing business. There is a risk involved but hoteliers should not be in fear of implementing this practice as, if done right, it can greatly help to optimize revenues. As long as the hotel does not find a large number of "walks" being done regularly, then this is something that must be worked into the overall strategy and even budgeted for.

## Stay Pattern Management

In addition to a demand-driven inventory control strategy, stay pattern management can further enable a hotel to maximize revenues. A reservation's stay pattern is the combination of arrival date and length of stay. When maximizing revenue you want to accept the optimal number of reservations for each stay pattern, not the greatest number of reservations for each individual day.

The reason for this is because taking as many reservations as possible for one day could preclude a longer length of stay that includes that day, thus losing potential revenue for the surrounding days. This lost revenue may not be made up by shorter lengths of stays running through those surrounding days.

*Example:*

Stay Pattern 1  Arrival August 10, one-night stay

Stay Pattern 2  Arrival August 9, three-night stay

If all available rooms on August 10th were sold to Stay Pattern 1 and then a request was received for Stay Pattern 2, the hotel would have to turn away Stay Pattern 2, thus losing potential revenue for August 9th and 11th.

A day's total unconstrained demand is the sum of room nights from guests wanting to arrive on that day plus room-nights generated by guests who would arrive earlier and stay through.

Stay pattern management works to achieve the optimal mix of stay patterns through each potential sold out date by limiting the stay patterns going through that date. Because the overall objective is to maximize revenue and not occupancy, it is possible to have a solution in which a potential sold-out day does not sell out and yet revenue is still maximized.

## Channel Management

Part of the inventory control strategy is determining the hotel's approach to channel management and how to manage the channels most effectively.

Channel management is one of the industry's biggest challenges. There are a multitude of different channels available for the consumer to book and for the hotelier to manage.

When addressing channel management the following are the key issues that are involved:
1. Pricing
2. Rate management
3. Availability

Effectively managing these three elements across all channels is not an easy task.

For the purposes of understanding how to update inventory, rates, and reservation content, the variety of channels can be broken down as follows:
- Electronic channels including the CRS, GDS, GDS-powered sites, third parties connecting via a CRS, and proprietary websites are the easiest to manage in terms of time. Typically any updates in the CRS will distribute through to the rest of the electronic channels. However, it is important to understand how it works specifically for each hotel.
- Manual extranets or third-party sites such as Expedia are the most time-consuming from a maintenance perspective. These typically require separate updates via each site's extranet. In some cases however, there are direct connects which make the updating much easier.

- Voice representation such as reservation centers (on property and off property) can vary depending upon how the technology is setup. Some companies have their on-property reservations department use their PMS for rate and inventory information. In that case, the PMS is then yet another system that must be updated at the same time as the others. For those who use the CRS for on-property or even off-property reservations, any updates made to the CRS will be applied. However, the selling order may be different than what the agents normally see in their system.

Most stay controls can be applied throughout the channels. However, it is important to understand how each of the stay controls works in the various distribution channels. Some of the controls do not apply the same way in all channels. For example, while the PMS will apply a minimum length of stay control as expected, the same control may appear as "closed" in some GDS systems. Therefore, as outlined in the stay controls example, the use of this control may have an adverse effect on the hotel's revenue in that channel.

Finally, the most important consideration to remember regarding channel management is to ensure each of the channels with which a hotel chooses to participate is managed appropriately and effectively. It can be detrimental to a hotel to participate in a channel and not to manage it effectively. In that case it would be better not to participate at all.

For more details about channel management and distribution issues refer to the HSMAI Foundation report, *Distribution Channel Analysis: A Guide for Hotels.*

## Overbooking by Room Type

As already referenced in the Pricing chapter, hoteliers commonly miss out on proper management of the inventory availability by room type allowing for complimentary upgrades. Managing room types based upon demand and availability needs to be handled according to the needs of the hotel and the customer's willingness to pay for a higher room type.

More specifically, how a hotelier manages the availability of overbooking room types in low demand may be more flexible than managing overbooking of room types in high demand times. This approach will need to complement the hotel's pricing strategy.

## Management of Group Blocks

Finally, for hotels that have group business, there should be a process in place that allows for the management of blocks to maximize and protect the hotel's inventory. As it relates to inventory, hoteliers traditionally follow a process that nets down or applies a "blind cut" from the total number of rooms requested and contracted by the group. This information is typically not shared with the meeting planner as it is an internal decision and internally communicated, and a way to maximize revenue.

At a 100-room hotel, for a group that requests 100 rooms per night, based on the sales manager's research, expertise, and communication with the meeting planner, the hotel may decide the group should be cut down by 10%. Therefore, the hotel will block 90 rooms per night for the group. This leaves ten rooms per night to sell to other paying guests. Should the hotel estimate incorrectly, they are still obligated to provide the contracted number of rooms to the group.

In the past, hotels could "blind cut" the group based on past performance at their and other hotels. However, that is no longer realistic because of the significant change in group performance over the past years. It is imperative that the sales manager have a trusting relationship with the meeting planner. This level of trust and solid communication will provide the sales manager guidance in blind cutting.

In addition to applying this theory at the time of analysis, it is just as important to continue watching the group's pick up. If the group is not picking up as expected, it may be necessary to further net down, or "wash," the group in order to release more inventory for sale. However, if the group is picking up more than expected, it may be necessary to increase the inventory maxing out at the total number contracted or possibly increasing the block if the hotel finds that this would be prudent.

Ensuring proper management of a hotel's group wash will have a direct impact on the accuracy of inventory management.

More about groups and their relationship to revenue management is explored in the displacement analysis sections of this publication.

## Questions for Review

- What are the seven stay controls outlined in this chapter?
- What are four or five key steps that are important to consider when performing a channel cost analysis?
- What are some key cost factors to include in a channel cost analysis?

# CHAPTER 10

## ROOMS-ONLY TO TOTAL HOTEL REVENUE OPTIMIZATION

### Learning Objectives
- To understand why and how revenue optimization is being employed beyond guest rooms
- To comprehend the considerations that must be addressed before diving into total hotel revenue optimization
- To know best practices for getting started applying revenue optimization practices to revenue centers such as restaurant and golf

In today's fast-paced and multi-faceted world, it is no longer enough just to manage revenue for guestrooms. In some cases, what begins as ancillary revenue may eventually become a main source of revenue for a hotel. For some hotels (especially in the resort space), non-room revenue may represent over 50% of their total revenue. This is an area with much potential for revenue and profit growth.

It is vitally important that hotels employ total hotel revenue optimization (THRO), which applies revenue optimization techniques and strategies to all revenue generating operations — from food and beverage to spa, golf, and more.

Hotels are still in the early years of expanding revenue optimization efforts beyond rooms. One reason for the slow adoption is that other profit centers often involve complexities not found in the rooms division, and some, such as restaurants, have high variable costs associated with them. This may require a shift from a focus on revenue to a focus on profit.

It is also important to note that the appetite to invest in non-rooms profit centers depends on the size of the hotel's non-rooms operations and the associated revenue contribution. Hotels with larger operations and larger contributions from non-rooms departments are the ones leading the way in terms of the application of THRO.

While most agree on its importance and potential benefits, so far only a few have experienced real success which continues to mark THRO as an important area for innovation in the industry.

### Defining Total Hotel Revenue Optimization

Total hotel revenue optimization (THRO) considers multiple revenue sources, demonstrates a deep understanding of customer value, and shifts the focus from top-line metrics to bottom-line measures taking into consideration distribution, acquisition, and operating costs.

Total hotel revenue optimization addresses the need to optimize revenues at every possible revenue stream at the hotel and impacts all departments and team members. As with rooms revenue optimization, the discipline integrates strategy with the unique variables related to the particular optimization opportunity, statistical data, understanding of customer behaviors, and partnerships with key constituents such as sales, marketing, and operations.

The biggest challenges when applying revenue optimization to revenue centers beyond rooms are mostly cultural and profit related. Other departments have traditionally been managed by operational departments focused on the guest experience and services, rather than price and profitability (at least more so than rooms). Also, due to higher costs involved in non-revenue departments, managing price and inventory in those areas needs to take into account cost and profit much more than is the case when working with rooms. This has made applying analysis and revenue management principles more complicated.

The following chart identifies some departments that could benefit from applying revenue optimization techniques along with benefit and risk considerations.

| DEPARTMENT | APPLICATION | BENEFIT and RISK CONSIDERATIONS |
|---|---|---|
| Rooms | ADR, Occupancy, Rooms Revenue | Product and customer service have a direct correlation to success and profitability. |
| Meetings & Events: F&B and Function Space | ADR, occupancy, rooms revenue, stay patterns, opportunistic yielding, optimize food & beverage, optimize function space | Increased ancillary revenues; stay pattern management and rooms-to-function space ratio have a direct correlation to success; increased space usage and limited empty function space; new revenue stream from charges such as a service fee, set-up/tear-down fee, or menu engineering fee |
| Restaurant | Increase average checks | Increased checks will improve profitability; food quality and service have a direct correlation to success |
| Golf course | Increase rate yielding and tee times | Increased volume and optimizing price per tee-time; average play time will have a direct correlation to success |
| Spa | Increase average spend | Increased average spend and optimizing high profit treatments during peak times; customer service and quality of treatments have a direct correlation to success |
| Front Desk | Upsell program at check-in, late checkouts, early departure fees | Increased ADR and usage of premium room types/suites; product quality will have a direct correlation to success |
| Reservations | Increase conversion | Increased bookings; quality of call, product type, and customer service will have a direct correlation to success |
| Other | Parking, club memberships, and condo rental pools | In hotels that have heavy club components this can contribute more to NOI than total rooms |

## Important Considerations

There are a few considerations that must be understood and addressed before diving into THRO.

First, the organization must determine who will lead the charge. While there is no current standard here, it is reasonable that revenue professionals would leverage their experience with and knowledge of rooms revenue optimization and take the lead role in optimizing revenues through all profit centers. This responsibility for integrating centers such as food & beverage, spa, golf, function space, and ancillary products/services expands on the revenue professional's traditional role, and challenges them to further advance the revenue optimization discipline. This arrangement has the potential to reap significant rewards for owners and operators.

Then, build the team. It is important to ensure alignment and buy-in with all stakeholders. Even a solid strategy will fail if the revenue team and all impacted team members do not have a common understanding of key issues, if they have not bought in to the overall vision of the effort, or if they have not set realistic goals.

Start by building a common understanding about the role of the following:

- The jargon being used — whether it is revenue optimization-related terminology or discipline specific language from other areas of the hotel (e.g., restaurants talk about covers, average check, party, turn, 2-top, push, hockey puck, stiffed, walked, upsell, etc.)
- Customer reviews and reputation management (For a deep dive on this issue, see the "Reviews & Reputation Management" chapter of *Hospitality Digital Marketing Essentials: A Field Guide for Navigating Today's Digital Landscape* — available at www.hsmai.org.)
- Quality of product and service (and their impact on customer reviews and reputation)
- The position of the hotel as it relates to its competitors (See chapter 5, Understanding the Market)
- Associated costs — fixed and variable, and cost controls
- Technology and tools needed
- Key performance indicators (KPIs)
- Training
- Tracking and monitoring
- Partnership with finance and IT
- The reality of the execution

Of the above factors in effective strategy execution, three of the most important and impactful are training, tracking, and KPIs. Lack of training can sabotage proper tracking. Without proper tracking, data about the initiative will not be accurate, and therefore not useful. What gets measured gets done, and the team needs to align on what KPIs will drive goals, the cadence for tracking and pivoting, and, ultimately, success.

As part of building the team, assuming the revenue professional is the lead on revenue optimization efforts throughout the enterprise, he or she must form a solid professional relationship with the departmental leaders in each profit center. Without strong relationships, it will be difficult to gain buy-in and cooperation for the implementation of revenue optimization techniques.

As part of the process of developing strong cross-department relationships, the revenue professional must work to develop a deep understanding of each non-rooms profit center. At a minimum, they should know the answer to the following questions for each center:

- What is the product or service being offered?
- What is the value of each product and/or service?
- What discipline-specific language/jargon is used?
- What are the current challenges?
- Where are the opportunities?
- What data is currently being collected and how is it being used?

For more details, see the following sections which explore several specific profit centers in depth.

Another important consideration is talent. The reality is that hotels continue to struggle with bringing new talent into the industry, and, more specifically, recruiting top talent into the revenue optimization discipline. See chapter 2 for a deeper exploration of this issue. What does this mean for a THRO effort? It means increasing the demands on a revenue professional's time and attention, which is often already stretched to capacity. The organization must carefully consider what gets added to a revenue professional's plate — and what additional staffing may be required.

Finally, considering data and analytics and their growing importance in THRO is essential. Being able to set and deploy sound strategies across profit centers requires access to plenty of timely and actionable information. A well-planned strategy for collecting and reporting

relevant data will increase the likelihood of identifying meaningful patterns in data, and improve the process of applying those patterns towards effective decision making. Avoid making decisions based on bad data. It will only lead to bad strategies and derail the revenue optimization efforts.

## Key Steps to Get Started

1. Review and plan for the important considerations described above.
2. Determine the best outlet(s)/avenue(s) to begin applying revenue optimization concepts. Start with one or two outlets, or go for all at once. There is no right way to do it, but a guideline that may help the team decide where to begin is to identify the department with the highest profit margin today and start there.
3. Select a lead for each identified department revenue center. Incorporate the leads into the hotel's regular revenue meetings.
4. List and clearly define all common terms for every revenue center and be sure of alignment among all players.
5. Be sure that solid relationships are in place with key constituents. If needed, invest resources in creating a forum for those relationships to form and/or grow stronger. The Director of Restaurants or Director of Golf needs to be comfortable and understand the Director of Revenue (and vice versa) for this to be successful.
6. Clearly define the goal for each department. What is the challenge today? What are you trying to accomplish or solve? For example, is the restaurant too slow? Too many empty seats? Or is the restaurant always busy with a line of people waiting?
7. Brainstorm how to address the challenges or how to generate incremental profitable revenue from each center. Prioritize the top three ideas.
8. Determine measurements or KPIs as a team. How will success be measured?
9. Identify what data is currently available and what data is missing. Create an action plan to close the gap on missing data.
10. Begin implementation of ideas. Ensure proper tracking is in place and all impacted team members are trained.
11. Evaluate progress and adjust as necessary.

## Meetings & Events: F&B and Function Space

The revenue optimization approach has grown in importance when it comes to group business – in terms of both food and beverage (F&B) and function space – because it provides tremendous value and opportunity for revenue growth.

Group business used to be considered good filler for the rooms that transient business did not occupy. Over the years, hoteliers have come to realize the importance of groups and the revenues that can be generated from them. Today for many hotels, group business is an important part of the overall strategy.

In order for hotels to be successful in the group arena they must ensure that they have the proper strategies and tools in place as well as a thorough understanding of the various needs of groups. It requires establishing measurements and value for function space, defining the total revenue contributions from each group, managing function space, and providing the sales department with the knowledge and tools they need to properly understand the group strategies.

### Pricing Strategy

Developing a pricing strategy for group business is just as important as developing one for transient business. The process of developing a group pricing strategy is also similar to that of developing a transient pricing strategy. A strategic pricing strategy for groups allows hotels to be proactive and provides guidelines and plans that allow the entire hotel sales team to effectively sell their products.

Group pricing guidelines will allow the sales department to effectively and confidently quote rates for the future. The sales team will know the price points for specific demand periods and specific dates; have the opportunity to work quickly with the customer without having to take the time to discuss rates with the revenue director before they can quote; and, ultimately be empowered to achieve their own sales goals. They will also have a solid understanding of the hotel's future outlook, peak demand times, and times of need.

One factor unique to group business is that the pricing guidelines developed are just that: guidelines. The pricing strategy for groups should act as a general rule for sales managers to use in their initial discussions and as a basis for group evaluation. Once the sales manager understands the full needs of the group, including the total spend, they can then do a full analysis comparing the total value of the group to the value of other potential business that may be displaced if the group is accepted. (See page 79 for more information on displacement analysis.) After the analysis is completed, the rate should be adjusted to add value to the group if needed or decreased if needed.

The group pricing strategy needs to be created with the entire revenue team. It must be a part of the overall revenue strategy of the hotel and reflect the guidelines of that strategy. Groups are unique, however, and hoteliers need to address group-specific elements.

| FACTOR IN GROUP PRICING | PURPOSE/CONSIDERATIONS |
|---|---|
| SWOT Analysis | As with transient pricing strategy, a hotel is only able to create a proper group pricing strategy when it has a solid understanding of the hotel's unique attributes, strengths and weaknesses for both services and products as they relate to groups. This SWOT analysis must be developed according to what is important and unique to groups and their needs, which may be different than the needs identified in a SWOT analysis for transient business. |
| Market Position | Every hotel must put together an analysis that allows careful evaluation of the hotel compared to its competitors with respect to group business. It is important to understand the market position of the hotel within the competitive set. This will be an important part of determining group pricing for the hotel. Some hotels may find their market position differs when evaluating their market position with respect to groups. |
| Seasonal Demand | One of the fundamentals for a pricing strategy is to first understand the market demand for the various seasons in the marketplace. Flexibility for seasonal rates must be taken into consideration. |
| Lose-it Rate | Determine the lowest price point that is acceptable for the hotel. Regardless of the occupancy, what is the absolute lowest rate the hotel is willing to accept? Set this as the "lose-it" rate. |
| Price Points | Determine the various price points for each of the group market segments. |
| Group Segmentation | Understanding the group segmentation that is specific to the marketplace AND to the hotel is critical. Every hotel must identify the target group segments that are appropriate and create price points that satisfy each of them. |

| Economic Considerations | Identify the future economic status for the time of the group request. Based on this information, this will be the price point that is appropriate in that year. |
|---|---|
| Special Need Periods | Identify the hotel's need periods and areas of opportunity. This may include holidays, special events in the marketplace or low demand times. Identify these times and create an action plan to target appropriate group segments. Make this a part of the overall group strategy, not an afterthought. |
| Room Types | Identify the room types that should be included in group pricing. |
| Room Costs | Understanding the direct and indirect costs associated with rooms is an important part of pricing. Knowing the costs and incremental costs will ensure that profits can become the focus and ultimately be incorporated as part of the pricing strategy. |
| Catering Contribution | Identify food and beverage contribution for each group. This can have a significant impact on the value of the group. |

## Displacement Analysis

Part of the process of analyzing the value of a group is performing a solid displacement analysis. A displacement analysis compares the value of different pieces of business to identify the one that brings the most value to the hotel. A group displacement analysis analyzes group business based on the total value of the business, and compares it with the total value of other business (transient or other groups) that would be displaced if the group business was accepted. The group value includes all food and beverage spending, meeting room rental, and any additional outlet spending, minus any costs involved.

The following is a simplified displacement analysis. It compares a potential group's business to the transient displacement that would occur if the group was accepted at the current values.

### Displacement Analysis Example

|  | TRANSIENT | GROUP |
|---|---|---|
| Rooms | 40 | 40 |
| ADR | $200 | $160 |
| Sub-total | $8,000 | $6,400 |
| Ancillary Revenues | $1,200 | $5,000 |
| Room Cleaning Costs | <$600> | <$600> |
| Catering Costs | $0 | <$1,000> |
| TOTAL | $8,600 | $9,800 |

The example above is simplified to provide a value comparison between group and transient business. It does not take into consideration transient length of stay and the impact that group acceptance will have on demand for room nights before and after the group block. It is also important to understand that this example can be applied

to displacement against other group business as well.

At first glance, it appears that the group would not be profitable because the room revenue from the transient business brings in $1,600 more than the group business. However, when the ancillary revenues are added, as well as the costs associated with both pieces of business, it turns out that the group is more valuable to the hotel by $1,200.

If an analysis indicates the group is not profitable and it is best not to accept the group, the hotel should consider offering alternate dates to the group. Dates with less demand will result in a more positive impact from the group. Another option that will increase the value of the group is to increase the rate offered. If you increase the rate and revise the analysis, the overall group value will increase.

In situations where "walking" would apply, that must also be considered in the calculation. This example assumes 10 transient guests would be "walked" for one night at a cost of $305 per room.

|  | TRANSIENT | GROUP |
|---|---|---|
| Rooms | 40 | 40 |
| ADR | $200 | $160 |
| Sub-total | $8,000 | $6,400 |
| Ancillary Revenues | $1,200 | $5,000 |
| Room Cleaning Costs | <$600> | <$600> |
| Catering Costs | $0 | <$1,000> |
| Sub-total | $8,600 | $9,800 |
| "Walk" Cost |  | <$3,050> |
| TOTAL | $8,600 | $6,750 |

When the possibility of "walking" is calculated into the equation, the group is no longer profitable for the hotel. Another element that should be included in the displacement analysis is the booking method. Below is the same scenario with the addition of the booking method and the costs associated with the different channels as outlined previously.

In the following example, the booking methods assumed for transient are ten each of GDS, on-property, third-party, and chain website bookings. The group assumption is 20 on-property and 20 chain website bookings.

| | TRANSIENT | GROUP |
|---|---|---|
| Rooms | 40 | 40 |
| ADR | $200 | $160 |
| Sub-total | $8,000 | $6,400 |
| Ancillary Revenues | $1,200 | $5,000 |
| Room Cleaning Costs | <$600> | <$600> |
| Catering Costs | $0 | <$1,000> |
| Sub-total | $8,600 | $9,800 |
| "Walk" Cost | | <$3,050> |
| Sub-total | $8,600 | $6,750 |
| Booking Method Costs | <$509.70> | <$368.40> |
| TOTAL | $8,090.30 | $6,381.60 |

In addition to the displacement analysis there are other elements that must be considered above and beyond being able to compare the numbers. Some of the other considerations follow.

- Consider the long-term potential that this group may bring to the hotel. Will this piece of business bring additional group or transient opportunities? If so, when do you expect them? Will they be during peak demand dates when the hotel does not need the business, or will they be during slower times when the hotel needs the business?
- Is this a regular event that the hotel wishes to capture?
- Is there known history for this group?
- Are there any other potential ancillary revenues that may be realized through this group?
- Does this piece of business bring any political advantages to the hotel?

- Is this a significant customer of the hotel company? Should the customer's overall value to the entire corporation be considered?
- Does the group have an attrition clause?

These are a few considerations that may or may not apply to the decision process. If they are applicable to a hotel or a specific piece of group business, then they should be considered and weighted accordingly. By combining the scientific analysis with human judgment, hotels can optimize the group side of the revenue equation and move toward a total hotel approach to revenue optimization.

The final step in accepting or rejecting a piece of group business is to follow up on the decisions and measure the results. This will help the hotel enhance decisions in the future and learn from any mistakes or oversights.

Always review your performance. When evaluating your group displacement analysis, and measuring actual results against the projections, consider whether or not the group met the anticipated revenue objectives:
- Were higher value rooms or function space opportunities displaced?
- Did the hotel turn away more valuable opportunities from other segments (group, transient, or local catering / events)?
- How did the hotel perform relative to its competitive set during that time period?
- Can you establish new thresholds for similar time periods to maximize future demand based on what was learned from this situation?
- What would you recommend now based on what was learned?

Profitable decisions will ensure that the hotel realizes maximum demand from all segments on all measures from occupancy and ADR to Revenue Per Available Square Foot (or Meter) (RevPAS).

### Food & Beverage (F&B) Optimization
The contribution from F&B (i.e., catering, banquets) can provide tremendous value and opportunity for revenue growth. While the terminology in this area differs around the globe, for the purposes of this publication consider that hotels have two types of F&B business:
1. Group catering, or group banquet, is the business connected with a group that is utilizing overnight guest rooms.
2. Local catering, or local banquet, is business that is not connected with any overnight guest rooms.

An example of group catering is a large corporate function where most attendees stay at the hotel and attend the events. All of the functions that result from this group, such as breakfasts, lunches, dinners, and receptions, are group catering functions. An example of local catering is a breakfast meeting of the community Rotary Club.

Group catering or banquet contribution is directly impacted by periods of lower group occupancy. Non-group, or transient, business has no impact on catering/banquet business. Hotels that make the decision to fill their meeting space with local catering run the risk of having to turn away potential group business. This is because many groups require both meeting space and sleeping rooms.

Basic guidelines must be established for a hotel to benefit from a total revenue optimization approach to catering/banquets. Following these guidelines and including the information in the analysis will make a big difference in the outcome:

- Catering Minimums: Define the required catering minimums that are specific for the hotel.
- Measurements: Understand how to measure against projected demand for the same dates and space.
- Demand by Segment: Understand the demand from all segments for all future dates in the strategy window. This will help the revenue team better determine if a piece of local catering business may displace group catering business which can make a larger overall revenue contribution.
- Group and Catering Values: Calculate the total estimated value of the group opportunity being evaluated. Consider meeting or function space rental, food and beverage, audio visual / Internet usage, parking, valet, and business center usage, and other applicable outlets.
- Average Catering Performance: Access and understand the average catering performance by meal period and by function space.
- Pricing vs. Customer Requirements: Have a solid understanding of the profit implications by comparing catering pricing requirements with the customer's requirements.
- Margins: Identify the profit margins, by outlet, of specific food items. For example, the profit margin on beef is different from that of chicken.

The profit for the same item sold to a large group versus to an individual in the restaurant can be different depending on the hotel's approach to ordering.

Typically, items ordered for groups make it easier because the complete menu and count are known. Therefore, ordering may be done in a more profitable way.

The final step in evaluating catering business is to follow up on the revenue team's decisions and measure the results. This will help the team learn from any mistakes or oversights, and make better decisions in the future.

Effective revenue management in the catering arena requires performance measurement:

- Revenue Per Available Square Foot (or meter) (RevPAS) measures the revenue that an event generates based on the amount of space used compared to the space available. RevPAS can be applied to both group catering and local catering events.
- Catering Contribution per Group Room Night measures the amount of catering a group produces in relation to the room nights they use. A local catering group's contribution per group room night would be zero.
- Revenue per Occupied Group Room (ROGR) can be used to compare the contribution value of two different pieces of group catering business.
- Other useful measurements may include an historical look at day-by-day revenue generated on a particular day or in a specific function room, profit per available square foot (or meter), or revenue per available seat hour.

As the team reviews performance consider the following questions:

- Did catering revenue perform at or above expectations?
- Did the hotel perform better by taking this opportunity?
- Did the hotel maximize revenue and profit?
- Did the hotel realize maximum demand from all segments?
- Were higher value rooms or space opportunities displaced?
- Would the hotel consider rebooking this event?
- What might the hotel recommend be changed for the future based on past performance?

- Can you establish new thresholds for similar time periods to maximize future demand based on what was learned from this situation?
- What would you recommend now based on what was learned?

### Function Space Optimization

Applying optimal revenue management to function space is rare for hoteliers. For all of the sophistication that is applied to transient revenue management, the industry is lacking in this area. Hotels' function spaces provide substantial income opportunities that can be enhanced by applying revenue management principles and techniques. For this reason, some major group hotels have reorganized their structures and included function space management in their revenue management strategies.

When it comes to optimizing function space there are multiple hurdles that may prevent some hoteliers from even attempting it. However, all of these challenges can be overcome by understanding the concept, defining measurements, and developing an internal process that includes the right tools and know-how:

1. There are no industry-wide KPIs to measure optimized function space.
2. While some industry partners have developed function space revenue management software tools, they are not widely adopted; therefore, most hotels lack technology that can help with the function space optimization process.
3. The industry does not have enough revenue experts with the knowledge and experience to properly and effectively optimize function space.

The following sections touch on the requirements in each of these areas along with recommendations for consideration in order to get started.

### KPIs for Space Optimization

An important factor for implementing function space optimization is understanding effective key performance indicators (KPIs) and ensuring that the hotel implements the right measurements and definitions.

There are two key KPIs to review and measure when optimizing your function space.

1. Space to Group Room Ratio (SGR): This is the amount of required meeting space compared to the number of hotel rooms your group will need. The hotel needs to determine the value of the function space by square feet per guest room by day (not by total stay). Example: A group requests 100 peak room nights and 7200 square feet of meeting space on their peak event days. It is determined by Revenue Management that the hotel has an optimal Space to Group Room Ratio of 72. The rooms and space pattern, as well as the related SGR by day is listed below:

| Day | RNs | Sq. Ft. | SGR |
|-----|-----|---------|-----|
| Sat | 25 | 0 | 0 |
| Sun | 50 | 3600 | 72 |
| Mon | 100 | 7200 | 72 |
| Tue | 100 | 7200 | 72 |
| Wed | 100 | 7200 | 72 |
| Thu | 50 | 7200 | 144 |
| Fri | 25 | 3600 | 144 |

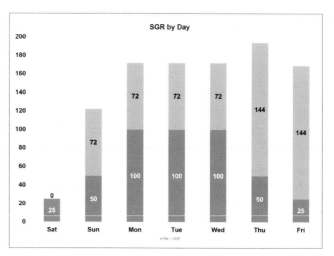

In this example, the hotel is optimizing the event space Saturday through Wednesday. However, the Space to Group Room (SGR) Ratio is twice as much on the last two event days where the room block decreases by 50% each day. This means that the hotel's space allocation on Thursday and Friday is only 50% optimal.

This leads us to the next KPI.

2.  Foregone Potential of Group Revenue (FPGR): If one group takes up too much space for the rooms booked, the hotel is unable to book another group requiring meeting space "on top of it" and optimize the hotel's revenue. This is the Foregone Potential of Group Revenue (FPGR). Using the same example as above, the group is displacing 50 room nights on Thursday and 25 room nights on Friday (50% optimization). If the hotel's average rate for this week is $200, the FPGR by taking this group is $15,000. [(50 + 25) x 200 = 15,000]

In these scenarios, there are three approaches the sales managers can use to optimize function space:
1.  Increase the room nights to align with the optimal SGR
2.  Lower the amount of square footage held on the less than optimal days, and/or
3.  Increase the proposed ADR to compensate for the FPGR

The key component to being successful using the above KPIs is that the revenue team must be very confident in the forecast that has been put together for groups and meeting space.

Jack Easdale, CRME, SVP, Revenue Management and Enterprise Analytics for Venetian Resorts, advises, "If you have adeptly and assuredly forecasted your future group room nights per day, then you believe the demand is coming. Be confident in your forecast and do not approve suboptimal groups (from a Space to Group Room Ratio perspective) that will put you in an upside-down position just because it's a 'bird in hand.'"

### Process for Space Optimization
Group sales typically have a group selling goal that is measured and rewarded on total revenue sold. And in some cases it also includes a specific amount of revenue that must be "on the books" by a certain time period. This completely negates the flexibility to focus on optimizing the space based on the demand and forecast according to the demand.

A robust space optimization practice includes ensuring that the space is sold or optimized based on the demand for the space versus the request for the space. This is where revenue management comes in.

Jack Easdale shared his perspective on this. "The person approving the meeting space allotment for a group ought to be a revenue professional, or at the very least be an individual who has the skill set to make an unbiased, articulate decision for the betterment of the entire property, not just a production goal. It can be someone with a sales background that knows how to optimize the space, but revenue optimization needs to have a hand in it."

If a group takes too much space compared to their rooms, then the hotel forgoes the opportunity to sell the remaining space to someone else. For example, take a hotel with 311 rooms. The hotel has forecasted a strong day-by-day rooms demand and the revenue team is very confident in the forecast and in the demand. Two hundred group rooms and 111 transient rooms are expected, which will fill the hotel to capacity. A lead from Group X requests 100 rooms and 70% of the hotel's function space. The hotel books the rooms and the space, and the sales manager feels great because she has met her room night goal.

Group Y, whose lead arrives chronologically later in the booking window, requests 100 group rooms but the hotel only has 30% of its function space left to sell. Group Y's meeting planner is not happy because the hotel has suboptimal meeting space to accommodate his needs. To compensate for the suboptimal space availability and ensuing less-than-ideal meeting experience, the sales manager discounts the guest rooms and the entire hotel loses as a result.

If revenue optimization principles were applied in the above scenario, the space could have been optimized initially with Group X based on the demand and the forecast for the overall space. Now the hotel is dealing with less-than-optimal revenue and will likely miss out on the hotel's overall financial goals for this time period. In this example, one solution to optimize the function space over these dates was for the hotel to calculate the foregone potential of group revenue (FPGR) of selling the space to Group X, and incorporate it into the offer presented to the meeting planner. In other words, Group X could have been required to pay for the amount of space they wanted to consume.

Another solution was for the hotel to provide different options to the Group X meeting planner for how the group could use less space more efficiently; thus leaving the hotel with optimal space to accommodate the next group request, optimizing the revenues for the hotel overall, and keeping the group's costs down.

Jack Easdale offered another sound recommendation. "Pieces of business don't grow on trees. Hoteliers need to optimize the demand they do have versus turn away things that are not absolutely perfect upon initial review. Work closely with your sales team to look for solutions to make them acceptable to the hotel and the meeting planner. Often a solution exists if sales and revenue management can partner to provide potentially viable solutions to the meeting planner that he or she hadn't thought of. In essence, be problem solvers. Ultimately sales and revenue management are on the same team with a shared objective. That objective is to fill the hotel with the most profitable business that doesn't impede future demand from matriculating."

If the meeting planner wants more space than what makes good sense for the hotel, hoteliers are wise to calculate alternative options instead of simply giving them what they have asked for. When sales is confident in what a group really needs and will realistically use, the hotel can calculate the value of any excess space utilization and include it in the room rate offer or find another way to make up the difference so that the hotel wins and optimizes the revenue. Revenue management needs to help sales calculate this amount to make it measurable and useful.

Hotels need to be better managers of the space they have. It is the same concept as with rooms — function space is a fixed asset and a perishable asset. So quantify what it is worth. There's always an opportunity to do better.

A robust function space optimization practice includes ensuring the space is blocked accurately to avoid downtime, performing audits of the space on a regular basis, and blocking space with straight line availability in mind as this allows for multiple-day bookings. This also helps with labor if the same set up is consistent. There are some common elements related to the management of function space in order to ensure optimization.

### Managing the Timing of Events
In high demand periods, the time needed to turn the function room around from one customer to the next can affect the hotel's ability to meet demand. Hotels that try to minimize the labor costs associated with function room set up and tear down often end up turning down business that could have been accommodated if the hotel had employed a sufficient number of employees to turn the room faster. For example, a hotel that requires a two-hour set up and two-hour tear down for all events would not be able to book a meeting that ends at 5:00 p.m. in the same room with a dinner that begins at 6:30 p.m. If more employees were assigned to speed the transition between events, the labor cost would be more than covered by the increased revenue associated with booking the incremental event.

### Program Flow
Understanding the configuration and needs for the program will help to layout the proper location for each event with the goal of optimizing any unnecessary downtime. Determining the optimal room and set up types such as classroom, theater, rounds, and so on will help ensure the most efficient use of space. Be sure to consider A/V needs and the number of attendees for each function.

## Restaurant Revenue Optimization
Restaurant revenue optimization is a relatively new discipline compared to efforts to optimize hotel rooms. Because of its newness, it can be difficult to get buy-in from all stakeholders and ensure full cooperation and commitment to execute the strategy.

Typically, one of the biggest hurdles to instituting revenue optimization in restaurants, and developing a culture that supports and promotes revenue optimization concepts, is the lack of coordination among the revenue team, the restaurant manager, and the chef. Improved coordination and teamwork can be supported with a focus on goal alignment, communication, trust, and respect for each team member's experience and contribution. It is essential that the revenue professional reduce all barriers possible for more creative, less data-minded chefs.

Applying revenue optimization concepts to restaurants is an easy transition from traditional rooms revenue optimization, as long as there is access to accurate data. There are important metrics which, when tracked and understood, can help the team make better strategic decisions and drive better promotions. The top three metrics, described in detail below, include:

1.  RevPASH (Revenue Per Available Seat Hour)
2.  Seat v. Table Occupancy
3.  Menu Engineering

### RevPASH
As with a hotel room, a seat in a restaurant is a perishable item. The difference between restaurant and rooms revenue optimization is the time component. The measurement of success for rooms revenue optimization is generally based on a per night calculation — how many

rooms were available for the night, how many were occupied, and the price for which each was sold. It is important to note that there are geographical exceptions to this as, in some places, such as Tokyo, it is common practice to charge by the hour. However, in a restaurant environment, the revenue generated by each seat is important, and it is calculated on a per hour basis; not per night basis like hotel rooms.

Additionally, the concept of through-put is critical to efforts to increase RevPASH, especially during high demand meal periods. Through-put is the maximum rate of production or the maximum rate at which something can be processed.

RevPASH is useful to measure the usage and revenue of a seat per hour, and it allows for better planning by the food and beverage manager. It is calculated by dividing total restaurant revenue by the product of available seats and available hours [Total Outlet Revenue / (Available Seats x Opening Hours)]. There is debate within the industry about whether RevPASH should be calculated based on the opening time of each check, or the actual duration of the meal. Just be consistent within your own efforts.

Cornell University explains it: "An essential measurement for restaurant revenue management is RevPASH, or revenue per available seat hour, which was introduced in 1998. This metric is useful, because it states revenue based on both time (hour) and capacity (seats). By tracking the RevPASH by day part, or even within day parts, the restaurant manager has a useful tool by which to measure performance and to guide his or her decisions to enhance revenue."[15]

## RevPASH Example

Comparing Restaurant A and Restaurant B, both restaurants have the same demand and pricing, and seat the same number of customers starting Saturday at 6:00 pm. The only difference between the restaurants is the length of time their customers are seated. Restaurant A's customer typically sits at the table for a longer period of time.

Restaurant A takes 1.5 hours to turn a table and get the next guests seated, while Restaurant B only takes 1.0 hour. Based on these factors, it is easy to see that Restaurant B will generate a higher RevPASH. Restaurant B is able to generate more revenue for the restaurant in a 1-hour time period compared to Restaurant A.

## Seat v. Table Occupancy

Another important metric for restaurants is maximizing seat occupancy compared to table occupancy as this can greatly influence RevPASH.

The following illustrates this concept using the same two restaurants as in the last example.

Restaurant A has 20 4-tops (20 tables that seat a maximum of 4 people), and Restaurant B has the same number of tables and configuration. Depending on how management matches party size to the optimal table configuration, one restaurant could end the night with 100% table occupancy and 100% seat occupancy, while the other could end up with 100% table occupancy but only 50% seat occupancy.

Again, with this example, maximizing the inventory to match the party size is critical during high demand. For some restaurants the ability to have flexible configurations is critical. If you have a booth for 6 versus 3 tables of two-tops that can be pushed together to seat 6, the ability to maximize seat occupancy becomes much easier when there is flexibility.

One could compare seat and table occupancy with maximizing each room type within a hotel. By not maximizing rooms types, it can be easy to oversell a standard room and just upgrade guests to a larger or more superior room without getting the maximum revenue potential.

Training the restaurant hostess on the principles of revenue optimization and its application to the seat versus table occupancy is critical to the success of the execution. It is similar to training front desk staff on room-type upselling. The same concepts are important for the waitstaff and hostess to know and understand.

## Menu Engineering

Menu engineering evaluates how items on a menu are selling (their popularity) and their profitability. It provides valuable data to ensure any menu changes are data-driven decisions with the goal of increasing profitability.

Depending on the restaurant, menu engineering can be broken down to examine each meal period and/or menu (including the bar menu, or even the mini-bar!), and can be updated and evaluated monthly or quarterly.

There are many free menu engineering worksheets templates available online, as well as software-for-purchase options. No matter what tool you use, the basic approach is the same[16]:

1. Select a time period.
2. Record menu items and number sold within that time period.
3. Record the item food cost, or exactly what you paid for that item.
4. Record the item sell price as it appears on your menu.

The data collected from these four steps allows the revenue team to access important metrics, chief among them are:

- Food Cost Percentage
- Item Profit
- Total Food Cost and Total Menu Sales
- Contribution Margin

Other metrics can be derived as well — some are simply interesting to know, some are immediately actionable:

- All Items Sold = sum of number sold
- Overall Food Cost = sum of total food cost
- Overall Menu Sales = sum of total menu sales
- Overall Contribution Margin = sum of contribution margin
- Average Profit Per Item = overall contribution margin / all items sold
- Overall Food Cost Percentage = overall food cost / overall menu sales

Visual representations of data are always valuable in revenue optimization efforts. In the following menu engineering example, the Thai wings are selling the smallest volume, and they are also the least profitable. Menu items in the lower-left quadrant are often referred to as "dogs." The upper-left quadrant contains items that are selling very well, but are not profitable. These are the "plow horses" — in this case the soup and salad. "Stars" (nachos) are both profitable and popular. "Puzzles" (calamari) are profitable, but not popular.

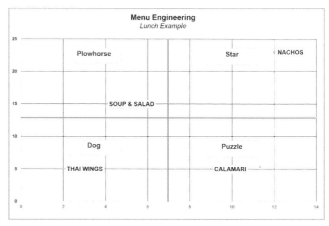

Special thanks to Heather Richer for providing this graph.

Once you have the data, the revenue team can think through it and make decisions based on it. Some questions to ask include:

- Can we raise the price of a plow horse and test if a higher price affects the volume?
- How are dogs and puzzles merchandised on the menu?
- Can we make a plow horse a star by reducing the portion size (and lowering the food cost)? With a smaller portion, would the dish still be as popular?
- Puzzles can be tricky — sometimes the only vegan dish on the menu falls into this category. It is an important dish to offer, but it will likely always have a more limited audience. Will customers who want a special dish be willing to pay a higher price?
- For stars that are profitable and selling well, is there an opportunity to raise the price and keep selling the same volume?

## Golf Course Revenue Optimization[17]

Golf courses can adopt the principles of revenue optimization to increase revenue. When bringing revenue optimization concepts to a golf course, you must think of its inventory as time during which a hole is available, not its physical inventory of carts and equipment. If a hole is not occupied for a period of time, that part of the inventory perishes without generating any revenue. Such time-based perishability is the key to a strategic framework for golf course revenue optimization. With time as the inventory that can be revenue managed, the performance measurement for golf courses is Revenue Per Available Tee Time (RevPATT).

Like other revenue centers, when applying revenue optimization practices to golf, the first steps is to understand the controllable and uncontrollable elements at play — impacting tee times in this case. In golf, uncontrollable elements include things like weather and daylight hours, which will vary. They also include unpredictable behaviors such as the amount of time it takes to play a round, timely tee time arrivals, the number of players that show-up, and no-shows.

Controllable factors include the length of a round of golf, the dispatching rule used on a particular course, maintenance, and the tee time interval. Unless golf course operators have a clear definition of the capacity, they will not be able to measure the performance.[18]

There are two strategic levers that can pulled to drive golf course revenue optimization: 1) round duration control, and 2) demand-based pricing.

For round duration control and demand-based pricing to be effective implements, accurate data is required and help forecast and determine how much to overbook the course at any given time. What is the history of no-shows? Walk-ins? Timely arrivals? Duration of play?

### Round Duration Control
Round duration can be controlled by reducing the uncertainty of when customers will arrive, reducing the variability of the length of the round, and/or by reducing the tee time interval. All of these factors may increase capacity and revenue — if the amount of time between parties can be reduced, more customers can be accommodated, and revenues will likely increase.

Consider a golf course that is open for 10 hours. If the course reduces its 10-minute tee time interval down to 8-minutes, the capacity of the course will increase by 25%. This tactic will not offend a departing customer and should please the customers waiting to play. However, this may cause congestion at some holes due to the variations in pace and expertise of players.

### Demand-Based Pricing
Golfers are generally aware that demand times and days fluctuate considerably. For example, demand may be at its highest on weekend mornings during summer months and at its lowest during a winter weekday. This is, of course, impacted by the geographic location of a golf course.

Like hotels, golf courses have a cost structure including high fixed costs and fairly low variable costs. The low variable costs provide a certain level of flexibility by giving operators room to reduce pricing during low-demand times and increase pricing during high-demand times.

Price golf tee times according to the demand. Applying differential pricing and logical rate fences can build demand during off-peak periods, and establish appropriate prices for busy periods.

Golf course optimization is an evolving field to which hotel revenue professionals can apply their knowledge and experience. To learn more, consider starting with the study "Applying pricing and revenue management in the golf industry: Key challenges" published in the Journal of Revenue & Pricing Management and available at https://www.researchgate.net/publication/265846695.

## Spa Revenue Optimization
"Spas are becoming influential assets for hotels and resorts given the increasing demand related to wellness and lifestyle programs....Examining the depth of spa and wellness performance has become a fundamental factor of strategic growth and valuation. Moreover, understanding how these assets are performing plays a critical role in core strategic planning, including ADR and RevPAR performance."[19]

And, just like rooms, golf, and restaurants, spa services can and should be revenue managed. The same basic principles apply.

Start by understanding all the spa's services and their associated costs — both fixed and variable. Then consider the profitability per service, and the demand per service. Know the spa's peak demand times and the low demand times.

Peak demand time is the perfect opportunity to limit the services to the highest profit margin services. Only offer the lower profit margin services during the low demand times. Decreasing the duration of service during peak demand times can be another way to increase the number of services in one day.

When applying revenue optimization to spa services, the key is to be knowledgeable about the range of services offered and to assess controlled and uncontrolled elements. Consider the space available (treatment rooms), but also consider the number of treatment providers and the amount of time each service involves. Be aware that the inventory is a combination of all three, which can add to the complexity of managing revenue and fees.

Like with hotel performance, measuring and benchmarking results is important. Consider measurements including:

- Spa Revenue per Occupied Hotel Room
- Spa Revenue per Treatment Room
- Average Rate
- Spa Departmental Expense Ratio

## Questions for Review

- Which departments can benefit from applying revenue optimization techniques? What are the benefits and risk considerations for each department to consider?
- Around which issues do all team members need to be aligned?
- What are the recommended steps when getting started in total hotel revenue optimization?
- Which three metrics can help the revenue team make better strategic decisions when it comes to restaurant revenue optimization?
- What are two strategic levers that can pulled to drive golf course revenue optimization?

# CHAPTER 11
## PERFORMANCE ANALYSIS

### Learning Objectives
- To understand the importance of key performance indicators that measure the success of a revenue optimization strategy
- To understand why it is important to align departmental goals around the revenue optimization strategy
- To learn what the key metrics for success should be for any hotel's revenue optimization strategy;
- To develop strategies to implement improvement action plans when key performance indicators are under achieved

It has never been more imperative for hoteliers to set objective metrics that accurately measure the effectiveness of their revenue optimization efforts. The scrutiny by management and investors on financial performance is accelerating the need for sophisticated measurements of revenue performance that are easily understood and directly correlated to the activity being evaluated. Revenue professionals need to have metrics that measure the success of the revenue strategies. Hotel companies have realized the importance of developing processes and sophisticated analyses to measure the revenue team's performance.

### "What gets measured gets done."

### "You cannot manage what you cannot measure."

These are two statements that are often quoted when referring to performance analysis.

Performance measurement plays an important role in:
- Identifying and tracking progress against organizational goals;
- Identifying opportunities for improvement;
- Comparing performance against both internal and external standards.

A revenue optimization organization can have a tremendous impact on the success of a company. Accordingly, many revenue optimization organizations are beginning not only to oversee the process, but also to measure the effectiveness of pricing and inventory control decisions with respect to the bottom line. This expanding role, coupled with robust performance measurement analytics, is leading to increasingly sophisticated metrics to measure revenue performance.

This chapter addresses the key metrics for successful measurements and key reporting methods, and identifies issues that may have an impact — both positive and negative — on performance.

It is important first to understand that every company has identified their own way of measurement and what is important within their environment. For example, some companies measure year-over-year performance while others base measurements on budget alone.

### Key Metrics of Success
It is impossible to manage what cannot be measured. The concept behind this is simple. If you can't measure the performance, you can't tell whether or not there has been any improvement.

There are many key elements that are recommended to ensure proper measurement of revenue optimization strategies and execution. Unfortunately, for a variety of reasons, many hoteliers do not measure success. The most common reason is a lack of understanding of what should be measured. Another is that they simply lack the knowledge of how to measure the result or lack tools that can help.

It is important to realize that an investment in technology may be required in order to effectively track and report success measures. Understand what is needed to do this right. It will be worth it in the end.

To have successful measurements, it is important to put together a solid framework on which measurements will be based. A good performance measurement framework should focus on four key areas:
- Internal Process Perspective
- Learning and Growth Perspective
- Customer Perspective
- Financial Perspective

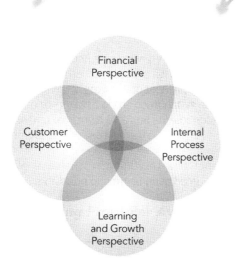

Financial Perspective

Customer Perspective

Internal Process Perspective

Learning and Growth Perspective

It is also important that performance metrics be:

- Meaningful, unambiguous, and widely understood
- Owned and managed by the teams within the hotel or hotel company
- Based on a high level of data integrity
- Such that data collection and proper tracking are embedded in the hotel's regular processes
- Reported and measured with regular frequency
- Able to be interpreted and explained within the organization
- Able to drive improvement
- Linked to critical goals and key drivers for the organization

There are four key steps in a performance measurement framework: the strategic objectives of the organization are converted into desired standards of performance, metrics are developed to compare the desired performance against the actual achieved standards, gaps are identified, and improvement actions taken. These steps are continuously implemented, reviewed, and improved upon.

Establish key goals → Establish metrics → Analyze performance → Implement improvement

If the above process is managed continuously rather than being reviewed once a year, the performance of the hotel will constantly improve. Additionally, any issues can be identified and corrected immediately rather than waiting for a year of poor performance.

In order for a hotel to perform at its best, the appropriate measurements must be tracked. Following are some of the recommended measurements to use in a performance analysis.

## Goal Alignment

Overall, it is important for senior management to establish the same measurements for all team members. Everyone needs to be working toward the same goal. Too often, hotels create different goals for different team members. By doing this, everyone is working toward different goals instead of working toward the same goal. For example, when sales managers are working toward a group production goal or corporate production goal and revenue professionals are working toward RevPAR, there is misalignment. In this case, the sales manager will only be focused on achieving their production goal regardless of how this impacts RevPAR. Success can be achieved if everyone works together and not against one other.

## Forecasting Accuracy

Accuracy in forecasting has a direct impact on the hotel's revenues. Therefore, it makes sense for the revenue professional to be measured based on the accuracy of the actual results compared to the initial forecast.

It is important to measure the performance results based on the initial forecast as this is the forecast from which all of the rate strategies are determined and, therefore, will have the biggest impact on results.

In order to be sure the measurement is being based on a realistic forecast that has a foundation in the business needs, the hotel must first define what that initial forecast needs to be. For example, those hotels that must create the demand forecast five years in advance do not want to use that forecast for measurement as it is highly likely that business needs will change over time. Basing the measurement results on the forecast created so far in advance will only be setting the revenue professional up for failure.

Each hotel will be different and must determine for itself what should be considered the initial forecast. This is likely to be based on an average booking window of two or three months in advance.

Additionally it is important that the expectation be realistic. Do not expect the accuracy of the forecast to be 100%, as this is not a realistic goal for anyone to achieve. Instead, each hotel should take into consideration the skill set and expertise of the revenue professional. If the revenue professional is skilled and very experienced, then the accuracy expectation can be higher; perhaps the actuals would have to be within five percent of the initial forecast. However, if the person is new and has limited experienced, then the expectation should be set to have more room for variance. Over time, as the individual's skill level improves, the hotel can close the accuracy gap and raise the expectations.

Another important factor in understanding a realistic accuracy goal for the hotel is the market in which the hotel sits. Markets with longer lead times and stable patterns are going to be easier to forecast. Other markets may have shorter or very last-minute lead times and erratic patterns will be much more difficult to forecast accurately.

As long as the forecast is created according to the appropriate guidelines such as business conditions (and not created to meet or exceed budget) then it is critical that the forecast have an accuracy expectation and measurement.

Too many hotels or hotel companies require changes to the forecast to meet budgetary goals instead of allowing the revenue professional to create a realistic forecast to meet business conditions. Requesting or requiring changes or enhancements to the forecast to meet other objectives not only puts the hotel in a situation of not being able to achieve optimal revenues, it also creates a no-win cycle.

This is a waste of energy and time for everyone involved. The end result is that the hotel will not achieve its potential for many reasons — the most likely of which is that their strategies were based on an unrealistic forecast.

## RevPAR

Both occupancy and ADR correlate to revenue optimization effectiveness, but revenue per available room (RevPAR) is a far better measurement because it includes both occupancy and ADR.

As touched on earlier, many hoteliers are still in the habit of measuring different staff members on different metrics. Occupancy and ADR are good examples of this. Many times the sales managers are measured (and incentivized) on volume of room nights or bookings and reservations staff are measured (and incentivized) on

ADR. RevPAR is a much better measurement because it is a good balance of both.

RevPAR can be deceiving depending on how it is used and compared. RevPAR is a valuable indicator of revenue efficiency when one is comparing an individual hotel's performance over time or to a well-defined competitive set.

## RevPAR Index (RPI) or Revenue Generation Index (RGI)

RPI and RGI are two labels for the ratio of the hotel's RevPAR and the RevPAR of the competitive set. A RevPAR (Yield) Index measures a hotel's fair market share of their segment's (competitive set, market, submarket, etc.) revenue per available room. If a hotel is capturing its fair market share, the index will be 100; if capturing less than its fair market share, a hotel's index will be less than 100; if capturing more than its fair market share, a hotel's index will be greater than 100.

To obtain this number, simply divide the hotel's RevPAR by the competitive set's RevPAR and multiply by 100. Fair share can be thought of as the subject hotel's "piece of the pie" in the market. For example, if the subject hotel's RevPAR is $50 and the RevPAR of its competitive set is $50, the subject hotel's index would total 100. If the subject hotel's RevPAR totals $60, its index would be 120, which indicates that the subject hotel has captured more than its fair share. If the subject hotel's RevPAR totals $40, its index would be 80, which indicates that the subject hotel has captured less than its fair share.

## Market Share Index

Market intelligence reports provide market share information, which includes market measurements such as market share, ADR index, and RevPAR index. An index measures a hotel's performance relative to an aggregated grouping of hotels (e.g., competitive set, market, submarket). An index of 100 means that the hotel is capturing its fair share. An index of more than 100 means it's capturing more than fair share and, conversely, an index less than 100 means it's capturing less than fair share.

Index balance (comparing the occupancy index with the ADR index) is an indicator of how well a hotel did in comparison to the market. Generally speaking, occupancy and rate indexes should not have more than a ten-point spread between them.

### Index Growth

The growth of a hotel's year-over-year index compared to the growth of the competitive set's allows a hotel to measure its ability to grow revenue, ADR, and occupancy compared to the growth of the competitive set year-over-year. If the market grows 10% and subject hotel grows by 5%, it is important to see this.

Consistent imbalances in indexes and index growth could be an indication of a misaligned competitive set.

### Gross Operating Profit Per Available Room (GOPPAR)

For hotels that are complex and sophisticated enough to focus on total hotel revenue optimization, GOPPAR may be a good measurement to use. This measurement allows the focus to be put on how well the hotel is managing the entire business.

More revenue professionals are included in EBITA discussions and are included in the overall revenue strategy discussions.

GOPPAR is derived from taking the gross operating profit (revenues minus expenses) and dividing it by the number of available rooms.

### Net RevPAR

Net RevPAR (Net Revenue Per Available Room ) has been talked about for quite some time but very few are measuring it accurately. Hotels can continue to increase top line revenues, but if costs are not understood and accurately measured, then owners will still be dissatisfied.

Net RevPAR is derived by taking the revenue minus all acquisition costs (commissions and sales and marketing expenditures) and dividing it by the number of available rooms.

A hotel can have a strong RevPAR Index and growth results, and one may believe that the hotel is performing optimally. However, once a true understanding of Net RevPAR is achieved, the performance of a hotel may look completely different.

Other metrics that are becoming more common include:
- Profit Per Available Room (ProPAR) which is based on operating profit and accounts for movements in both revenues and expenses

- TRevPAR, which measures the total revenue per available room from all revenue centers
- RevPAG, which helps hoteliers understand the total revenue per available guest

Regardless of the measurement a hotel uses, there are reports that need to be integrated into the daily operation of the hotel so performance can be measured effectively. The following section provides some direction on what types of reports should be considered in order to attain proper and useful measurements.

## Key Elements of Reports

It is important to design a reporting process and identify the key reports or required information that will be needed in order to effectively analyze the hotel's performance.

That process should:
- Determine the process for data collection and reporting;
- Create clear expectations and write clear definitions;
- Agree upon a method for establishing performance;
- Agree upon the data formats;
- Identify sources of benchmark information;
- Determine the reporting calendar;
- Establish roles and responsibilities;
- Detail training requirements (if any are needed to perform tasks or measurements);
- Validate with process stakeholders.

Establishing the right reports is critical to properly measure the performance of revenue optimization. The following are types of technology, third party vendors, and reports that hoteliers can look to for collection of information.
- Property management system;
- Revenue management system;
- Central reservation system;
- Sales and catering system;
- Customer relationship management system;
- Data service provider;
- Market intelligence or business intelligence companies;
- Representation companies;
- Benchmarking reports;
- Market share reports;
- Corporate account and travel agency performance & market share reports.

## Discovering Issues Impacting Performance

Understanding performance measurement metrics and how to effectively implement and manage them is important. However, it is just as important to understand the issues that may have an impact on performance and performance measurements.

Hotel senior management has a responsibility to ensure the proper revenue-focused culture is created and cultivated throughout the entire company or hotel. Success begins at the top.

The following are critical factors that must be in place to ensure success:

- Strong leadership and a commitment to supplying the appropriate support and tools needed;
- Good planning and a sound implementation strategy;
- Appropriate employee involvement to ensure understanding and buy-in;
- Simple measurements and evaluation (do not overcomplicate it);
- Constantly striving for improvement;
- A culture that encourages risk-taking and redirects appropriately when mistakes are made;
- Proactive rather than reactive leadership (do not react to every change in the market with drastic changes to the plan or to expectations);
- Aligned departmental goals;
- Rewards for employees for achieving revenue goals and successfully implementing the revenue optimization strategy.

## The Front Desk

It is often not fully understood by operations leaders the impact that the front desk has on the revenue success. The front desk must embrace the revenue strategies and the tactics needed to achieve the revenue goals so that they may properly support them.

A common practice that negatively impacts revenue success is the front desk holding "fake" rooms so that they do not have to worry about "walking" or overbooking situations. While their intent is never to have a negative impact on the revenues achieved, these practices are often done out of pure survival because they do not understand the overall strategy and everything that goes into achieving it. Therefore, it is important that front desk is included in the discussions, has input, and is on the same page with the estimated "wash" factor. This will go a long way toward ensuring that they work together with the rest of the team to achieve the revenue goals.

## Questions for Review

- What are the four key metrics of success when it comes to performance measurement?
- Why is it important to ensure goal alignment within an organization? What benefits does it bring?
- Why is it important to ensure accuracy in forecasting? What benefit does it bring?
- What are some of the recommended measurements to use in performance analysis?
- What are some critical issues to ensure are properly handled to ensure successful performance?

# CHAPTER 12
## PUTTING IT ALL TOGETHER

## Learning Objectives

- To understand how to create a successful revenue optimization strategy
- To learn the key elements in effectively communicating a revenue optimization strategy
- To understand how to implement a strategy once it has been created
- To understand how to measure the success of the strategy once it has been implemented

A revenue strategy should aim to capture the optimal profitability and business mix from projected demand. While it is important to have a clear strategy and direction for revenue optimization, equally important is how the revenue team*, led by the revenue professional, discusses, develops, and supports the goals for the hotel, then articulates those goals and manages the strategy throughout the hotel.

The revenue strategy should permeate the entire organization. It should be clear, actionable, and measurable. Each department should be held accountable, as well as be rewarded for the success of their component of the strategy. A successful strategy will incorporate the perspective of every department of the hotel or company. When developing a strategy, it is important to consider all input from all stakeholders — from line-level employees to executive-level managers. This will help maintain existing revenue sources and drive incremental revenue.

*See chapter 3 for more information on developing and managing effective revenue teams.

## Developing a Revenue Strategy

The first step in developing a revenue strategy is to ensure that the entire revenue team is included, prepared, and attending regularly scheduled meetings. To be successful the entire revenue team needs to provide their input and fully buy into the strategy. This is the only way to ensure all perspectives are taken into consideration and that there is across-the-board agreement. Moving forward, everyone needs to be working from the same foundation and goals.

It is also important to understand that the development of a revenue strategy may take one long meeting or several shorter meetings. Therefore, plan accordingly and make sure everyone has the same understanding and expectation.

Include the following elements in every revenue optimization strategy:

| ELEMENT TO INCLUDE | PURPOSE |
|---|---|
| Demand Targeting | Determine the most appropriate segments and identify which ones will deliver the greatest profit or value to the hotel. This must be done for the entire year and be broken down by season. |
| Acquisition Planning | Determine a communications plan and a sales plan that outlines how to reach each of the targeted segments to achieve the goals. |
| Customer Retention Plan | Identify the method(s) by which the hotel will retain customers. How will the hotel work to communicate directly with the customers to capture their next booking? How will the hotel target the appropriate customers directly? |
| Revenue per Available Customer Value | Identify the types of customers who provide the most value to the hotel. Factors to be included are the total spend, the time-of-year or day-of-week the customer typically stays with the hotel, and the method of booking. Once the team has a good idea of the revenue per available customer, create a plan to target the customers with higher value. |
| Channel Costs | Determine the cost to the hotel for each channel. This allows the team to understand the most profitable channel through which to receive bookings. |
| Channel Shifts | Once the team understands the most profitable channels, develop a plan to target specific customers or customer types to shift their bookings to a lower cost channel as appropriate for each customer. For example, for those customers who currently book through a higher cost channel such as a third-party site, provide an incentive for them to book via a lower cost channel like the hotel's website. It will not be appropriate to shift all customers to another channel, but it will benefit the hotel to shift those that are appropriate. |
| Acquisition Costs | Understand how much the cost of customer acquisition is by channel and by segment. |

All of the decisions and factors must be documented and distributed to all revenue team members, including the following:

- Specific and detailed action plans created in support of the strategy.

- Assigned responsibilities for all action plans. Remember, the revenue strategy is led by the revenue professional, but can only be successful through collaboration across disciplines/discipline owners.
- Assigned timelines or specific dates for all action plans.

The last step in the development of the strategy is to set follow-up meetings to review the progress, discuss challenges, and identify resolutions. These meetings will allow the revenue professional to ensure everyone is doing what they should be doing to stay on target.

## Managing Demand

Managing demand is a key factor in revenue optimization strategy, and requires an understanding of unconstrained demand, which is a measure of how much demand a hotel would enjoy in the absence of any pricing and inventory constraints. In other words, if one room could be built for each additional request for a room, the total would be the unconstrained demand for that hotel.

Applying restrictions (e.g., pricing, rate fences, stay patterns, etc.) constrains the demand for a hotel. In some cases, this is good and needed. There are definitely times when they are called for. For example, if a hotel sells out all the time, it is possible that the rate was not set optimally. So, achieving full sellouts is not always the best possible result.

Full sell outs often have a negative impact on their shoulder nights. While you cannot force demand for them, low-occupancy nights can be better managed through the use of restrictions. When a hotel sells out on specific evenings – especially if it sells out too quickly or too early – it misses revenue opportunities from guests who would have stayed through the sold-out night on the shoulder nights.

Another way to look at it is, when evaluating unsold rooms on a night during high-demand times, you might initially think that a length-of-stay restriction hurt results. Before jumping to that conclusion, look at the bigger picture — you may find that, because stay restrictions were applied, the hotel actually optimized its revenue opportunity over the course of multiple days versus just that one day in question.

Keep in mind that it is possible for a hotel to overuse restrictions and end up hurting its revenue. An automated revenue management system can help manage optimal revenue restrictions and rates; however, the revenue professional often has information about their hotel, market, and competition that an automated revenue management system does not. Therefore, it is critical to continually "teach" the revenue management system and never adhere to a "set it and forget it" mentality.

## Communicating the Strategy

Once the revenue strategy is developed and properly documented, it is critical to communicate it to all key stakeholders. "This must be done in a well-planned and thorough manner in order to obtain a high level of 'buy-in' of the current goals and objectives of our organizations," said Jack Easdale, Senior Vice President of Revenue Management & Enterprise Analytics at Venetian/Palazzo/Sands Expo. "Thoughtful management at all levels must lead in these endeavors in order for the corporation to survive and thrive in today's disquieting milieu."

All members of the revenue team must receive a final copy of the strategy. Be sure to distribute the final copy to all team members by the predetermined due date.

A communications plan must be created and executed to ensure proper understanding, support from the field, and success. Each department and level of staff or management has their own role in ensuring success. Therefore, they will need to understand varying parts of the strategy to support it and do their part. Remember — one size does not fit all. The communication will need to be tailored to each audience member. For example, what the general manager needs to know may be different from what the front office manager needs to know and will certainly be different from what the reservation sales associates need to know.

It is very important that the revenue professional (or whoever is responsible for the communication) manages the communication to all team members. The communication of the strategy can ultimately determine its success.

Consider the following recommendations which may help manage the communication of a revenue strategy to all stakeholders.

1. Prioritize the information that needs to be shared.
2. Educate the players.
   - Provide the specific information each department needs to know.
   - Outline the specific ways each department plays a role, and show them how they are fit in the overall strategy.
3. Be specific about what is needed from each department.
4. Create an action plan with each department. Be specific, and assign due dates and responsibilities.
5. Set follow-up meetings to ensure ongoing communication and buy-in.

The following sections outline the varying roles and responsibilities of each key stakeholder along with recommendations on how to target each appropriately.

### Communicating to Ownership or the Corporate Office

One of the key points in communicating the strategy, or any information, to a corporate office and ownership is the fact that the information that is most appropriate for them will be different in many ways than the information that is appropriate for others.

It is first important to identify the key points that are most important for the ownership or the corporate office to know and understand. It is also important to understand the existing knowledge level. For example, does ownership understand the complexity of distribution channels and the costs associated with each? Do they understand strategic forecasting? Understanding their level of knowledge will help you in putting together the information. It may require straight forward information in some areas where there is a high comfort level and some supporting educational information in other areas where the comfort level is lower.

Owners and corporate offices typically have the same areas of focus — ROI, bottom line revenue, profitability, procurement, and development.

The information that will be provided to this audience will need to take into consideration all of the above points. Additionally, be sure that the information provided is specific and to the point, supports their overall goals, and includes supporting data where appropriate.

The method of communicating this information will vary based on several factors:
- Your relationship with them
- Their preferences
- The type of information to be communicated

The method of communication may include some face-to-face meetings along with supporting documentation and a formal presentation or simply a formal document sent via email. This must be assessed by each company to determine their specific preferences.

### Communicating to the General Manager

It is vital that the general manager has a solid, high-level understanding of the revenue strategy and the tactical plans to execute it. It is important that the general manager does not undermine the strategy by focusing on short-term results, demanding constant changes, or requiring implementations that work against the original strategy. If this happens, no one will be successful. The general manager needs a full copy of the strategy and someone to walk through all of the high-level points with him or her. Ideally, the general manager will have been involved in the development of the strategy, but depending on the hotel structure this is not always possible.

### Communicating to Sales and Marketing

Revenue optimization and sales have a long history of not always seeing "eye to eye." Because of this, it is vital that there is a strong level of communication between the two.

Sales and marketing professionals need to have a good understanding of the revenue optimization strategies — both short- and long-term. Without this understanding, it will be difficult to ensure that everyone is on the same page and working toward the same goals.

There are many ways or approaches to communicating the revenue optimization strategies and providing information that will help sales and marketing know specifically what they can do to impact the goals — both negatively and positively, as well as both long-term and short-term. It really is all about the communication and information shared that will bridge any gaps between these departments or disciplines.

It is critical to provide them with an overview of the various demand periods with the supporting rate strategies. Ensure that sales and marketing both have a solid understanding of specific dates and time periods for when business is needed. Discuss specific items that can help to fill the slower times with more business. Hotels that are corporate focused may consider ideas such as GDS marketing campaigns, consortia campaigns, or value-add promotions to offer during these dates. Hotels that are leisure heavy might consider an email promotion or online promotions. The point is, identify all possible options to help drive more business during the "need" times based on the customer type that makes the most sense for the hotel and timeframe.

It is equally important to ensure that the sales team is included in the strategies for high-demand time periods. A good example for a corporate hotel is to ensure that everyone knows how corporate contracted business will be yielded to accept longer lengths of stay versus one-night stays.

One of the ways to ensure buy-in of the strategies and open communication is to make sure everyone is working toward the same goals. Sales managers should be measured by profitability, not by volume. Ensuring the optimal communication and understanding as described will ensure proper buy-in by all.

> In addition to communicating the revenue strategy to sales and marketing stakeholders, consider continuing education and training for them in revenue optimization topics. HSMAI offers online training on revenue optimization specifically designed for non-revenue professionals (e.g., sales, marketing, and operations).

### Communicating to Operations

Communicating the revenue optimization strategies to the operational departments is just as important as communicating with the sales and marketing department. Unfortunately, the operational departments are often forgotten. The operational departments such as front desk and reservations are critical to ensuring the success of the revenue optimization strategy. These are the departments that are dealing with customers on a daily basis, receiving feedback and questions, and are selling the products and services.

These departments need to understand the general strategies, the purpose for these strategies, and how the revenue team came to their decisions. Additionally, they need to understand management's expectations on how to "sell" the product, and they need to have guidelines for

overcoming objections or resistance in their efforts to sell the product.

This can be achieved through several communication opportunities:

■ Ensure the appropriate department heads are included in the meetings at which the strategies are set.
■ Ensure the appropriate department heads are included in the ongoing revenue meetings (see recommended revenue team members).
■ Attend the appropriate departmental meetings. This will be extremely helpful in providing information directly to the line staff and answering any questions or concerns they may have.

Another point critical to success is providing the operations team with an understanding of how they can impact the results directly. Ensure that they are provided with the tools and training to know how their activities have a direct impact on achieving the revenue goals and adhering to the revenue optimization strategy. A whiteboard in the back office outlining the monthly revenue goals along with a daily status update of what is on the books is a great way to keep them informed.

Remember, good communication is the key to maintaining successful relationships.

## Implementing a Revenue Strategy

The next step is to ensure a successful execution of the revenue optimization strategy. This is where many hotels drop the ball. There are several things hotels can implement to ensure the strategy is executed successfully.

The first and most critical is to ensure everyone's incentives are created so that every team member is working toward the same goal. Create the incentives to focus and reward based on profitability. This does not mean the incentives must be the same across the board. Instead, just be sure the incentives created are appropriate for each individual and allow their focus to be on the same end goal as everyone else.

The next step is to ensure all appropriate departments understand their role in the strategy and tactical plans. Each department should have a specific plan of action that is appropriate for their department and positions. Review these plans with each department. Follow up periodically with one-on-one meetings to work through any challenges and give recommendations. This follow up is key to ensuring everyone stays motivated and continues moving forward.

## Measuring the Success of a Revenue Strategy

Measuring the success of a revenue strategy is just as important as developing it. Without measurements one would not know the outcome and what needs to be changed for the future.

One of the key indicators of whether or not a revenue strategy worked for a hotel is how many times the revenue team wanted to or tried to make significant changes without an extreme market change. Did the team implement tactical plans that conflicted with the overall strategy? Did this happen often? Was everyone questioning the strategy over and over again? If the answer is yes to these questions, then there is a strong possibility the overall strategy was not developed to work realistically for the hotel and the market conditions. It is also important to drill down further and review each element and how successful each one was throughout the year.

Each department's role must also be reviewed. Did the department implement their specific action plans? What worked? What did not work? What were the challenges? What was done to overcome these challenges? Was it the specific actions that were failing or not appropriate, or were they neglected? Was it human error? Was it process error?

## Adjusting a Revenue Strategy During Extreme Market Changes

Effective strategies are the outcome of expert analysis and evaluation. Strategy setting is an ongoing process. Through excellent management, it will become obvious when to change and when to maintain the current strategy.

Anyone can have the best laid plans, but the reality is that extreme market changes can cause a need to adjust a revenue optimization strategy. Hoteliers have faced the reality of major unexpected events significantly impacting revenue optimization strategies. Events such as 9/11, the 2011 tsunami in Japan, Hurricane Katrina in New Orleans in 2005, and Houston's Hurricane Harvey in 2017, and so many more, have forced hoteliers to quickly readjust their plans.

It is important that, if a hotel company uses a revenue management system, the system can quickly recalibrate to take into consideration the new market conditions when establishing revenue recommendations, pricing, and inventory controls. If a hotel company does not utilize a revenue management system, it is equally important that the hotel is able to make quick changes in all channels to respond to an extreme market change.

Additionally, data from past time frames in which there were extreme market changes should be examined to determine what worked well, what didn't work well, and what adjustments produced the best results. A plan that considers major demand-impacting events must be created and executed quickly. For example, after 9/11 many companies realized they had to do drive campaigns with organizations like AAA, because many people stopped flying. During those times, it is crucial to be aware of changing travel patterns and create a plan to address the new reality.

## Questions for Review

- Which elements should be included in every revenue optimization strategy?
- To whom and for what purpose should the strategy be communicated?
- How can a revenue professional determine if a revenue strategy is working for the hotel?

# PART TWO:
# CROSS-DISCIPLINARY
# PARTNERSHIPS & THE ROLE
# OF REVENUE OPTIMIZATION

**Today, to drive optimal revenue and optimal profitability, other revenue-impacting elements (beyond the fundamentals covered earlier in this book) are often being added to the revenue professional's responsibilities.**

Therefore, it is not possible to talk about revenue optimization or its related strategies without addressing owners, strategic distribution, marketing, data analytics, business intelligence, or information technology (IT).

These specialties are extremely interdependent — regardless of how it might seem when looking at a hotel or hotel company's organizational structure. If they are not being directly added to the revenue professional's duties, the revenue professional is certainly expected to have a solid understanding of them and to work collaboratively with the individuals and teams looking after them.

At the same time, to be more agile and achieve better results, hotels need to break down the silos between revenue-generating disciplines. This means that all functions — sales, marketing, revenue, branding, loyalty, and reservations — must collaborate and operate as one team. To achieve this holistic approach will likely require a new perspective on well-established processes and a willingness from all to change. Appendix D offers a case study of this collaboration in action with an example

of what revenue optimization and marketing can accomplish when they are aligned.

The traditional roles of marketing and sales have been to generate and capture demand while revenue management tactically executed product distribution, yielding, conversion, and optimization of that demand. Today, revenue optimization professionals are intimately entwined with demand drivers, creating even higher expectations.

It is not news that the better collaboration, the more profitable and successful the enterprise. With this in mind, some hotel companies are now moving toward an integrated approach to their organizations, with one person with oversight responsibility for all commercial functions (sales, marketing, and revenue optimization). The intent behind this type of structure is to support proactive business mix planning and more effective deployment (or realignment as business demand drivers indicate the need) of revenue-generating resources.

This chapter provides a high-level overview of the interdisciplinary issues between revenue optimization and technology operations, marketing operations, and data analytics. Chapter 14 examines owners. Chapter 15 is a deep dive on issues related to strategic distribution. Chapter 16 covers marketing, with an emphasis on managing it in the digital world.

## Technology Operations

More often than not — in hotels and across industries — technology responsibilities fall under the information technology (IT) discipline. Hoteliers, however, have begun to look at "technology" in two different categories.

First is overall technology, including technical installation and set-up, networking, security, and ongoing maintenance. The second category — equally as important for hoteliers to understand — is technology operations. This includes system selection and the operational set-up from the perspective of the business need and practical application of the system, which has a direct impact on the data output and interfaces with other systems. It requires careful thought and a strategic approach in how technologies are selected and set up.

Often during a new system installation, hoteliers rely on the technology vendor to train them on how to use the system. While that vendor's perspective is important, it certainly does not provide the full picture. They will share the standard technical or transactional approach on how to use the tool, but they are not in a position to identify the most critical component: the technology operations strategy in terms of how the hotel or hotel company will use the system to support optimizing revenues. Business

stakeholders' involvement is critical in order to minimize business disruption, optimize system set-up, and use the tech to its fullest extent.

There are often nuances to a hotel's revenue strategy that a technology provider does not understand. On top of that, complex systems such as PMS, CRS, and RMS typically require a degree of custom set-up specific to the hotel's strategies.

The initial set-up of a system including the use of fields, parameters, integration with supporting systems, data flow, efficiency, and more, is important to ensure that it will support the desired output. The set-up will have a direct impact on resulting data and the usefulness of it. It will also impact data flow between systems which can impact the optimization of other systems already in use or newly installed.

The point is that hoteliers would be wise to ensure the right resources are dedicated to fully understanding the optimal system set-up based on the needs of the hotel and/or hotel company. Otherwise, changing the set-up later can be extremely painful. Investing time and financial resources up front will be well worth the investment and prevent lost opportunity in the future.

The following graphic demonstrates the complexity of various technology components and integration between and among them, and illustrates the importance of making sure the initial set-up is done properly. Keep in mind that this is just an example. Every system, company, and offering is different when it comes to terminology and integration approach.

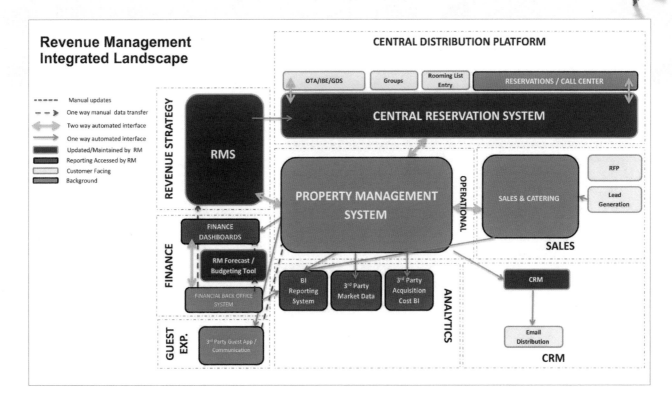

Revenue Management
Integrated Landscape

The next graphic shows, at a high-level, the configuration elements that must be set up in most systems. Again, the terminology differs from system to system, but the general concept is the same in most. The key takeaway is that all the decisions and details in the configuration will ultimately impact the decision output, and, potentially, the revenue optimization strategy.

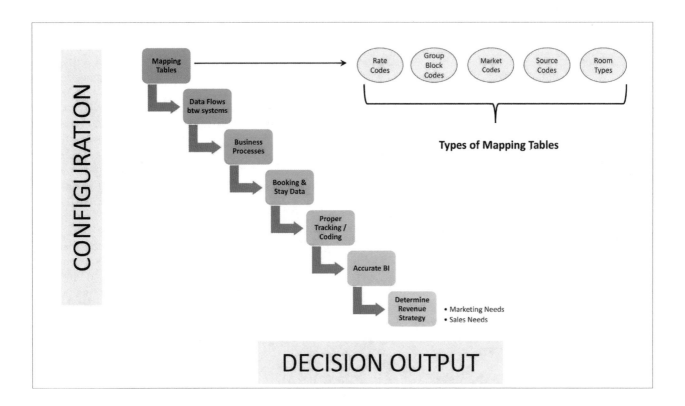

The next graphic demonstrates the different systems that must have proper mapping tables defined and set up properly. Each system has its own types of mapping tables impacting the decision output.

This is a very common area overlooked or not understood by many hoteliers. Often times the end users of the system are not aware of the mapping tables, or have not been fully exposed to the set-up and impact.

Without the proper set-up, understanding, and accuracy of the mapping tables, the integration between systems is not optimal. The resulting product will require significant manual work on the part of the user. That is exactly the opposite of the intended result of leveraging technology to support revenue optimization (or any other function within the hotel).

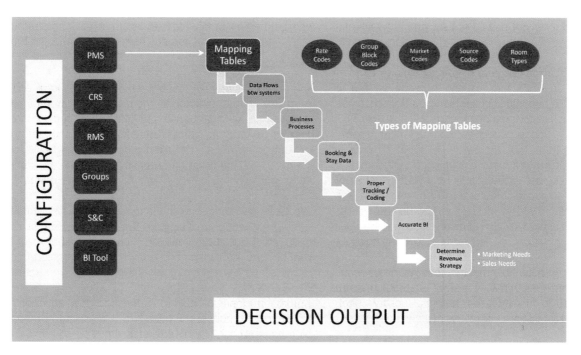

The other areas equally as important, but often not fully embraced or understood, are the supporting revenue-related business processes. The next graphic illustrates a few critical business processes that will impact revenue if not handled properly.

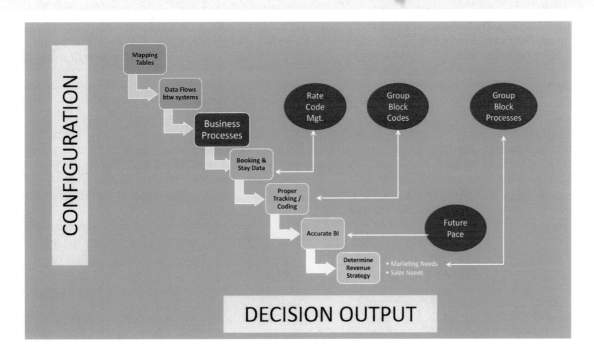

## Group Block Example

Setting up a proper group block can have a significant impact on a revenue strategy — for hotels that focus on large or on small groups.

When creating a group block in the system of record, be sure you understand the technology's functionality within the group block. (The system of record can vary by hotel or company, but for many hotels it's the PMS.)

In an ideal world, the group block should be set up in the system to hold rooms by room type (not run of house), and the total number of rooms being held should be "netted." That means that if a group contracts for 100 rooms, it is the hotel's responsibility to ensure that a "net" amount (versus the "gross" amount) of rooms are held out of inventory.

Most groups will not pick up or actualize the gross amount originally contracted. If the revenue team believes that the group will only pick up 90 rooms out of that 100, only 90 should be held out of inventory. Leave the remaining 10 rooms in inventory to continue to sell. This practice will help with forecasting accuracy further out.

## Marketing Operations

Just as technology is impacted by technology operations, marketing also has an operational element which needs to be better understood by revenue professionals.

When a marketing campaign is created, there is a need to support the campaign in various ways that are specific to each channel, and will likely differ by channel. To ensure proper execution of the campaign and optimize results, operational needs are best documented and clearly outlined.

For example, a promotion with a voice channel component requires that the reservations department, or call center agents, must understand the operational implications in order for them to find and book the promotion. Deliberately identifying and planning for the operational components of marketing efforts make the difference between a seamless call with the customer and one that is fragmented because the agent does not have all the information needed to support the caller's interest and questions.

Knowing booking codes, how and where to find the promotion in the system, how to book and code the reservation, and other information needed to effectively "sell" the offer are critical to a smooth process. It is also critical in order to accurately track the results of the offer.

Taking a detailed approach to outlining all pertinent information for each campaign will help increase the ROI for each campaign. Detailed layers of tracking are critical to providing clarity across the organization. Consider defining and using campaign-specific terms for channel, source, sub-source, rate plan, rate category, and rate code.

As noted below, if coding and tracking are not set up with a cohesive and defined approach, the data extracted and the data output will not be useful to anyone. Making decisions based on bad data will only lead to bad strategies and thus to lack of optimization.

To better plan for operational components of marketing, start with understanding all the offline and online tools available to hoteliers, many of which fall to the revenue professional to manage. Further details regarding the online components are in chapter 16.

## Data Analytics

The importance of having data easily available cannot be understated as timely, actionable data is essential for setting and deploying sound strategies. Revenue professionals are under increasing pressure to extract knowledge and insights from vast amounts of data to enhance business strategies and optimize the customer experience.

While revenue professionals have unprecedented access to data today, many still struggle to gain the "right" data. Most understand that the data extracted from their technology tools is only as good as the data entered into them.

The focus of this section is to help hoteliers understand how to properly set up a solid foundation to prepare for tracking of accurate data analytics. Prior to being able to use any type of sophisticated analytics system or even extract simple reports from the PMS or CRS, there are a few steps that hoteliers must first understand and embrace.

Like with technology operations and marketing operations, proper set-up with desired data results is essential and will have a direct impact on results.

Start by very clearly defining every field. If fields are not clearly defined, users may enter the "right" data but may not enter it into the "right" field. This requires a collaborative partnership among the technology operations team, the data analytics team (or expert), and the revenue optimization team. Ensure that every field and every data point is clearly defined so that it is fully understood and embraced by all departments — from marketing and sales to reservations, front desk, and other departments that are part of the overall revenue optimization strategy.

If coding and tracking are not set up with a cohesive and defined approach, the data extracted and the data output will not be useful to anyone. Making decisions based on bad data will only lead to bad strategies and thus to lack of optimization.

In order to have long-term integrity in the data, hoteliers would be wise to ensure that there is a dedicated department that is held responsible for the data integrity. This typically is someone in operations such as the front office manager or director of operations.

It is important ongoing education and training take place for existing staff, and that there is a process to educate and train new staff members. If someone understands the reason behind the fields, how they are used, and how their role impacts this data, that person is more likely to focus on getting it right.

Have some type of tracking or scoring for the data integrity or data accuracy. What gets measured, gets done. Without ongoing measurement of data collected, the focus on ensuring accuracy may be lost.

# CHAPTER 14
## OWNERS

Understanding ownership's point of view is critical to help revenue professionals manage expectations and ensure alignment.

Owners come in all shapes and sizes — institutional owners such as pension funds and private equity funds or REITs (Real Estate Investment Trusts); a group of individuals that has formed a single purpose entity (SPE) joint venture in a hotel asset; a family investment; and management companies that both manage and own hotels. But one thing is certain, all owners are looking for the same thing — return on their investment.

Expected investment returns will vary from owner to owner, but will likely include either:

- an expectation, or even need, for immediate cash flow;
- a strategy to build asset value over time and get the return when they sell the asset. Many investment timeframes are between three to five years or five to seven years. This is not a hard and fast rule as there are many other variations.

There are also many examples of owner-operator partnerships. Some owners work directly with the hotel team or operator while others hire asset managers to manage the operator relationship and asset results.

Regardless of the set-up, in recent years owners have taken an active role in how their hotels are managed. This is especially true when it comes to the revenue optimization discipline, as owners see the significant value this discipline brings to their asset's profitability growth.

Profit growth is realized when the dollar value of the change in revenue exceeds the dollar value of the change in expenses. Hoteliers have long used the growth of RevPAR to measure the growth of profitability for an asset. According the CRBE's "2017 Trends in the U.S. Hotel Industry," there has been an 86% correlation between the annual changes in RevPAR and gross operating profit from 1960 to 2016 (in the U.S.).[20] This implies that changes in RevPAR do provide a very strong indication of changes in Gross Operating Profit (GOP).

"The strong relationship between changes in RevPAR and changes in GOP becomes evident when analyzing data from the 2017 [CRBE] report. From 2015 to 2016, the entire sample of 3,331 operating statements averaged a RevPAR increase of 2.6 percent, while GOP for the sample grew by 3.7 percent. However, when stratifying the sample by the magnitude of RevPAR change, we see a linear relationship between RevPAR change and GOP change."[21]

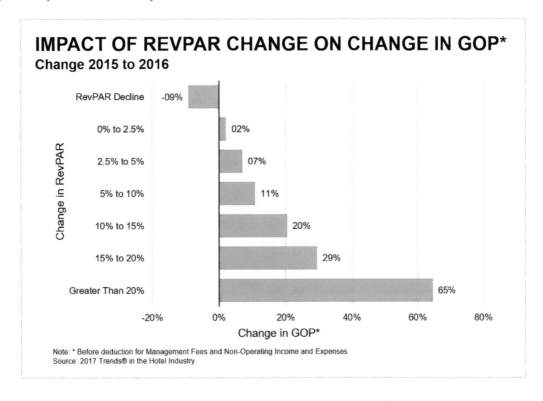

**IMPACT OF REVPAR CHANGE ON CHANGE IN GOP***
**Change 2015 to 2016**

Note: * Before deduction for Management Fees and Non-Operating Income and Expenses
Source: 2017 Trends® in the Hotel Industry.

## Optimizing the Partnership

Both owners and operators will best be served by understanding the others' needs and quickly figuring out the best way to partner together. Owners need to be confident that their asset is being managed by experienced operators who will produce optimal results. Operators need to know that their teams have the appropriate resources (financial, human, and technology), and reasonable autonomy and flexibility to be successful in achieving the goals.

If all players can create and work from this foundation of mutual understanding and respect, the relationship is more likely to be positive. Operators — including the revenue professional — should keep the following advice in mind to cultivate healthy and productive partnerships with ownership.

- Always take a partner-like approach. Think about what the other needs to best do their jobs.
- Understand the HMA (Hotel Management Agreement). This ensures that everyone knows the guidelines established in the HMA and the performance expectations outlined.
- Understand the value of the asset.
- Ensure that all constituents are working with the same understanding of and beliefs about the hotel's positioning, competitive set, and market conditions. Ensure that these factors are being examined from a realistic point of view, not a personal preference or gut-feel point of view.
- Communicate the short- and long-term strategies, expected results compared to budget and the forecasts, and the risks involved. Always do it in a timely and thorough manner. Communication is key.
- Communicate any anticipated short-falls to budget or forecast well in advance, along with supporting initiatives already in place to try to mitigate the short-fall. Do not wait until the last minute to communicate the short-fall. Waiting until the last minute, or even worse after, can and will likely destroy trust.
- Establish regular owner meetings and calls to review past results, future expectations, anticipated variances, supporting strategies, and what is needed from the owner. The frequency of these meetings and calls can be determined in partnership with the owner. Some prefer frequent (weekly or monthly) meetings or calls while others are comfortable with less. Identify what

works best for all involved. Be flexible and adjust as needed.
- Determine what information to share with the owner in advance of any meeting. Make sure that the information you send is useful to the owner and identify any gaps in information they may need. Once you know what you'll share, ensure timely delivery based on the owner's expectations. This will avoid an overload of ad hoc requests for "other" information.
- Listen to and seek to understand the owner's point of view.
- Take advantage of the opportunity to collect market data from those owners who have multiple hotels in the same city.
- Take advantage of the opportunity to understand the ideas and proven successes from those owners who have multiple hotels.
- Voice your opinion, as long as it is backed by data and experience, even if it conflicts with the owner's opinion about the revenue optimization strategy. Share supporting information, along with potential performance-impact concerns. Owners hold operators responsible for results, so it is important to identify, embrace, and execute the best possible strategy to achieve the goals.

Owners will be well-served to keep the following advice in mind to cultivate healthy and productive partnerships with operators.
- Always take a partner-like approach. Think about what the other needs to best do their jobs.
- Ensure that the operators have all the appropriate resources (financial, human, and technology) to effectively do their jobs to reach optimal results.
- Assuming there is a trusting and respectful relationship in place, give the operator reasonable autonomy and flexibility to reach goals in the way they determine is optimal.
- Ensure that all constituents are working with the same understanding of and beliefs about the hotel's positioning, competitive set, and market conditions. Ensure that these factors are being examined from a realistic point of view, not a personal preference or gut-feel point of view.
- Support realistic goal setting, including budget expectations. Asking for some "stretch" is acceptable, but too much can be demotivating and set the team up for failure.

- Encourage two-way communication. Some operators will be hesitant to voice a difference of opinion. Be open to what they have to say and ensure healthy discussions.
- Listen to and seek to understand the operator's point of view.
- Offer (instead of dictating) ideas and suggestions.
- Respect the operator's time by providing advance notice (when possible) of any special or unscheduled requests. Ad hoc requests will happen but try to avoid too many of them as they will disrupt the team's focus and ability to effectively operate and drive strategy for the hotel.

## Understanding Asset Value

The following illustrates the negative impact to asset value with the decline in a hotel's monthly Revenue Generation Index (RGI). Eight out of nine months have declining year-over-year (YOY) RGI. This equates to $900k in rooms revenue, implying lost asset value of over $6.4mm, assuming 50% flow to the bottom line and a 6% cap rate.

**Monthly RGI, YoY % Change**

| TTM Valuation Reassessment | | | | | |
|---|---|---|---|---|---|
| | Jul-12 Jun-13 | Jul-13 Jun-14 | Jul-14 Jun-15 | Jul-15 Jun-16 | Jul-16 Jun-17 |
| NOI w/ FEE | $9,511,802 | $8,470,029 | $8,336,383 | $7,133,114 | $5,834,347 |
| Change in NOI | – | ($1,041,773) | ($133,646) | ($1,203,269) | ($1,298,767) |
| Gain/(Loss) in Asset Value @ 6% Cap Rate | – | ($17,362,883) | ($2,227,433) | ($20,054,483) | ($21,646,117) |
| Aggregate Gain/(Loss) in Asset Value | – | ($17,362,883) | ($19,590,317) | ($39,644,800) | ($61,290,917) |

**Aggregate Asset Value Loss @ 6% Cap Rate**

### Pain Point: Profit Margins

The distribution and digital environments have changed the way consumers find hotels and changed the way hotels acquire customers. See chapters 15 and 16 for more details. These changes have come at a high cost to the hotel industry, significantly eroding profits. Therefore, owners and operators are under extreme pressure to find ways to increase the profit margins.

The revenue professional is uniquely positioned to drive not only the top-line revenue but also lead efforts to identify the optimal future strategies to achieve highest profitability. Many different elements play into these efforts including costs of acquisition, optimal business mix, and a focus on applying revenue optimization to all other revenue centers.

### Pain Point: Cost of Acquisition

"The cost of customer acquisition continues to rise unabated ranging from a low of 15% to as high as 30% of guest paid revenue. Customer acquisition costs will continue to spiral out of control if left unchecked. Hoteliers must manage acquisition costs with a rigor similar to that with which they learned to manage labor costs."[22]

Performance success is more and more often being measured based on RevPAR, revenue, and/or profit minus acquisition costs, which includes everything from commissions and transaction fees to all sales and marketing expenses.

Hotels must understand how to manage these costs before they put a painful squeeze on profits. This requires, in part, determining the hotel's optimal channel mix based on its competitive positioning and demand in the market.

### Pain Point: Optimal Business Mix

Hotels need to become selective when it comes to the channels in which they invest, which requires determining their optimal business mix and then allocating the budget accordingly. "The days of 'putting your hotel on every shelf' are over; no one can afford that anymore."[23]

Determining the optimal business mix for a hotel is a key factor in the development of a cohesive revenue optimization strategy. Today, hoteliers have good market data available to help make decisions about business mix.

## Best Practices for Managing Owner Expectations

Many operators spend a significant amount of time responding to owners' questions and requests for information and updates, which is time taken away from running the hotel, selling the hotel, optimizing revenue, etc. At the same time, more owners and asset managers want to be more involved in the revenue optimization strategies and tactics.

In addition to the best practices outlined in the prior "Optimizing the Partnership" section, the key to efficiently and effectively managing owner expectations is preparation. Start by demonstrating confidence in the revenue team by proactively managing the strategic direction and execution of the hotel's revenue optimization strategy.

It is generally not a good idea to include owners in the revenue team's weekly meetings. While some owners ask to join so they can better understand the strategies, and others seek to control the strategies. Either way, the owner's presence can hamper open and meaningful conversations among the team as many revenue team members will not speak freely in front of an owner, nor will they disagree with him or her even if they have the data and experience to back up their opinions.

The purpose of the revenue meeting is to give the team an opportunity to outline the needs, gaps, challenges, and opportunities, and work together to design the strategies to achieve the goals. When the team cannot speak freely, the end goals will not be achieved and opportunity will be missed, and money will be left on the table.

An alternative to their involvement in revenue meetings, and responding to frequent ad hoc requests and inquiries from owners, some hotel teams schedule monthly, or even weekly, calls with owners to review results against the strategies deployed, future expectations, and future strategies with expected results. These calls can address what is working and what is not working, along with alternative strategies to offset what is not working.

A regular meeting or call between the owner or asset manager and operating team — general manager, director of revenue, and director of sales and marketing — can help to ensure proper communication and understanding of the strategies, and to set expectations. This is a manageable and useful investment of everyone's time. This approach ensures full transparency between ownership and management teams and helps build confidence and trust between the owner and operator. See the sidebar below for a sample revenue-focused owner meeting agenda.

Bilal Chamsine, Executive Director at DCA Hotels & Resorts, summed it up, "The main objective of this meeting is to provide additional information that would give a strong reflection of the past, current, and future position of the hotel and ... to be able to relay a clear picture and informative reports to the owner."

### Sample Revenue-Focused Owner Meeting Agenda

#### MTD Performance
- Overview of MTD performance
- Business on the Books

#### Business Forecast
- Review of 3-month rolling forecast
- Competitive review and analysis
- Review of market segmentation performance
- Review of rate strategies and results
- Review of current hotel ranking vs. comp set (STR Report)
- Additional data showing hotel's future pace and positioning against competitors
- Sales leads, prospects, tentatives, cancellations
- Market dynamics
- Event calendars, market demand, weather, major disruptors, changes in competitive environment

#### Sales and Marketing Activities
- Overview of sales and marketing activities
- Overview of promotions

#### Next Steps
- Follow up information to be provided (and by whom)
- Next meeting date

Sometimes an owner will insist on dictating certain rules or guidelines, or even a very specific strategy. This is a very challenging situation for the operator and can end up hurting revenues in the end. For example:

- An owner creates pricing guidelines without proper data, insights, or market intelligence because of their belief that the hotel should be aligned with an aspirational price point as opposed to a realistic one. The hotel will likely sit empty resulting in an unhappy owner and demotivated hotel team. It is easy to imagine that cost-cutting measures would be put into place, and that staff would leave to go elsewhere in such a scenario. It is likely that the hotel team will shoulder the blame for a failed strategy.
- An owner directs the revenue team to shift away from OTA business because the monthly commissions are too high, or the channel is not delivering the "right" type of customers. Without a replacement for this business, the hotel will again sit empty…and the same results as the previous scenario will follow.
- An owner demands that the revenue team follow an occupancy-driven strategy only. While this may work in some situations, it is typically not a sustainable long-term strategy as a full hotel – and its staff -- takes a beating, and all for very little profit as margins are not optimal. Burned-

out staff will leave for new opportunities, the owner will not be happy with the bottom line, and again the hotel team will likely blame shoulder the blame.

These are a few extreme, but far too real, situations where owners put the hotel team in a position of executing strategies that are less than ideal. Unfortunately, owners can blame the management team for the failed strategies when in fact it was owner that dictated the strategy from the beginning.

The hotel leadership would be well-served in these situations to explain why a different strategy is a better, more profitable, and sustainable option to get the hotel to its end goals. This is not easily done, but it is definitely worth the energy and time investment.

Proactive communication and information are key to success in remaining focused and staying the right course in managing owner expectations and positive relationships. The following illustrates a visual way to think about the different stages and steps involved in fostering effective and efficient owner-operator relationships.

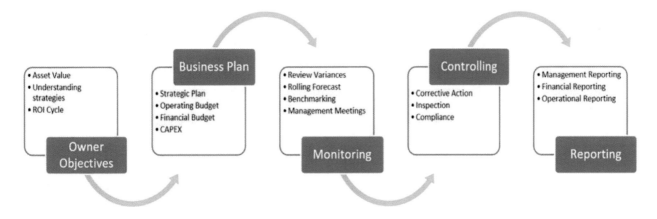

Special thanks to Bilal Chasmine

# CHAPTER 15
## STRATEGIC DISTRIBUTION

Distribution plays a critical role in a hotel's revenue optimization strategy. It encompasses all the ways in which inventory, rates, and products are sold, and includes the process and connections through which hotels provide inventory, rates, and products to consumers. Examples of distribution channels include GDSs (Global Distribution Systems), OTAs (Online Travel Agencies) and other third parties such as wholesales/tour operators and bedbanks, voice (call centers), and hotel websites.

As the cost of acquiring customers continues to climb, and with third-party commissions significantly higher than the cost of sale through a direct channel, it is imperative that revenue professionals (and the rest of the revenue team) understand the strategic ramifications of their distribution-related decisions. Focusing all stakeholders on obtaining a profitably channel mix is the first step to ensuring that you are optimizing revenues at the lowest costs.

## The Distribution Landscape

If there has been one constant in the world of hotel distribution over the past several years, it is change. Over the past few years, hoteliers have undertaken more aggressive efforts in driving consumers to book through direct channels, while more and more third-party intermediaries continue to emerge, and existing platforms transform their business models, all in an effort to capture the consumer's booking.

On top of constant changes, the distribution landscape is further complicated by regional differences in key distribution players, platforms, connectivity options, payment options, data rules and other regulatory issues. For example, rate parity is a concept that has been ruled illegal in the EU, payment needs are far broader in Asia, and different online players are far more prevalent in specific markets.

Additionally, consolidation — on both the hotel and distribution channel sides — continues to add complexity and change. As hotel companies grow larger through consolidation, they seek to create economies of scale when it comes to negotiating agreements with providers. With pressure on margins, distribution channel providers have expanded their business models to now offer home share and other alternative lodging sources side by side with the hotel product.

Consolidation among some of the major online travel agencies (OTAs) has created three behemoths in the space. As of April 2018, Booking Holdings, Expedia, and Ctrip owned more than 80% of market share in the OTA category globally. Additional consolidation is ongoing. For example, in 2018, TripAdvisor acquired Bokun, a tours and attractions booking engine. Around the same time, Airbnb announced a technology agreement with SiteMinder, giving boutique hotels the opportunity to list their properties on Airbnb and connect directly to its customer base. And more recently, AirBnb acquired Hoteltonight.

Understanding the distribution environment — that of where your hotel is located and that of your source markets — and how it may be changing, is critical developing and managing your revenue strategy. Many hoteliers find it difficult to keep up with changes in distribution and to understand the impacts to their business. It requires constant attention so that you can make any necessary adjustment to revenue practices and strategies to optimize opportunities and avoid potential negative impacts to revenue.

### Special Challenges

Other current and evolving challenges in the distribution space include:

1. **Onward distribution** of wholesale and net rates. If you give a rate to anyone, assume that it will eventually make its way onto the internet. Today's transparency of information and rates has made it far more complicated for hoteliers to control inventory and rates that would otherwise be available to a limited audience such as FIT. Some FIT partners have made it a common practice to resell their contracted secured rates on other online third party sites, many times lower than published rates, creating rate parity issues. It is a daily struggle for hotels to track how some rates are being distributed and sold on third-party sites. That ultimately could impact search results positioning on OTAs and impacts revenue negatively.

2. **Deceptive online practices.** Online booking scams, fraudulent and misleading travel websites, and companies that mislead and confuse consumers are major frustrations for hotels and consumers. According to AH&LA, 23% of consumers report being misled by third-party traveler resellers on the phone or online — translating to 28.5 million hotel stays and $5.2

billion in fraudulent and misleading hotel booking transactions in 2017[24].

These third-party travel resellers use a variety of marketing tactics to mimic hotel websites and call centers but are not, in fact, affiliated with the hotel. These fraudulent and misleading transactions cost both consumers and hotels real time and money.

This is an issue in many parts of the world, and there are numerous initiatives in play to attempt to address it. For instance, in February 2019, the UK's Competition and Markets Authority (CMA) "moved against six booking agencies to end hidden charges, pressure selling, misleading discount claims, and a lack of transparency on how commissions affect the display of rooms online."[25] As of March 2019, the Stop Online Booking Scams Act (SOBSA) is under consideration in the U.S. Congress. "This legislation would prohibit third-party online hotel reservation sellers from charging a consumer's credit card or financial accounts in an Internet transaction for a hotel unless they disclose: a description of the offered good or service, the cost, and other material terms before the conclusion of the transaction; that the third-party seller is not affiliated with the hotel owner or an entity that provides the hotel services or accommodations; that the third-party seller is not an exhibition organizer, a meeting planner, or the official housing bureau for an event at the hotel; and the brand identity of the third party online or over the phone."[26]

3.  **The digital marketplace.** New entrants, new business models, and new players have become the new normal today. The challenge is keeping up with who is who, how to control and track the originator of the booking, and how to control the cost.

    Mobile was a game changer for consumers. Voice may be the next big influencer changing how the consumer is searching and booking travel. Additionally, metasearch has seen significant growth, offering consumers a similar booking experience as with an OTA, but ultimately funneling the consumer back to the hotel site for the final booking.

4.  **Rate parity.** Rate parity is the maintaining of consistent rates for the same product in all distribution channels. Often hotels' contracts with OTAs demand rate parity in all channels. These agreements restrict hotels from offering lower rates on brand.com or through any other public channel, and have come under scrutiny in the European Union with several countries, including France and Germany, making them illegal.

    An uneasy relationship often exists between OTAs and hotels when it comes to this issue. On one side are the OTAs and wholesalers, who frequently push out disparate rates in an attempt to drive bookings through their sites.

    The landscape has become even more complicated as wholesalers often re-sell their contracted rates via OTAs, and other multiple layers of unknown intermediaries pushing hotels out of parity without any faults by the hotelier. Not only does this often cause hotels to lose OTA prime placement which can have a direct impact on revenue opportunity losses, but it also creates an additional load on the revenue professional to chase down the offender.

    On the other side are hoteliers, trying to maintain parity in order to increase the number of direct bookings and control costs. (Since every channel has its own unique costs, the same rate will net differently to the bottom line depending on the channel through which it is booked). For more information on channel costs and inventory control, see chapter 9.

    One of the most important nuances of rate parity is the challenge of managing rates across all distribution channels. It is critical for revenue professionals to have a solid understanding of the various distribution platforms and their optimization requirements.

    When evaluating potential new distribution partners, closely review the features and functions to understand how a rate will be distributed through that channel or partner. For hotels that use BAR by Length of Stay or

Daily BAR, this is especially important as not all distribution partners are created equal. Some do not support complex rate and revenue structures like BAR by Length of Stay while others do support it. That means that, if a hotel distributes BAR rates by Length of Stay, and one or two partners do not support that strategy, the rates will be out of parity.

For ongoing maintenance to ensure rate parity, consider investing in a rate shopping tool. These tools are helpful for capturing real-time rate parity issues through alert-driven notifications. See Appendix C for examples of this type of tool.

Rate parity differs throughout the world. Enforcement of rate parity by OTAs is now illegal in certain countries including Germany and France, and it is in the process of being reviewed by many other countries. Conversations around rate parity are quite passionate no matter what the position or perspective. But while the future of rate parity is still unknown, one thing is certain — parity will continue to be an important piece of the discussion for hoteliers and OTA partners.

The only certainty is that the industry will continue to see more disruption on the distribution front.

## Practitioner Perspective: The Evolving Distribution Landscape
by Andrew Rubbinacci, SVP, Distribution & Revenue, Omni Hotels & Resorts

The changing distribution landscape has had a profound impact on how the industry needs to manage channels versus accounts. Before everything was connected and consumers had full transparency, hotels could work with an account like an OTA or a wholesaler to optimize that account and gain some additional share. This worked as each account was targeting different customer pools and there wasn't much cross over. Examples would include, offering a special with a German wholesaler to gain better access to the German leisure customer who was buying vacation packages. Alternatively, you could give a promotion to a Japanese OTA targeting customers in Japan, knowing that both language barriers and their audience would limit the offer to targeted Japanese consumers.

What has changed in the past few years is that any special or promotion is loaded onto the Internet, backend wholesale portals, the GDSs, and all metasearch sites. This reality means that we should change our approach if we are to optimize a hotel's revenues. Now when you optimize an individual account, the increase in revenue comes at the expense of the other accounts and/or channels.

One such example is giving better conditions or pricing to a wholesale account. That account will invariably sell more rooms for your hotel. What we need to understand is how they will do that. One way is on the backend travel agent systems and GDSs. When an agent selects your hotel, they will be shown a list of prices for the dates and room type selected along with the commission the wholesaler will pay. The agent will just pick from the list with the best rate and commission combination for them and their client. This list could include corporate negotiated rates.

This will result in the wholesaler with the best rates to drive the most rooms becoming one of your best accounts. It may get to the point where they ask for even better rates because of the volumes they are driving. All this will do is shift business away from other wholesalers or negotiated rates to a less profitable one resulting in the account being optimized, but the hotel's revenues being diluted. Alternatively, if you stopped working with a wholesaler or two, you would still be on the shelf. The trick is to optimize the entire channel and hotel, not individual accounts.

Another example would be to give an exclusive promotion to an OTA. The metasearch sites make it extremely easy for a consumer to find and compare rates. That means you should see the OTA drive more revenue. The issue is that you are primarily shifting share from other OTAs and your direct channels. The bottom-line result is you will optimize the OTA account, but you will dilute revenues and increase costs, thus reducing hotel profits.

Remember it is in the best interest of the sales manager or the account itself to optimize the production of the individual account. It is revenue optimization's role to optimize the revenue of the entire hotel. All the channels, segments, and accounts are connected to one another and only by managing the total picture can you truly optimize revenues.

## Hotel Distribution Technology

To make strategic distribution decisions, it is helpful to understand the various technology platforms involved in distribution, and how different channels and models work with and connect to the technology platforms.

Understanding hotel distribution technology can be challenging — especially as new technology providers are introduced frequently. And, existing providers are regularly evolving their business models to capitalize on revenue opportunities. Ongoing mergers and acquisitions of these companies adds another level of complexity.

The "Hotel Distribution Technology Chart"[27] below illustrates the relationships between and among many of the technology providers involved in hotel distribution.

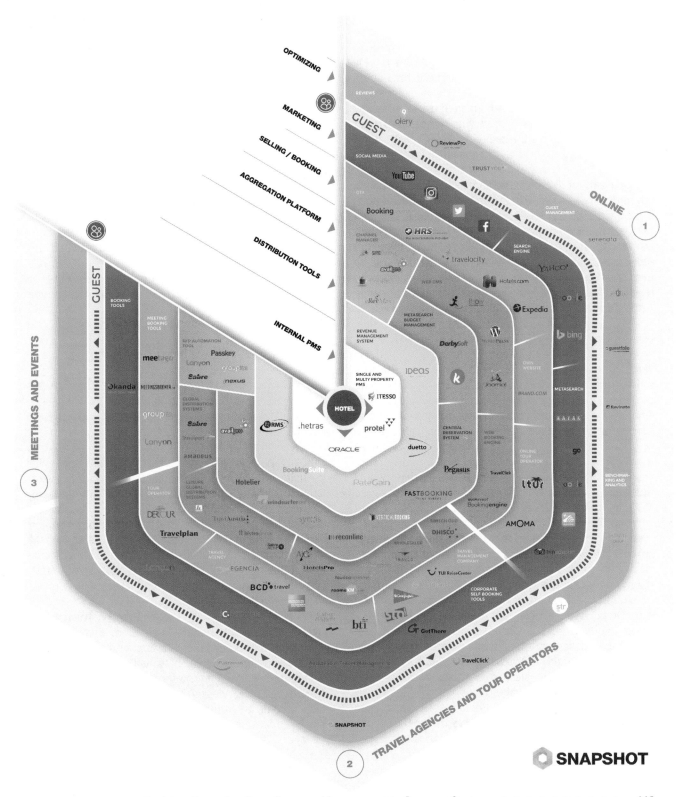

Starting with the hotel in the center of the chart and moving toward the customer on the perimeter, the following section explores each layer in the distribution ecosystem.

### Internal PMS
The internal PMS layer is a relatively simple component to understand as most hotels have some type of automated property management system (PMS). The PMS typically interfaces with various distribution tools in the next layer. It is the following layers that get a bit more complex, and can be quite confusing.

### Aggregation Platforms
Aggregation platforms include software such as a central reservation system (CRS) or channel management tool. The role of an aggregation platform is to take the hotel's inventory, rates, and availability and format them in a way that can be distributed onward to others for sale.

The original aggregation platform for hotel distribution technology was the Global Distribution Systems (GDS). The primary objective of the GDS was to facilitate the delivery of the hotel's data from the CRS.

To garner additional exposure outside of the leisure travel agent segment, RFP management tools were created to capture more business from corporate clients and major travel management companies (consortia) and consulting intermediaries.

Through distribution technology evolution and the demands of guests wanting the ability to obtain records without manually submitting a request to a travel agent, web booking engines were developed enabling guests and hotels to deliver real-time hotel data including availability, rates, and inventory. The true merchandising of the web booking engine is through the web CMS (Content Management System). The web CMS is the consumer facing platform elevating hotel branding, rich media, and personalization while monitoring the site performance of the booking funnel.

Most recently channel managers have been introduced and provide hotels with the ability to streamline the management and delivery of availability, rates, and inventory to the "selling brands" and "booking brands."

### Selling and Booking Platforms
Consumers use both selling and booking platforms to make travel arrangements. It is essential to understand the differences between these platform types.

A selling platform is one where the guest data is owned by the hotel. It typically has a lower cost of distribution even though bookings that come in through it will have operational and technology costs associated. The best example of a selling platform is brand.com, a hotel's website.

A booking platform is one where the guest books through, and their data is owned by, a third-party. Typically, minimal guest data is provided to the hotel at the time of booking. The booking will have a margin or commission associated with it in addition to operational and technology costs, depending on the connectivity. A good example of a booking platform is an OTA.

### Marketing Platforms
Marketing platforms drive traffic or demand to a selling platform. There are a variety of different models and methods but regardless of the method or cost, the guest data is owned by the hotel and the hotel pays a third party for the lead generation.

### Optimization Platforms
With a clear understanding of the distribution technology landscape in place, the next step is optimizing those platforms with streamlined integration of all the technology.

> For a deeper understanding of the ins and outs of distribution today, see HEDNA's calendar of upcoming educational opportunities at www.hedna.org.

## Third Parties in Distribution: Online Travel Agencies (OTAs)
Part of an effective distribution strategy typically means working with OTAs in some way. Consumers using OTAs are generally brand agnostic and often price-conscious, searching for a cheaper way to book their travel. Determining which OTAs will provide your hotel with incremental revenues at long-term sustainable cost requires a thorough understanding of the models and specific OTA marketing efforts.

There are four primary business models for Online Travel Agencies (OTAs) — retail, merchant, opaque/auction, and metasearch. It is critical for hoteliers to understand the differences of each so OTAs can be appropriately incorporated into the hotel's overall revenue optimization strategy.

Be sure to review chapter 16 for more information on online intermediaries beyond OTAs.

### Retail Model

Much like a traditional travel agent, the consumer books through an intermediary and pays the hotel directly on checkout. The hotel then pays the intermediary a commission (or margin), typically 10-20%. This model is also sometimes referred to as the "published" or "agency" model. Room revenue for retail OTA bookings is captured on the hotel income statement as a gross rate, or what the consumer paid. In an example with a room revenue of $200 and a commission rate of 20%, the income statement would look like this:

Room revenue = $200

Commission paid (@ 20%) = $40

Net room revenue = $160

Booking.com is the leading site worldwide using the retail model. Expedia's Hotel Collect or Expedia Traveler Preference (ETP) model also employ this method of reservation and payment. Typically, this model also operates more like a traditional reservation which the guest can cancel until the day of the reservation (or with a longer lead time if the hotel utilizes a stronger cancellation policy), which often results in high cancellation rates. Marketers and revenue teams need to monitor these cancellation rates as they plan their sellout strategies, as markets with long lead times or days to arrival (DTA) can be impacted by retail model cancellations.

### Merchant Model

The merchant model was created by former wholesale tour operators and later adopted by OTAs, most notably Expedia. Initially, OTAs would negotiate room blocks just like wholesalers and guarantee payment for those rooms, but today that practice has largely gone away. Here, the traveler pays the OTA by credit card directly upon booking, so the OTA becomes the "merchant of record" hence the model name. The OTA charges the traveler a room rate, which is a combination of the hotel's net rate and the OTA's commission (or margin). The net rate is the actual revenue the hotel receives for the room while the margin is the negotiated fee that the OTA charges for its service. Typically in this model, the guest will pay the OTA up front on their credit card and, after the traveler's stay, the OTA pays the hotel the net rate via their own credit card or other payment processing system.

Under the merchant model, a hotel provides OTAs net rates that are typically 12 to 25 percent below published levels. The OTA will then generally offer the hotel's room rate at the published rate.

A variation of the merchant model is the package model. In the package model, the consumer is offered a bundled price where the hotel rate is combined with a rate for another travel product such as an airline ticket or car rental. OTAs often require a deeper discount (an additional 10% or more) for package rates versus hotel-room-only rates. Packages are typically booked farther in advance, for longer lengths of stay, and are often chosen by guests who will have higher incremental spend.

Room revenue for merchant OTA booking is captured on the hotel income statement at the lower net rate. As a result, the amount of the OTA margin does not show up on the income statement directly, which some call a hidden marketing expense. In our example with a room rate of $200, the net room revenue is still $160 but the commission paid at 20% ($40) is kept by the OTA up front. No marketing expense shows up on the hotel's P&L.

Since merchant model reservations are pre-paid, typically their cancellation rates are much lower than the retail model.

### Opaque/Auction Model

This model involves the consumer not knowing the name or brand of hotel chosen until after booking, hence the term "opaque," as the consumer doesn't know which hotel he is selecting until after the booking is made. In 1997 Priceline invented the "Name Your Own Price" opaque model, which employed an auction model wherein consumers could bid on discounted airline tickets. Priceline quickly expanded the model to include hotel rooms and other verticals. Hotwire launched its version of opaque travel products in 2001 using a posted price rather than a bidding model. Opaque/auction sites are popular with price-sensitive travelers who are not concerned about the brand they use.

In exchange for the 'opaque' nature of the transaction, typically hotels will offer much deeper discounts to these sites (20% - 60%). Most hotels using these channels only do so to yield last-minute revenue when they are not going to fill, or over future slow period dates. Hotels must be mindful of using these channels, and ensure that they are truly opaque and that consumers are not 100% certain of which hotel they will get when making a booking. Analysis of reports provided by the opaque site will give the hotel insights about the opacity of their property.

In the opaque model, the consumer makes a non-refundable commitment to purchase based on the rate offered within a given competitive set which is defined as a specific star rating and a general location (e.g., 3-star hotels in Midtown Manhattan). Once the consumer has clicked "buy," the opaque site will select which of the hotels in the comp set with which to secure the booking. While this model is radically different relative to the traditional OTA model, from a transactional perspective it can be considered a variation of the merchant model, as the customer pays the OTA directly and the hotel bills the OTA for payment on a net rate basis.

Priceline continues to be the market leader in opaque hotel sales, and morphed its model to also include a posted price (yet still opaque) offering in 2012. Through its parent company Expedia, Hotwire has sometimes offered its inventory on Expedia, Hotels.com, and Travelocity. Recently the opaque model appears to be waning somewhat in consumer usage due to more sophisticated hotel revenue optimization systems and policies, and the availability of other last-minute booking channels like the mobile-only app HotelTonight (which was acquired by Airbnb in 2019).

### Metasearch

A metasearch engine is a search tool that queries content and pricing from multiple online sources and delivers it to the consumer in one comprehensive display. Metasearch continues to mature and impact how consumers purchase travel. Today the major metasearch engines in the travel arena offer multiple paid media options, thus blurring the line between media partner and travel agency/OTA partner.

Common metasearch sites include TripAdvisor, Kayak, and Trivago.

- Subscription Model: The most well-known subscription model is TripAdvisor's Business Listings. This is an annual paid subscription that allows a hotel to list and link its hotel website, phone number, and hotel deals to TripAdvisor. There are also some back-end tools that hotels can use to further optimize its listing.
- Cost Per Click (CPC) Model: This is a bidding model hotels use, often with the help of a hired agency, to bid on improved search result placement. Others, such as booking platforms, can also bid against a hotel on hotel terms which often drives up the bid costs.
- Cost Per Action (CPA) Model: This is where a hotel pays the metasearch agency a commission for realized bookings sent to the hotel's booking engine.
- Cost Per Impression (CPM) Model: This is similar to a traditional form of advertising. Hotels can pay for advertisement on a metasearch site.

It is important for hoteliers to understand how metasearch works so that it can be used to their advantage to support revenue optimization strategies. Working with metasearch is not a "set it and forget it" exercise. Because the rules of meta constantly change (like everything else in the online travel landscape), hoteliers must stay on top of new developments and adjust content and strategies to optimize results. Using meta correctly can improve the value proposition for a hotel compared to its competitors, thus optimizing the revenue potential.

### Third Parties in Distribution: Group Intermediaries

The process of sourcing group bookings has historically been highly manual. In the past, meeting and event planners struggled with finding the right venue to meet their event needs; and hotels found it difficult to target their marketing dollars to book incremental group business.

Over the past several years, planners have increasingly shifted from the traditional means of venue sourcing and moved toward online sourcing methods because of the time and cost savings they offer. As a result of this shift, hotels are receiving more group business and group leads than ever before via online channels. That means that hoteliers must rethink their approach to group marketing and merchandising.

Hotels must invest in building a strong online presence targeted to groups within the online sourcing platforms such as Cvent and Meetingsbooker.com. Revenue teams must also assess their hotel's overall sales approach when it comes to groups. Today, many sales professionals spend a significant amount of time responding to online RFPs versus more traditional sales activities that put them in direct contact with clients.

Consider organizing the sales team with less experienced team members managing the straightforward online group sources and RFPs so that more experienced sales professionals can uncover new sources of business, maintain relationships with current clients, and bring a more strategic sales approach to the hotel.

At the same time, there are many offline third-party intermediaries in the group space. Another of the biggest challenges that hotels face is the sheer scope of services that are now considered third-party intermediation. There exists a staggering variety of intermediaries, including third-party planners, full-service agencies and planning firms, site-selection companies, incentive planners, housing companies, travel-management companies, association-management companies, hybrids, and many others. And under the current model, everyone wants to collect the same 7-10 percent — sometimes on the same piece of business.

The sales profession and the professionals in sales continue to evolve in the face of this issue. HSMAI's Sales Advisory Boards globally are working to help hotels:

■ Reduce cost of sales/customer acquisition to improve profitability, and fight commoditization of hospitality services in the purchaser's mind so that hoteliers are not just selling on price.
■ Implement innovative talent development practices that enhance sales force business acumen, increasing productivity and improving the buying-selling process.
■ Develop efficient sales practices, including aligning sales with operations, revenue management, and ecommerce, while reducing costs. This includes implementing effective performance measures (e.g., conversion, speed, filling need periods, profitability, etc.) and simplified reward systems that keep salespeople focused on the goals of the overall enterprise.

## Third Parties in Distribution: Alternative Accommodations

Peer-to-peer websites (e.g., Airbnb, HomeAway) offering alternative accommodations are enticing consumers out of traditional hotels and into people's homes or spare rooms, and are causing controversy in the hotel industry.

For several years, the industry has debated the question of whether or not these peer-to-peer sites should be considered distribution channels. Recently, hoteliers have more widely accepted them as a means to distribute inventory. Adoption is happening, but at a fairly slow pace mostly due to the lack of connectivity to manage these sites. OTAs are keeping a close watch on this because of the difference in commission models compared to the traditional OTAs.

It is expected that these platforms will continue to grow in popularity as distribution channels for consumers and hotels alike. Consider the acquisition of HotelTonight by Airbnb for example.

## Rising Costs of Customer Acquisition

For a thorough review of the many issues involved in the rising costs of acquisitions see:

■ Distribution Channel Analysis: A Guide for Hotels, published by the HSMAI Foundation. Download a PDF at no cost from www.hsmai.org/trends/Book. cfm?ItemNumber=5016.
■ Demystifying the Digital Marketplace: Spotlight on the Hospitality Industry, Parts 1, 2, and 3 — available at www.kalibrilabs.com/demystifying-the-digital-marketplace.
■ Book Direct Campaigns 2.0: The Costs and Benefits of Loyalty 2018 — available at www.kalibrilabs.com/bookdirect.

The rising cost of customer acquisition is top of mind for many hoteliers — owners, asset managers, marketers, sales professionals, and revenue professionals. It is no secret that the cost to acquire customers is rising while hotel margins are shrinking. This is not a sustainable model.

As more and more entrants come into the picture, each one wanting a "piece of the pie," existing players continue to create new ways to drive customers to book through them. Today there are more pay-to-play ways to distribute hotel inventory, acquire new customers, and drive traffic to brand.com than anyone could have ever imagined.

Approximately 15% to 30% of guest-paid revenue is spent acquiring customers.[28] All of this comes at a cost: hotel profitability.

Every operator is dealing with this issue as it consistently comes up in budget meetings and owner reviews. There is no silver bullet to completely turn the tide of rising acquisition costs, but there are a variety of strategies hotels are instituting to help. A combination of strategies may lead to increased margins.

## Leverage Metrics

Most owners and operators use RevPAR index growth as an important measurement of success for a hotel. This is a useful tool that helps them understand how a hotel compares to its competitive set based on top-line room revenues. But it does not take costs of acquisition into account.

Cindy Estis Green, author of the Distribution Channel Analysis and Demystifying the Digital Marketplace reports referenced above, has offered new metrics that she proposes will help owners and operators get the best possible data in order to make smarter strategy decisions in the future.[29]

- Hotel Collected Revenue: Reflects the top-line revenue the hotel collects and appears on the profit-and-loss (P&L) statements. This does not include transaction costs or commissions, expenses, and markups.
- Guest Paid Revenue: Reflects everything paid by a guest to a hotel or third-party for a hotel stay and includes the mark-up to account for Merchant (net) rates — this is the real rate the guest is willing to pay.
- COPE Revenue (Contribution to Operating Profit and Expense): Reflects the Guest-Paid Revenue after removing all direct acquisition costs such as commissions, transaction fees, and channel costs.
- Net Revenue: Reflects the bottom-line revenue after additionally removing sales and marketing expenses.

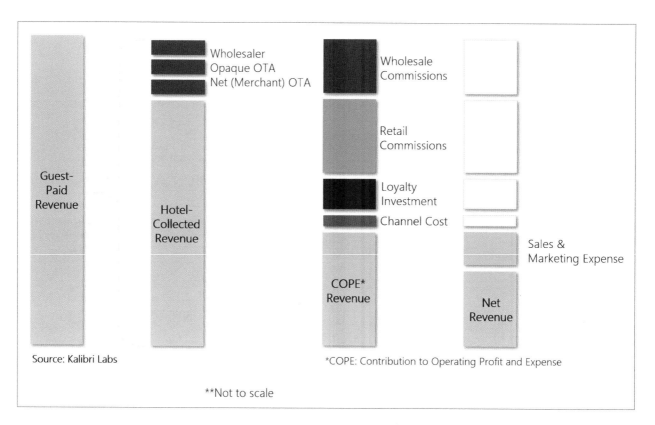

Guest-Paid Revenue

Hotel-Collected Revenue

Wholesaler
Opaque OTA
Net (Merchant) OTA

Wholesale Commissions

Retail Commissions

Loyalty Investment

Channel Cost

COPE* Revenue

Sales & Marketing Expense

Net Revenue

Source: Kalibri Labs

*COPE: Contribution to Operating Profit and Expense

**Not to scale

## Know the Cost of Commissions

Commission costs are nothing new for hoteliers. However, the rising commission payments hoteliers see on P&Ls today are a cause of angst. But what about the costs of commissions that do not show up on the P&L? How are they being accounted for?

One of the largest overall reservation cost drivers is "... bookings where the revenue is collected by third parties, such as wholesale, opaque, and merchant model OTA, [where] the commission is taken 'off the top' which means that only the portion paid to the hotel by the third party is recorded on the P&L, but not the fees paid that were included in the total rate the guest paid to the third party. Since the commissions are taken out of the rates paid by the guest, these mark-up commissions represent a customer acquisition cost from the hotel's perspective and must be tracked and considered."[30]

Few hoteliers would ignore an expense item that equals 15% to 35%. That's why it is important to thoroughly monitor and examine acquisition costs by channel and then determine the most optimal channel mix possible.

At the same time, it is important to know all of the costs required to drive direct bookings —paid search, programmatic display media, affiliate marketing, metasearch, social media, etc.

## Determine the Optimal Channel Mix

In an interview with HSMAI[31], Cindy Estis Green shared that, "Hotels have spent so much time optimizing the overall revenue stream that it is a new way of thinking to optimize sub-sets of that overall business volume by channel. This will require some attention on the channel mix patterns and trying different methods to test which ones yield the best results in different market conditions."

Finding optimal channel mix requires several factors:
1. Knowledge of the demand patterns in a market for each channel and segment
2. An understanding of consumer's perception of the hotel, and how it compares to its competitors
3. A realistic assessment of how well each channel performs and is evaluated by consumers compared to the same for the hotel's competitors (e.g., website, call center, GDS)
4. An understanding of the costs of varying channel mix combinations to calculate how much contribution there is toward operating expenses and profit

Once a hotel puts a stake in the ground regarding its channel objectives, the revenue team can carefully track costs to be sure they are moving toward an optimal mix. Determining the optimal channel mix happens in seven steps, given the constraints of the market.[32]
1. Forecast demand
2. Review the gap
3. Choose the opportunities
4. Establish the net revenue objective
5. Select a spending target
6. Measure performance
7. Evaluate success

## Focus on Flow-Through[33]

Hoteliers need to understand the flow-through for the bookings coming into the hotel.

The goal of the analysis is to evaluate different parts of business in relation to each other to get insight into profits. Different sources have different flow-through to profit, so hoteliers need to analyze them with all costs in mind.

Part of that analysis relates to under what circumstances hoteliers should and should not take low-margin business. Hoteliers should consider taking low-margin business in the following instances:
- To create a base for compression
- To bring in business when it would otherwise not come in
- When ancillary spend is high
- To fill a hole
- To hit a threshold
- To cover cash flow

On the other hand, hoteliers should not take low-margin business in certain scenarios. For example, it is best to steer clear of low-margin business when:
- It becomes too large a percentage of the property's overall channel mix.
- It diverts financial or staff time and resources from finding higher-profit business.
- It erodes the overall rate strategy of the property.
- It feeds a downward price spiral in the comp set and does not bring in enough demand to make up for the rate reductions.
- It reroutes customers who would otherwise book through higher-profit channels.
- It is promoted close to arrival and trains

customers to wait until the last minute to book for the best deal.

"Determining flow-through for each type of business helps a hotel operator calculate the profit contribution for the planned mix of business," Estis Green said.

Like strategic distribution, digital marketing plays a critical role in a hotel's revenue optimization strategy. It too has undergone, and continues to see, fast-paced and large-scale changes in the technology, business models, and players involved. Understanding marketing in a digital world, embracing its importance and impact, and keeping up with it as it evolves is critical to the success of every revenue professional, revenue team, and hotel. At the same time, it is important to acknowledge the crossover and reliance between revenue and digital, and bring these disciplines closer together on and above property.

In today's multi-channel, multi-device world, when consumers interact with brands – regardless of location or channel – they expect a seamless experience. For this to happen, revenue teams must work with marketing teams to holistically plan and align strategies from ideation to implementation, across traditional and digital channels.

## Certified Hospitality Digital Marketer (CHDM)

Created by hoteliers for hoteliers, the CHDM recognizes digital marketing professionals for their expertise in leveraging digital channels to maximize online revenues. CHDMs are the digital marketing experts hotels need today.

This is the certification for hospitality sales, marketing, and revenue optimization professionals who want to:

- demonstrate their proficiency globally
- expand their current role or move into a digital role
- upskill and become more proficient
- better understand how digital marketing intersects with and impacts their areas of responsibility

The study guide for the certification is *Hospitality Digital Marketing Essentials: A Field Guide for Navigating Today's Digital Landscape*.

Learn more about the certification, or get your copy of *Hospitality Digital Marketing Essentials*, at www.hsmai.org/chdm.

## The Digital Marketing Trifecta

There is so much overlap between different areas of digital marketing that dividing topics into understandable chunks can often become overwhelming. One example of this would be social media. When discussing social media, we need to discuss paid media, review sites, engagement, influencers, website integration, on-property activation, and so on.

With this in mind, this chapter will focus on where specific tactics or strategies fit within these three buckets:

1. **Paid Media:** This includes any media that requires that you pay the "publisher" for that media unit. This includes paid search, display advertising, social media advertising (including "boosting posts"), subscription services (e.g., Trip Advisor Business Listing), and the myriad of other paid advertising vehicles.

2. **Earned Media:** It is called "earned" media because it often requires effort and know-how to get it; you can't buy it – you must earn it. In a traditional sense it might be PR or word of mouth advertising but in the digital world this becomes mentions in blogs, posts, websites, review sites, and so on. While it takes effort (and sometimes cost) to garner earned media, it is often among the most powerful because it is deemed by consumers as "unbiased" information.

3. **Owned Media:** This is any media that is directly controlled by the hotel. The most obvious is your website but can also include social sites, database/email marketing, blogs, and so on.

The following diagram illustrates how different marketing vehicles fit into this structure.

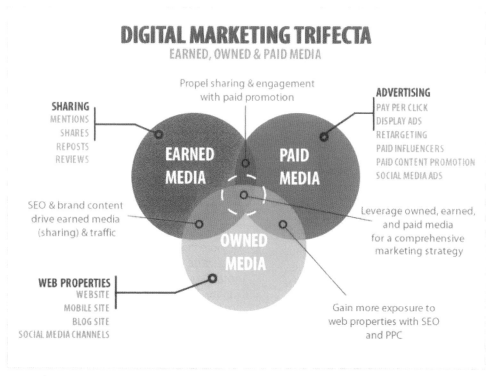

## DIGITAL MARKETING TRIFECTA
### EARNED, OWNED & PAID MEDIA

Propel sharing & engagement
with paid promotion

**SHARING**
MENTIONS
SHARES
REPOSTS
REVIEWS

**EARNED MEDIA**

**PAID MEDIA**

**ADVERTISING**
PAY PER CLICK
DISPLAY ADS
RETARGETING
PAID INFLUENCERS
PAID CONTENT PROMOTION
SOCIAL MEDIA ADS

SEO & brand content
drive earned media
(sharing) & traffic

**OWNED MEDIA**

Leverage owned, earned,
and paid media
for a comprehensive
marketing strategy

**WEB PROPERTIES**
WEBSITE
MOBILE SITE
BLOG SITE
SOCIAL MEDIA CHANNELS

Gain more exposure to
web properties with SEO
and PPC

Source: https://www.titan-seo.com/newsarticles/trifecta.html

### Why Revenue Professionals Should Care

Understanding these categories will help the revenue professional better determine how to use the variety of options available, ultimately leading to more success in using them to drive revenue and achieve goals.

Everything the marketing team does should be for a reason; once the goal is determined then you can consider your options and determine how you will get your message/rate out. For example: Hotel A has a soft period in the next month and needs to do its best to fill those rooms. As part of the revenue optimization strategy, three key questions must be asked:

1.  What, if anything, should we do in paid media?
2.  What, if anything, should we do in earned media?
3.  What, if anything, should we do in owned media?

Several aspects of digital marketing are especially relevant to revenue professionals because they have can have a significant impact on the success of the revenue optimization strategy. A high-level understanding of how all the drivers work together is important, but a deeper understanding of them is recommended. HSMAI's book,

*Hospitality Digital Marketing Essentials: A Field Guide for Navigating Today's Digital Landscape,* provides that detail and is available at www.hsmai.org/chdm.

The remainder of this chapter highlights the most pertinent components, and most common best practices, for revenue professionals today.

### OWNED MEDIA: Website Optimization

Hoteliers have a lot to gain when the consumer books directly. Not only does it provide a direct relationship with the consumer, allowing a better understanding of the customer and opportunity to communicate directly, but it is also one of the most cost-effective ways to receive a booking for hotels.

Optimizing every opportunity to ensure highest conversion and ease of booking on a hotel's website is a critical piece of any revenue optimization strategy.

Currently, the hotel website represents the best opportunity for high-volume, low-cost bookings. It is your most valuable owned asset in the digital landscape.

Properties must ensure that their hotel websites are optimized for search engines, best represent their selling points, and are geared to an online customer.

There are essentially three types of websites:

1. **Brand.com** – If your property is part of a brand, in all likelihood, your property will be included in the brand website and booking engine; the property will have some level of control over content and rates but for the most part control is with the brand.

2. **IndependentHotel.com** – Hotels that are not part of a brand, in all likelihood, will build an independent website and utilize a third party or homegrown booking engine for their property.

3. **VanitySite.com** – Sometimes also called microsites, these sites are sometimes created by properties that already have presence on a brand site but for some reason have decided that having an additional property-specific site is needed. Reasons include uniqueness of property that cannot be represented on brand.com, language needs that may not be represented on brand.com, search engine strategy, etc. While vanity sites may be a good option, they should be carefully considered as there are also drawbacks to having these sites. Please note that different brands have different guidelines as they relate to vanity sites; some may allow them while others strictly forbid them.

> "When I started in the hotel business 52 years ago, the first impression customers had of our hotels was the lobby when they walked through the front doors. But in this digital age, often the first impression comes when they visit Marriott.com. It's our digital front door." —Bill Marriott

Once the investment decision is made to build (or re-build) a website, there is a finite list of must-haves to ensure your website is user friendly, search engine friendly, and booker-friendly.

What began in the early '90s as simply a digital brochure has evolved into a complex collection of marketing content, keywords, meta tags, visual images, widgets, and booking engines. Within this platform, you are not only telling your story to your potential guests through visuals and text, there is a lot more going on. Your website – and social presence – should communicate a specific vision that speaks to search engines, Google, Siri, your customer's and their friends and family, other influencers, and of course, your owners. And these elements exist for two reasons – to acquire and convert more customers.

The first step in any hotel digital marketing strategy should be a review of (or creation of, in the case of a new hotel) the hotel website. Today's hotel website carries the burden and responsibility of generating or initiating a large percentage of online bookings for the property. The property website has become the backbone of the hotel marketing mix and is the primary digital asset of any hotel. In this age of multi-channel marketing, any type of hotel marketing initiative (from search engine marketing and banner advertising to email and social marketing) ultimately drives travel consumers to the hotel website. In short, the best ROI can currently be found by creating or maintaining a well-optimized, user-friendly, mobile optimized, booking-friendly, property-specific website.

### Independent vs. Franchise/Branded Properties

Each brand or franchise has a website typically referred to as its brand.com site. For example, when you franchise a Holiday Inn, your property has an individual presence on the IHG.com branded site. For these branded hotels, maintaining an up-to-date branded site should be the primary focus and centerpiece of your online presence. In some cases, a stand-alone site, often referred to as a "vanity site," may be a necessary supplement. In the case of independent, non-branded properties, a stand-alone site is a necessity.

While in some cases branded hotels will also create and maintain a stand-alone ("vanity") website, hotels should always discuss this with their brand to be sure they understand the brand's position on vanity websites, as well as possible issues this may cause versus the potential benefits.

### Brand.com

Typically, hotels that are part of a large brand (such as Marriott, Hilton, IHG, etc.) are automatically provided a website on the brand.com site. These sites follow the brand templates (design, color schemes, and navigation), and have many of the important features already built in, including booking widgets and other appropriate technology, textual content, and imagery placements as well as additional marketing components.

While the brand provides the framework, it is the responsibility of each hotel to ensure their hotel site is well maintained from a content perspective, including:

- Well-written and effective textual content from both a marketing and SEO standpoint
- Up-to-date, professional hotel and room imagery, and proper room descriptions
- Use of other ancillary components offered by the brand for promotions & deals, additional hotel information, "product" highlights, and other "news and updates" for the hotel

### IndependentHotel.com (also for branded properties with stand-alone websites)

The decision is simple for an independent hotel or resort – a website is an absolute necessity. The primary strategic decision in this case is the level of investment appropriate for the vanity site based on projected returns. In order to determine the level of investment you should make, consider the following factors:

- Does your website have the most accurate descriptions of your hotel product and services from both a textual content and imagery perspective?
- Are your year-over-year (YOY) website booking contributions growing, level, or slipping? How does that compare to industry benchmarks and within your market?
- Are your website traffic and search rankings deteriorating? When was your website last re-optimized for SEO?
- Is the website integrated with the hotel's social media profiles?
- Does your website include a blog (and are you posting to that blog)?
- Does your website support open graph tags (snippets of code that cause your selected picture and marketing text to appear when users share content from your site on Facebook, tweet links to your content, or post to Instagram)?
- Does your website have a robust Content Management System (CMS) to allow you to manage visual and textual content, set up new specials and packages, post events and happenings, create new landing pages, and push fresh content to your social media and mobile site? Does your CMS support social media integration, such as updating Facebook from within the CMS?

- Is your website responsive? In other words, is the site built in a way that automatically adapts to the various devices and screen sizes used by today's consumers? Most search engines, such as Google, are now favoring responsive sites in their ranking algorithms. In fact, Google penalizes websites that are not mobile friendly.
- Do you find that you and your staff like the websites of your competitors better than your own?
- Do you have any staff capacity and capability to manage the site in-house, or will you need to outsource the site management?
- If your hotel website was last redesigned more than two years ago, remember that the rate of change in the industry is high. In the last few years we saw the deployment and adoption of schemas, open graph tags, and new algorithm updates including penalties for non-mobile friendly sites. Change is continuous and rapid. Hoteliers no longer have a choice of whether to redesign their website. A website redesign is a must and should be considered in the upcoming budgeting season if not budgeted for the current year.

### VanitySite.com

For branded properties, a number of factors must be considered prior to electing to allocate resources for a vanity site.

First, it pays to understand the chain/brand policies regarding property vanity websites. Several brands discourage their franchisees from creating stand-alone sites, preferring the resources be channeled through a central brand site or other online marketing activities. This enables product consistency, and in some cases is the wisest decision for a property. In either case, the best practice is to review your chain/brand's policies and recommendations regarding vanity websites before investing time and resources. Maintaining current information on a branded site is time consuming, and regardless of whether a stand-alone site is needed, this should be a priority for any digital marketing strategy. Keeping photos, information, keywords, and market niches up to date is primarily the responsibility of the property.

Before making the decision to invest in a vanity site, consider the following questions.

- Does the chain/brand provide adequate marketing exposure and promotional support for all of your key customer segments? Typically, branded hotels have similarities. Residence Inn is known for extended stays. Hyatt is known for meeting and catering space. If your hotel matches your brand's typical profile, it is likely their branded site will provide you the support you need. However, if you are a hotel with an unusual ratio of meeting space, have unusual or different facilities outside the brand norm, or are in a location near a strong demand generator, the branded site may or may not support your needs.

- After analyzing property location and composition of visitors (e.g., leisure, business, group, etc.) to your destination, is every significant visitor segment sufficiently addressed by the chain/brand site? Sometimes resorts and full-service properties in primary markets may not be adequately supported by a brand site. There are resort brands that support their properties perfectly, but a resort property is often unique in that it targets a very specific mix of customers due to its location and activities. This may necessitate a more specific targeted approach to the website than the brand can provide.

- Does the chain/brand provide adequate marketing exposure for your property in your main feeder markets? More specifically, do you know where they are marketing your hotel? Most brands run extensive search marketing campaigns, but it is the responsibility of the property to communicate your targeted feeder cities to the brand.

- Does your hotel offer packages and special offers that can't easily be accommodated on the brand site? If so, a vanity site can help in featuring and selling these packages and special offers better than the brand site.

- How competitive is your location on the chain/brand website? If you are in a primary or even secondary market with a strong brand presence – meaning multiple properties flying the same flag – a vanity site may be necessary to stand apart. Also, as noted previously, if your property has a non-standard brand component, a vanity site may be necessary to target your right customer mix.

- Are your booking contributions via the web competitive – are you receiving your fair share of online bookings? Bottom line, if you are receiving more than your fair share on your branded site, is a vanity site necessary? If, on the other hand, you see that your share is lagging, a great boost would likely be a new or upgraded vanity site.

- How easy is it for a customer to find your specific hotel on the brand site? In some cases, there are franchise naming issues – Hotel X airport south, airport southeast, etc., that may be confusing to consumers, and a vanity site may more clearly differentiate your property.

- What is the referral process of your brand site? If your hotel is sold out, what properties will be recommended? When will you be recommended?

- What investment does the brand require of you to support the website and what investment does the brand make in local search efforts? The percent of spend on organic versus paid search should be relatively easy for a property to discover. Again, look at your return – are you getting a reasonable ROI?

## Best Practices: Textual Content

You and your brand may have invested a lot of time, effort, and budget into driving traffic to your website...now that you have a possible customer on your website, it's time to effectively market to and convince them that your hotel is the best choice for their trip. Once the consumer arrives at the website, the content – both written and visual – are key to keeping the attention of the consumer and eventually converting them into a booking.

Content should be written, first and foremost, with the customer in mind. It is also important to understand when creating content WHY the customer is considering your hotel and, thus, how you should market to them. There are obviously large differences, for example, between a city center hotel, an airport hotel, and a resort hotel. Each has a different audience, a different reason for "being" (trip purpose), and various amenities and services. Your content should best relate to those differences and speak in the appropriate "voice"...allowing visitors to quickly understand who and what you are...and what impression you wish to give of your hotel.

One way to approach this is to think of your website in terms of how a Director of Sales (DOS) markets the hotel. Does your website reflect the demand generators that bring customers to your area? Are you appropriately featuring proximity to local attractions, amusement parks, stadiums, etc.? Are you a venue for weddings, family reunions, etc.? Make sure your website reflects the reasons why consumers travel to you or your area.

Best practices to optimize website content include the following:

- The revenue team should work with the sales and marketing teams on content creation. Much of what is described on the site should support sales, marketing, and revenue teams' efforts reflecting how the hotel is sold and marketed.
- Define the audience by segment and create content according to the needs of each different customer type.
- Write the content in the right "voice" according to the hotel personality, and targeted customer type.
- Consider the various demand generators for the market or hotel. What content will be best to capture and satisfy those needs?
- Consider the various local attractions in the content creation. Does the hotel cater to any of these needs or partner? Be sure to appropriately represent any content needed in this area.

### Best Practice: Keep It Brief

As you write your copy, keep in mind that web copy is a very different animal than print copy. Web copy is "scanned" or glanced through…not "read" in the traditional sense. This is even more true on mobile platforms, which will soon be the primary source of your online traffic and where visitors have much shorter attention spans. Most consumers will not read your website content word for word but look for appropriate "keywords" or phrases.

You should ensure that all text relates important features and selling points quickly and upfront and avoids long lists and heavy-handed, overly-promotional content that visitors won't read. Content should be easily scannable and paragraphs and sentences kept short and concise so visitors can find what they're looking for quickly. Your most important points should always come first, whether written in paragraph format or bulleted lists (for branded hotels, the formatting is typically pre-determined at the brand level template).

In addition, it is best to avoid needless repetition, jargon, and unnecessary words in your copy…keep it as simple as possible. As effective online copywriting can be seen as an "art," some properties will choose to hire professional copywriters or vendors to handle this area for them. Check first with your brand to see if they have any internal services or vendor recommendations.

### Best Practice: Keep It Fresh

The "freshness" of your content is also extremely important, both from a marketing and an SEO perspective. All content areas should be up-to-date and include the latest information on the hotel itself, new services and amenities, and the most recent local area content. Not only is this important from a consumer perspective, but it is also extremely important from an SEO perspective as Google and other search engines weigh the "freshness" of content in their ranking algorithms.

Also, all promotional or event dates should be constantly updated (e.g., is your website still promoting a New Year's Eve event in February?). While content should always be reviewed and refreshed on a regular basis from a marketing and business perspective, especially when your property's facilities and amenities are changed or updated, the question is tougher when it comes to SEO. For SEO, it can be important to keep the addition of new content at a steady pace, keeping your page dynamic and continuously offering fresh content when and where possible. You should consider updating at least once to twice a year on key pages (those pages with the highest visitor view rates). For branded sites that include customer reviews, the constant addition of customer reviews also helps in this area as it is technically new content (as are responses by the hotel to those reviews).

It is important to have proper room descriptions as these will help drive conversion and upsell the customer into paying for a premium room.

In summary, is your website offering what your potential customers are looking for, is it current, and can they find it quickly (at a glance)?

### Best Practices: Imagery

Imagery sells…and can make all the difference. Strong photography may be one of the most important aspects of your digital presence and your hotel website. Numerous studies show that photography is one of the primary influencers of bookings on a hotel website and, aside from price and location, ranks with reviews as one of the most important aspects in the customer decision-making process. Imagery should be professionally shot, using a photographer experienced in architectural photography.

Your hotel website photo gallery and header images should contain images representing all architectural features of the hotel, including the exterior, meeting space, lobby, fitness centers, pools, recreational areas, business centers, etc., and should provide the website visitor with enough visual knowledge to understand the offerings and services provided by the hotel. Pictures can tell a story, and a single image, if shot correctly, can convey information faster and more effectively than a paragraph of text.

Room photography is especially important. At the end of the day, the room is what the customer is "purchasing." It is important for them to understand the features of the room, the size of the room, and the differences between various room types. If you are selling a suite, focus on the size and layout of the room. If you are selling a "view" room, show the view.

Too often, hotels simply repeat the same images (typically a bed shot) across various room types, in essence telling the customer that regardless of description and price, the rooms are all the same. We know that this is not the case and should show the rooms accordingly. This will assist in both conversion as well as upsell opportunities. If you can show a visitor how much bigger the "Junior Suite" is than a "Standard" room, or what that "City/Ocean View" looks like versus the "Standard" room through imagery, a customer will be much more likely to respond to upselling opportunities.

Effectively impact revenue generation through imagery.
- Tell the whole story with professional architectural photos. Be careful of over-staging, unnatural lighting, or props.
- Display a minimum of 2-3 images for each room type. The more high-quality images of the rooms and the hotel, the better; and trends have shown the number of images has an impact on customer engagement and bookings.
- Document the space with the best angles to give guests the visual information they look for when booking a room...show context.
- Capture the "benefits" of the room to show layout, features, and amenities...and, yes, bathroom shots are important as well.
- Document what is unique about a room type and visually represent the differences.
- Ensure that new photo shoots are scheduled as soon as possible during the opening process or after major renovations and enhancements.
- Avoid any stock hotel imagery. If customers realize you are showing them stock images and not actual images of the hotel, they will lose trust.

- If the website has the capability to show videos, 360's, and more immersive type imagery the property should take full advantage of this, as video (in particular) has been shown to have a big impact in the guest's purchase decision.
- Be honest...do not "trick" customers through the use of photo cropping or Photoshop type enhancements, etc. Color correction, cropping for size, etc., is one thing...but providing false impressions of facilities to guests will result in lost trust or, worse yet, very unhappy customers at a hotel.
- Consider the impact of including people in the imagery. Remember the audience and tailor the photography to that audience. If the hotel caters to conventions and business travelers, avoid photos of families and children splashing in the pool as it will provide the wrong impression to the targeted audience.

### Best Practices: Ancillary Content
In addition to textual content and imagery, many brand. com sites offer additional opportunities for adding ancillary content on your hotel website. These may include the ability to add "product" pages to the website (think spa, golf, restaurants, meetings, historic, etc.), additional promotional pages or elements beyond the typical "deals" listings, various timed marketing messages, renovation and new hotel alerts, and posting of PDF/informational items (menus, A/V service listings, directions, etc.). Be sure to check with your brand to ensure you are aware and knowledgeable on all available enhanced products for your website.

### Best Practices: User-Friendliness
Website user-friendliness refers to the quality of the user experience on the website (i.e., the website usability). In human-computer interaction, usability usually refers to the elegance and clarity with which the interaction with a computer program or a website is designed.

Website user-friendliness encompasses several key components that are crucial to the user experience, including:
- site architecture and page layout for both desktop and mobile usage
- tiered navigation structure (e.g., top/main navigation, subnavigation, actionable navigation, footer navigation, etc.)
- logical flow of information

- content addressing all of your key customer segments
- rich media, videos, and quality imagery
- page download speeds
- design aesthetics
- on-page/internal links
- call to action
- quick links

Every page should have a clear and easy way for visitors to make a reservation. Some sort of "Book now" or "Click here to make reservations" should have a prominent position on every single page. It may seem redundant, but the primary function of your hotel website is to generate bookings, and you want to make it easy for the visitor to make the reservation whenever they feel they have enough information. It may be once they visit your home page, or once they see the restaurants you offer onsite, or directions from the airport – make it easy to book.

The same principle can be applied for those hotels that focus on group business. Prominently include clear navigation to information about event space and sales contacts so that meeting and event planners can find the information they need no matter how they have come into your site.

Redundant navigation is important. Show the main content areas across the top and duplicate them in text on the bottom of each page. Don't make the visitor scroll too far to find what they are looking for. The most relevant information should be top left, then top right. If you have a call to action (other than to make a reservation) give it a clear spot near the top. Don't bury it in the content.

Make sure your pages load quickly – if it's too slow, your visitor will move on. This typically means you have to carefully determine the number of images per page. And for every image, determine if it is inviting, and is it worth the load time? And remember, mounting evidence suggests that mobile users are even more impatient than desktop customers. With mobile, page load time is just as, if not more, important than the image.

Another opportunity doesn't have as obvious an ROI, but it has a potential cost of noncompliance. Making your website accessible to users with disabilities is critical. Threats of lawsuits for noncompliance aside, some marketers feel that Google is rewarding sites who are trying to focus on universal accessibility factors. To learn more, search for the topic at www.hsmai.org or visit the Web Accessibility Initiative website at https://www.w3.org/WAI/. There are some simple best practices to implement immediately.

- Provide sufficient contrast between foreground and background.
- Don't use color alone to convey information.
- Ensure that interactive elements are easy to identify.
- Provide clear and consistent navigation options.
- Include image and media alternatives in your design – create visible links to transcripts of any audio you have, visible links to audio described versions of videos.
- Include text along with icons and graphical buttons.
- Provide a caption and description for each table and image.

### Best Practices: Travel Booker Friendliness
The booker-friendliness of a hotel website is a direct result of how well the hotel website handles a whole range of complex issues that can influence the purchasing behavior of the website users.

Build trust and credibility. Visitors are savvy; they will search between 17 - 22 sites during the booking process. How is your rate integrity? If you offer any sort of lowest rate guarantee, place this in a prominent position on your website, repeatedly. A Best Price guarantee is all you may need to build some trust. See chapter 15 for an overview of rate parity issues.

In addition to best rate guarantees, there are other tactics hotels can leverage to convert more visitors into bookings. Deliberately test these options one at a time to understand the ROI impact. Trying everything at once will not give you a clear indication of what works (and doesn't) to drive conversion. It can also create a lot of "noise," leaving visitors with a poor user experience which can affect their view of the hotel and/or brand.

While OTAs have outpaced hoteliers in applying these conversion tactics, many brands have also implemented similar functionality on their websites.

### Create a Sense of Urgency
Create a sense of urgency during the booking process – get the consumer to feel that they may miss out on an opportunity or good deal if they don't book now.

- Most CRSs offer functionality to set an allotment for a specific number of rooms or special rates left to be sold. Indicating a finite number that is available for sale can create a sense of urgency for the consumer to make the booking right then and there.

- Display the number of visitors currently viewing the hotel's website.
- Display the number of bookings made within a specific timeframe.
- Employ slash-through pricing.
- Format content and pricing with bold text, highlights, boxes, and other "bells and whistles" to highlight specific features.

### Combat Shopping Cart Abandonment

Taking a cue from retail, hotels have become more sophisticated about tracking and engaging with lookers who don't make it all the way through the booking process.

First, track the percent of your visitors who go to your booking engine, and then the percent who actually make a reservation (or request an RFP if that is a goal). If you have a high abandonment rate, you should research to find out why. Is it a technical issue, or a rate parity issue?

There will always be a percentage of prospects who will go to your booking engine and then change their mind. Employ a trigger screen that appears as they try to close out your website. A popup can appear that offers a further special, or invites the visitor to sign up for a newsletter. Send a follow-up email later the same day or the next, again with a special incentive to return to complete the booking. Retargeting (aka remarketing) is a paid media option – an ad for your hotel will appear when the visitor is on another site.

Recover lost sales by re-engaging with the consumer who abandoned the site after starting the booking process, using targeted communications. For example, send an email within a defined period (e.g., same day or next day) offering a special incentive to return and complete the booking. Or, when a guest signs up for your loyalty program, send an email to explain the benefits of booking directly through the program.

All these methods can increase your ultimate conversion rate, but the key is to understand why your visitors are leaving in the first place. If it is cumbersome to book online, they may pick up the phone to call or simply go to a competitor's site. If your rate is not in line with what they have seen on the OTA sites, they will likely leave to find the better deal. In both of those cases, the traditional shopping cart abandonment practices will not be effective.

### Merchandising

Merchandising involves presenting your content — text and visuals — in an appealing and persuasive manner designed to encourage guests to consider and book your destination and property.

- Put a reservation widget on your home page and include it as part of the global navigation of the site. Use a customized look-and-feel design that "mimics" the website design. When a customer clicks to book your property, are they worried they have gone to another site because the look and feel is different? That doesn't help with trust and credibility. Most usability studies and industry best practices suggest that the booking widget should be placed at the top left of the page. This is where you will find most widgets on brand websites for example. If your reservation widget is located on the right-hand side of the page, lower down on the screen, or in a difficult-to-find place, you will pay a penalty in revenue and conversions.
- Highlight dynamically changing special offers on the home page to showcase specific opportunities. Keep these offers up-to-date and have a specific call-to-action to make it easy for the visitor to make a booking.
- Highlight offerings or benefits that guests receive if they book directly on the hotel's website.
- Connect web content according to the visitor's origin, preferences, and interests. A resort, for example, should understand that a guest who found its website through a golf blog will be interested in golf content as opposed to spa content on the main page. Customize content to your user's preferences to improve engagement and ultimately conversion.

## OWNED MEDIA: Mobile Websites & Marketing

Coupled with a well-planned revenue optimization strategy, mobile can help the hotel capture last-minute bookings and fill up last-minute inventory that might otherwise sit empty.

On average, one third of hotel bookings in North America and Europe are made on mobile devices. This figure increases significantly in Asia and the Middle East where approximately 49% and 53%, respectively, of hotel bookings are made via mobile.[35] Transactional growth in mobile is only part of the shift in the travel marketplace. Increasingly, consumers see their mobile devices as an extension of their overall travel experience, whether it's preparing for their trip and creating activity agendas, looking around on-site for activities or restaurants in the area, or finding ways to include their social network in everything they're doing while they're on their trip.

Hotel revenue and marketing teams shouldn't view mobile and desktop in silos, but rather as a consistent consumer experience across channels from the dreaming stage of travel planning all the way through post-purchase activity. By considering how users use mobile technology at each stage of the process, hoteliers can integrate their content seamlessly into the guest's experience, rather than forcing the guest to conform to the hotel's experience, delivering amazing personalized guest experiences that can lead to better vacations, increased brand loyalty, and more bookings over the customer's lifetime.

It is strongly recommended that revenue professionals develop a solid understanding of mobile platforms and the opportunities they present to hotels. The best place to start is HSMAI's book, *Hospitality Digital Marketing Essentials: A Field Guide for Navigating Today's Digital Landscape*, which covers this topic in-depth including:
- The differences between mobile optimization and compatibility; mobile apps versus mobile websites; and responsive versus device-specific design.
- When and where mobile devices are used – what drives the decision of the device and the activity, and how it is relevant for hotels.
- Best practices for mobile optimization.

A sampling of best practices in this space include:
- First ensure that the objectives are clearly defined, and identify the key performance metrics to use as a measurement for success.
- Display redeemable special offers. (e.g., Ensure offers or promotions are easily redeemable by linking them directly to the booking engine, including the appropriate booking code already populated.)
- Make booking easy. (e.g., Always include a "Click to call" button, as there are always people who would prefer to ask questions or simply talk to a person when booking.)

- Leverage mobile marketing techniques:
  - Segment and target your strategy and messaging for mobile devices.
  - Run mobile-specific campaigns that have ads, landing pages, and content targeted to the needs and behaviors of the mobile user.
  - Target mobile users through Mobile Pay-Per-Click (PPC) via the major ad networks and in conjunction with your regular PPC campaigns.
  - Extend geolocation and location-based marketing by "pushing" ads or offers to consumers via SMS (requires opt-in) as well as through geolocation specific applications like Swarm (Foursquare), Facebook, Google+, and Yelp.

Remember, mobile usage is growing at a pace faster than adoption of all previous technology advancements including social media. Hotels that approach mobile marketing from a consumer-centric position will gain a competitive advantage and build stronger relationships with the online visitors and onsite guests.

## EARNED MEDIA: Social Media
Social media creates an incredible opportunity for interaction between consumers and brands, transforming conventional messaging into a two-way conversation. Anyone can create and share content – and almost everyone does. Social marketing makes the most of all this user-generated content via consistent participation on networking platforms, publishing sites (blogs), micropublishing sites, review sites, message boards, and groups. With this in mind, it is easy to see how social media is an important aspect of any revenue optimization strategy.

As social beings, we are drawn to interesting stories. When we find a compelling story, we instinctively want to share it. In traditional marketing, hotels fed stories to consumers. It went one way. Today, consumers share stories with hotels and with other consumers. In lauding all the statistics about users and uploads, it's sometimes easy to forget the "social" part of social media – the sharing and connecting between individuals, businesses, brands, and more, worldwide.

As social media channels have matured, they've become increasingly driven by visuals. YouTube, with its millions of videos, has always been visually driven, but Facebook, which was once mostly text-driven, has evolved to include ever more photo and video sharing features. While Twitter remains mostly the province of 140-character info-bites, it now fosters more photo and video sharing. In fact, re-tweeting links to videos is one of the most popular activities on the site.

Best practices for the hospitality industry have emerged for several of the most commonly used social media platforms. Use them to tell your hotel's story, and attract and engage potential guests.

### Best Practices: Facebook

Facebook is the largest and most well-known of the social networks. More than 50 million businesses use Facebook pages[50] and one-third of Facebook users engage with brands regularly[51]. Consider the following when building and maintaining your property's page.

- Make use of the cover photo feature. Your cover photo is a great way to establish your brand in a big, bold way. And given its prominence on your page – and the simplicity of updating it – you can change it regularly to tie in to promotions or to give seasonal views of your property.
- Take advantage of the Facebook app infrastructure. There are more than 7 million apps and websites that integrate with Facebook. Using apps is a great way for you to leverage the Facebook platform while telling your story the way you want to tell it – and the way that engages your customers most effectively. With apps, you can customize your Facebook experience to your hotel's brand, display multi-media, promote loyalty programs and offers, enable booking, and more.
- Be responsive. More and more, people are using social media as a support platform. If you have guests and prospects asking questions on your wall, write back promptly -- and politely!
- Study your community. Analyze and better understand your Facebook audience and their interests – align Facebook content to better resonate with your community.
- Be human and authentic. Be approachable and honest, and personalize the page so it is consistent with your brand/property.
- Get existing customers and prospects to be fans by emailing to your opt-in list, blogging about your page, sending out Tweets, linking it to your email signature, and posting a link or badge on your website.

- There are advertising options that target specific demographics. Facebook Polls can be used to get input and opinions, and Facebook's built-in analytics lets you track valuable metrics such as page views, wall posts, discussion threads, and photo views.
- DO NOT...constantly change your "profile" picture. This is the image users see in their news feed every time you're active on Facebook – it should be something recognizable and familiar, so that everyone knows right away who you are.

### Best Practices: YouTube

YouTube revolutionized online video sharing with its introduction in 2005. Quickly bought by Google, YouTube now sees more than 1 billion unique users – watching more than 6 billion hours of video – every month.

Ensure hotel videos are posted on channels that make sense for your personality, style, features, and amenities. Some brands are successfully creating YouTube channels to syndicate their content for the benefit of the grander marketing objectives.

- Consider the global audience. YouTube is localized in 56 countries and 61 languages worldwide, and 70% of the site's traffic comes from outside of the U.S. Include videos that have global appeal to attract worldwide travelers. The beautiful thing about imagery is that it requires no language translation.
- Share videos other than your own. You might not have the resources to create new videos every week, but that doesn't mean your YouTube channel page should sit idle. Consider the types of videos your guests and followers might like; showcase local events and other travel videos.
- Listen, monitoring all mentions of topics relevant to your brand/property, to better understand customer sentiment. Use YouTube Insights and comment/discussion sections to monitor customer concerns or misconceptions of the brand/property.
- Link channel videos on other social mediums. Integrate other social media properties. For instance, add your YouTube content to your Facebook fan page to better unite social media efforts and raise the relevancy of your content in search.
- Maximize SEO opportunities. Title and tag videos and channel appropriately to maximize

their SEO value for consumer searches. Be sure to brand yourself by displaying brand/property information, URL, email, and phone number in every video and post links to your videos on social networks.

- Tag videos with relevant keywords.
- DO NOT...share completely unrelated videos. While it's tempting to share the latest hilarious video you see making its way through social media, be careful not to dilute your message: stay on brand and give your visitors only the videos that relate to your property's image and identity.

### Best Practices: Twitter

Twitter launched its mobile photo filters feature on iPhone and Android in December 2012. Twitter's quick bursts of information are ideally suited to our time-crunched, on-the-go, increasingly mobile society. They've recently embraced more visual storytelling features as well, including header photos, photo streaming/swiping on mobile apps, and new photo filters for mobile uploads.

- Use your background. Use an image that says something about your property, or that shows off what you have to offer. Consider the way your background image "splits," with your timeline in the middle. Why not have a photo of your hotel on the left and photos of your pool, business center, and restaurant on the right?
- Re-tweet. As with other social sites, sharing is a huge part of Twitter. Follow local businesses and other Twitter users that may be relevant to your guests, and re-tweet anything you think has value.
- Add photos to your tweets. To engage visually, augment your tweets with photos – of your property, of your guests enjoying themselves, of your chef's latest creation. And while Twitter no longer supports Instagram, the company's new mobile filters allow you to add a similar retro-like feel to your images.
- Use hashtags. Hashtags are used before a relevant keyword or phrase to categorize tweets and help them show more easily in search. They are a great way to join an existing conversation or even start your own. A great example of hashtag use and success is #discoverIHG hashtag. It's also important not to overuse them. Hashtags are intended to add value to your tweets, so use them sparingly and respectfully. A good rule of thumb is to use no more than two per tweet.

- Keep tweets short to allow room for your followers to give you credit when they "retweet" and share with their friends. Always include a link within the message, ideally at the beginning, since it will increase the likelihood that followers will click on it. Twitter also allows an image to be added to each tweet.
- DO NOT...worry if your tweets don't get a response. Avoid focusing on measuring retweets; instead, focus on making your content engaging and relevant to your followers.
- #dontmakeyourhashtagafullsentence. They are simply too hard to read, and no one will ever hashtag that again, and therefore no conversation will happen.

### Best Practices: Pinterest

Pinterest is a perfect platform for visual storytelling.

- Stay organized. Pinterest makes "pinning" cool photos a breeze, but your board can quickly become cluttered. Keep your pins neat and streamlined by creating different boards for different aspects of your property, such as rooms, guests, the grounds, local attractions, and events. Since sharing food ideas and recipes is one of the more popular activities on Pinterest; consider a board showcasing your property's restaurant or bar offerings, or local restaurants.
- Be a content curator. Remember that social media is a two-way conversation, and be sure to upload and repin relevant images that others post about your hotel and surrounding area to contribute to your hotel's story through the eyes of guests.
- Draw people to your content. Put a "Follow Me on Pinterest" button on your website and periodically post Pinterest content to your other social networks to create awareness and interest. You can link to specific boards which gives you an opportunity to segment your followers in ways relevant to your business.
- DO NOT...ignore the past. If you have old photos lying around, put them to use. Nostalgia drives many pin boards. Your guests might enjoy seeing what your property looked like over the years, before and after renovations, or seeing how the neighborhood around you has changed.

### Best Practices: Instagram

With its retro filters and snap-and-upload simplicity, the mobile photo-sharing phenomenon Instagram has proven extremely popular with users. Originally launched on Apple's iOS, Instagram has expanded to the Android platform and continues to grow rapidly.

- Show visitors the human side of your property. While you never want to make your marketing all about you, it never hurts to show off the faces behind your business. It can help humanize your hotel and remind potential guests that it is more than just a brand.
- Show off the surrounding area. Unless you're an inclusive resort, your visitors want to know what else your neighborhood offers beyond the hotel doors. Using Instagram's filters and special effects, you can convey how much your local restaurants and attractions have to offer.
- Take lots of photos. While you want to keep your Facebook albums tight and focused, Instagram is all about photos. Your followers will expect regular updates, or they'll quickly forget why they follow you.
- DO NOT...get too personal. While it's great to show your staff hard at work and your guests enjoying your property, you never want to embarrass anyone. Awkward and embarrassing photos will create a negative image of your property in a consumer's mind that you may not be able to shake.

## Best Practices: Snapchat

Snapchat, a mobile app that's all about pictures and videos, is wildly popular amongst teens and young adults. Snapchat is inherently ephemeral -- Snaps are viewable for about 10 seconds before they disappear; Snapchat Stories, about 24 hours. With some 150 million daily users creating 9,000 Snaps every second, now is a good time for brands to get on board.

- Make your profile public and make "everyone" your friend.
- Create original geofilters for your hotel and/or for special events there.
- Make it snappy. Snaps should be brief and easy to read in about 10 seconds.
- Link individual Snaps together to create a Snapchat Story.
- Stories should last only 1-2 minutes.
- Go vertical. Snapchat is used via mobile phone, so vertical content is easiest to view.
- Fill your space. Make sure images take up the whole frame.

- Go for contrast – white text on a dark background, for example.
- Make liberal use of emojis.
- Engage followers with Snaps about contests, coupon codes, employee bios.
- Be responsive. Reply to snaps and connect with influencers.
- Don't play solo – allow employees, influencers, even guests to "take over" your account or host a snap-based Q&A.
- Selfies were made for Snapchat.
- You cannot share links on Snapchat but you CAN cross-promote on other social channels.

## Best Practices: Connect with your global customer through social media

Before booking hotels, reserving restaurants, or choosing attractions to visit, most consumers take to the web. They've become accustomed to reading travel reviews and recommendations on portals such as TripAdvisor, Expedia, and Kayak. This familiarity with portals has accelerated consumers' use of social networks — like Facebook, Twitter, Sina Weibo, Wechat (China), and VK (Russia) — to get destination information and peer recommendations.

There's an important difference between portals and social networks, however. Through recommendations, photos, and travel experiences posted directly by friends and family, social networks offer a greater level of trust. In fact, Social Media Today noted that "84% of Facebook users admitted in a PRSA Travel & Tourism poll that viewing their friends' post actually influenced their own future travel plans."

This trend holds true for global social network users. So, what should you do to join and influence conversations? And when those conversations span many social networks and include multiple languages, how do you stay connected?

The following are helpful tips on where to start:
- Recognize that not all social networks are the same, and develop a global social media strategy accordingly. For instance, if your audience is primarily in China, use Sina Weibo or Wechat to reach those customers.
- As with any conversation, there are two parts: listening and engaging.
- Use social listening to gain an understanding of your consumers' sentiment.

- Support social engagement with a local community engagement manager to answer questions, defuse issues, and be a trusted part of the conversation in real-time. Customers increasingly expect customer service on social networks.
- Once you've tracked conversations and gained insights, plan to deliver localized and targeted content, promotions, and information around popular topics.
- If you're using a social network's advertising platform, be sure to localize ads accordingly so they stand out to your targeted consumer.

### Best Practices: Measuring Social Media

There are a variety of social media marketing tools and an almost infinite stream of data available. Remember though, there's no magic potion to turn your social media activities into dollars. The social sphere is and always will be a rapidly evolving marketplace. Understand the role of social media in the shopping journey so that you can keep your eye on how it's helping you achieve your larger marketing objectives. So, what should you measure and why? Following are nine time-honored metrics[52].

1.  **Share of Voice**
    The number of mentions of your brand versus competing brands on the social web. Your Share of Voice can be a good indicator of the consumer awareness of your brand as compared to your competitive set. It essentially shows how much of the social conversation your brand has earned or is currently earning.

2.  **Brand Volume**
    The total number of brand mentions over a given period of time. If this number isn't growing, your campaign probably isn't working. Tracking brand volume week-over-week and month-over-month can be a good way to measure the overall health of your social presence.

3.  **Engagement**
    The overall number of times a user talks to your brand on social sites. You can push out all the content in the world, but if no one cares to reply or discuss it, what's the point? Social media is a conversation, after all. The more highly engaged your followers and fans are, the more likely they are to be brand-loyalists, or become influencers

and evangelize your products or services on their own personal networks.

4.  **Interaction Per Post**
    The number of replies or comments you receive on a given post, tweet, or update. Similar to the engagement metric, the more times a user makes the effort to comment or reply, the more likely it is that they will grow to care about your brand and what you have to say.

5.  **Sentiment Analysis**
    The process of determining how the people who talk about your brand on social media actually feel about your brand, products, or company. Although P.T. Barnum famously said, "All publicity is good publicity," it's an obvious problem if your hotel is consistently being trashed on social media. Also, if the sentiment is mostly neutral, that could be a sign your marketing is not making a big enough impact, and no one cares enough to have a strong opinion either positively or negatively.

6.  **Social Click-Through Rate**
    The number of times a user clicks on a link to one of your owned web properties (e.g., your hotel's website) shared via social media. Typically, one of the goals of a social media campaign is to drive traffic to a brand's website, microsite, or other owned media, thereby creating consumer awareness and subsequently bookings. The growth in the number of click throughs can be one of the indicators of a successful, engaging campaign.

7.  **Key Influencer Mentions**
    The number of mentions by users you've designated as "key influencers" due to their substantial and loyal social media following. Having influencers discuss your brand and serve as brand ambassadors is an extremely powerful way to organically extend your reach within key communities. While having anyone mention your brand on social media can be proof your tactics are working, mentions by key influencers are considered more valuable since they have a deeper reach or more pull/influence with your target demographic or communities.

8. **Platform Reach**

   The number of social platforms that your hotel appears on, or the social "reach" across various online networks. Your brand might be a hot topic of discussion on various forums, but your Twitter mentions are low. Whether this is a problem depends on the social networks your targets actually use. After all, having a popular Pinterest page, which has a predominantly female user-base, doesn't really help if your brand is trying to target teenage males.

9. **Mobile Mentions**

   The number of mentions of your hotel on mobile social sites. Social media is an increasingly mobile form of communication, and posting updates while on the go is quickly becoming part of nearly everyone's lifestyle, thanks to smartphones and tablets. If consumers aren't bringing your brand with them via mobile apps, this could be a sign you are getting left behind. It is especially important if your campaign involves mobile coupons, QR codes, or anything else that's tied into the Android, iPhone, or Windows phone operating systems.

## PAID MEDIA: Paid Search

Paid search should be an integral part of any internet marketing strategy. However, it can be costly and is not sustainable as a singular strategy for promoting hospitality websites in search engines since paid search does little to create demand. A balanced strategy that includes paid search in addition to organic optimization, paid linkage, online media, social media, and email marketing yields the best results over the long term.

Paid search, due to the inherent immediacy of its results and control of the message, lends itself to the tactical promotion of specific rates, packages, and promotions. With a good understanding of booking lead times, paid search campaigns can be executed with precision and coordination with the revenue strategy of your hotel. The strategic use of paid search can supplement a solid organic optimization program.

### Best Practices: Keyword Research & Analysis

Any marketing program or campaign should start with clearly outlined goals and objectives and should be complementary to the overall digital marketing strategy. By ensuring this at the outset, the results will be more

quantifiable, and for Paid Search specifically, it is critical in the development of an appropriate keyword strategy as well as in writing ad copy.

Begin by making a list of words and phrases that describe your hotel by its location and unique selling points (USP). Where is your hotel located? What would the consumer have in mind when looking for a hotel in your location? Asking yourself why the consumer would be traveling to the destination can be helpful. Consider including modifying words like the city, state, or country, as well as the neighborhood and surrounding landmarks.

The major search engines have access to a huge amount of data about what keywords people search for every day. For instance, Google has a keyword tool within its AdWords interface that will provide additional keyword suggestions based on a list of keywords you enter. By leveraging the tool, you can understand not only the potential of your keywords but also related terms that you might want to use in your Paid Search campaign. This same tool can be utilized to estimate the required budget. Each keyword or keyword group will provide an estimate of the number of impressions you will receive, and from this you can anticipate the budget required to fund your campaign.

Include long and short tail keywords as part of your strategy. See chapter 2 of Hospitality Digital Marketing Essentials for additional information on these particular keyword types.

Organize your keywords into related or similarly themed groups. These will become "Ad Groups" in your final campaign setup. By approaching the keywords in this manner, you can optimize the use of ad copy and descriptions. Many campaign management tools utilize this concept to organize the keywords and manage budget. Otherwise, you will need to identify a keyword, then a description, then a headline repeatedly. If you can group similar words, you can write less copy, and the smaller sample will enable you to test your headlines a little easier. Tightly themed ad groups also help to ensure that the most relevant ad copy is being served for all keywords within the group. As a rule of thumb, groups of 10 to 15 keywords work well.

### Best Practices: Campaign Set-Up

The implementation of a successful paid search campaign involves several elements.

## Ad Copy & Headline

Your ad copy and headline should be brief, and, in conjunction with the keyword utilized, provide a compelling reason to click through to the landing page. It must be succinct due to the character limitations imposed by the search engine. It should communicate your unique selling proposition (USP), what you are promoting, and encourage a call to action in a small amount of space. Think about these issues when you create your copy:

- Include keywords in your ad copy whenever possible as this will assist in continuity and relevance.
- Why should someone click on your ad? Consider your USP and use this as the ad headline or the call to action.
- Create a sense of urgency and a call to action (example: Book now!) to trigger the desired action (which is to click through).
- Include rate, percent off, or value adds if applicable as these are strong compelling messages.
- Consult search engine guidelines for rules about ads to ensure you don't violate any editorial policies, or have ads disapproved by the engines.

## Keyword Group

Develop the ad copy to correspond with the ad groups created to ensure that the ad copy is relevant to what users may be searching for.

## Consider the Competition

Some simple searches of your keywords should show you what your competition is doing and what you are competing against. The intent here is not to copy the competition, but to position your ads and messaging well. However, being aware that your ads will display alongside these is a key consideration. Knowing what your competition is doing can help you modify your ad copy to stand out, and help you decide whether to bid on certain keywords at all.

## Keyword Matching

Keyword matching is a method the search engines use to serve ads based on keywords that might be similar to what you selected as targets or similar to what the consumer has utilized. Understanding this allows you to determine how broad or narrow you want to set your campaign. It is important to understand the difference between a "keyword" and a "search query." A keyword is the word or phrase you choose to bid on in paid search. A search query is a word or phrase that a consumer actually types into the search box of the search engine. Matching helps you refine your keyword list so you don't have to bid on and manage every possible keyword combination. While the details of use vary by search engine, there are some general concepts that apply to all of them.

- EXACT MATCH: The search query must be the same, or very similar to your keyword to trigger your ad. This works well in situations where you want to tightly control the type of traffic your ads generate.
- PHRASE MATCH: Your ad will appear on searches that include the words in your keyword phrase, in the same specific order, but the query can also include other words before or after the word or phrase you are bidding on.
- BROAD MATCH: Casts the widest net and is the most difficult to control. When using Broad Match, your ad is shown on queries containing similar phrases and relevant variations of the keyword. This will generate a lot of activity, some less relevant.
- MODIFIED BROAD MATCH: This match type is offered by most search engines and is a more targeted approach than simple Broad Match. By utilizing a plus sign (+) in front of a word within a Broad Match keyword, you ensure that your keyword will only match to queries that contain each word that you've marked with a plus sign.
- NEGATIVE MATCH: Used to ensure that your ad does not show for any query that includes the terms you specify. Think about phrases containing words like "free" or "cheap," inappropriate content, customer reviews, and news-related terms (like robbery, bedbugs, fraud, etc.), competitors' brand names, etc. Do you want to show up in these searches or not?
- DAILY CAMPAIGN BUDGETS: These can be set in most search engines and allow for managing your budget and spreading it across the campaign period.
- AD DISTRIBUTION: Allows you to control whether your ads appear only on Search Engine Result Pages (SERP), or also on display network sites like news and blogs, mobile apps, etc. You will want to consider that users on other websites may or may not be as likely to click as those directly searching on a search engine.
- AD ROTATION: Allows you to have several different ads that are eligible to serve on a

rotating basis based on keyword match. You can have them rotate evenly, or in an optimized rotation.

- GEOGRAPHICAL AD DISTRIBUTION: Allows you to pinpoint where you want your ads to be displayed based on the physical location of the consumer, or the location that they are searching for. This can be particularly useful if you understand the major feeder markets for your hotel, or if a campaign is intended to focus on a specific market.
- LANGUAGE: Language settings allow you to target the consumer based on the language they have specified in their internet browser settings. This is a key consideration as your campaign can be more effective if you also have keywords translated into the preferred language of your target audience. Adding multiple languages to a campaign can allow you to target a larger set of consumers, but can also add to the cost of the campaign.

## Best Practices: Measuring your Campaign Performance

Paid search metrics for hotels include:

- CONVERSIONS: When a person who clicked your ad completes an action on your website, such as booking a room, buying something, signing up for an email list, or requesting more information.
- CONVERSION RATE: The percentage of clicks that resulted in a conversion.
- COST PER CONVERSION: Total conversions divided by total cost.
- ROAS (RETURN ON AD SPEND): Also called ROI (return on investment), this metric measures how profitable your advertising is.
- As well as revenue, ADR (Average Daily Rate), room nights, and market share.

Additional cross-industry metrics include:

- IMPRESSIONS: How often your ad is shown. Each appearance of your ad equals one impression.
- IMPRESSION SHARE: The percentage of impressions you received divided by the estimated number of impressions you were eligible to receive based on your targeting, bid, and other factors.
- CLICKS: The number of times a user interacts with your ad by clicking on it.
- COST: Total cost that you have spent with each search engine or campaign.
- AVERAGE COST-PER-CLICK (CPC): How much you

paid for each click on your ad. Can be calculated by dividing cost by the number of clicks.

- CLICK-THROUGH RATE: Expressed as a percentage, this metric is the number of clicks divided by the number of impressions.
- AVERAGE AD POSITION: A statistic that describes how your ad typically ranks against other ads. This rank determines in which order ads appear on the page. Position one is the first ad on the page.

## Best Practices: Campaign, Bid, and Budget Management

Managing your paid search campaign involves the fine tuning of your keyword strategy, ad messaging, bids, and available budget. By manipulating these elements, the budget can be managed to allow you exposure all day or during the key hours you want to be displaying. Keep in mind that when the daily budget is depleted you will no longer be rotating and have no presence until the new budget period begins. The optimization of the campaign will come through changing ad copy and the keywords being utilized – in and of itself this process is a series of tests to find the correct balance of exposure and return.

Quality score affects your cost per click and ad position and therefore is a key component of the management of the optimal campaign. As a way of rating paid search keyword relevance, quality score ranks relevance on a scale from 1 to 10, with 1 being the worst and 10 being the best. The components of quality score are your CTR (click-through-rate), ad relevance, landing page quality and relevance, and expected impact from the use of extensions and ad formats. It is important because it is used to:

- Determine the actual cost per click (CPC) that you pay.
- Estimate first page bids.
- Determine if a keyword is eligible for the ad auction.
- Rank your ad against other advertisers in the auction.

Quality score will directly impact what you pay for a click, where you appear on the list of ads, and therefore how effectively your budget will be consumed.

## Best Practices: Testing

Testing is an indispensable component of any marketing strategy. A challenge for certain channels, like email or direct mail, is that they take more time to test in setup and to receive test results. PPC tests can take only days. While nearly every element of Paid Search can be tested, following are some of the most common tests.

### Keywords
Which keywords draw the most traffic to your page? But also important is to measure if those visitors are staying and converting.

### Headlines and Description Line
Changing one word in a headline can alter performance dramatically. Not unlike headlines in direct mail, certain words seem to compel action, like "new," "limited," or "free." The usage of rates, discounts, or other numerical ad components can also significantly improve your ad's performance. Again, it's important not only to measure traffic but the results of the traffic. Once you find the headline that works the best, that becomes your control and then test other headlines to see if they can beat it. The same is true for ad copy. A/B testing or split testing is a method of testing marketing strategy by which a baseline control sample is compared to a variety of single-variable test samples to improve response or conversion rates. You can change the settings to rotate ads evenly to ensure clean results.

### Landing Pages
You can easily create multiple landing pages and see which has a higher conversion rate. More images? Fewer images? Placement of your call to action?

Testing can be an arduous process but it is worthwhile as paid results can be expensive. In order to maximize your investment, always be testing and changing your purchases or copy based on results.

The data gathered from a test can be applied to all elements of the digital marketing strategy, but specifically it is most useful when developing organic optimization of keywords and even website content.

## PAID MEDIA: OTA Paid Media
Many of the OTA's have paid media models where you can purchase "media assets" that will try to drive bookings (in most cases within the "walled garden" of the OTA). These are helpful in need periods but one must be careful as the cost for acquisition needs to be calculated as your margin plus the media cost divided by your revenue. OTA paid marketing programs include:
- Travel Ads (Expedia) or some version of this, where you pay for top placement on the page in a

PPC bidding model.
- Genius Program (Booking.com) or some version of this, where you pay an extra % in margin to get preferred placement.
- Display Advertising which is targeted display advertising within the OTA driving guests to your information.
- Click Off Campaigns – Though not common, sometimes OTA's will allow you to buy display advertising that enables you to send clicks to your own website.

## OWNED MEDIA: Email Marketing
The primary goals of email marketing today include moving the guest along their digital journey from awareness through the booking process and after the stay by encouraging brand advocacy. It is an integral part of the hotel's direct online channel strategy and marketing mix, and is crucial to digital customer relationship management (eCRM).

There are three primary categories of email today – transactional, relational, and promotional. Where your customer can be found along the journey to purchase and beyond will drive the type of email that should be utilized.

### Transactional Email Examples
- reservation confirmation
- confirming loyalty membership
- sending receipts post stay
- loyalty account creation
- newsletter subscription confirmation
- support tickets
- password reminders
- unsubscribe confirmations

### Relational Email Examples
- new subscriber (to loyalty club or newsletter) welcome
- gated content delivery
- newsletter/blog
- confirmation
- survey/review
- social updates
- contest announcements
- referral requests

### Promotional Email Examples
- promotional content

- new gated content
- flash sale announcement
- new product announcements – renovations, new services, etc.
- loyalty program updates
- event announcements
- trial offer
- upgrade offer

## Best Practices: Growing Your Email List

Consider the following best practices for gathering new email addresses and maintaining your relationships with your fresh, new leads:

- Opt-in via a collection form on your website: Make sure you provide leads with a place to indicate what they are interested in receiving (e.g., golf specials, dining offers, etc.) so that you can cater to those interests with your marketing materials later.
- Upon making a reservation: Whether a new reservation comes in through a phone call or a reservation request online, aim to capture guests' email addresses. Whatever your tactics on this front, be sure to understand and comply with GDPR (General Data Protection Regulation).
- Upon check-in: If a guest is part of a group or booked through an OTA, you may not have had a chance to collect their email prior to their stay and can certainly do so when they check in at the front desk.
- Upon check-out: If the guest's email address still hasn't been secured by the time a guest checks out, make sure that you request a valid email address so that they can be sent a follow-up email after their stay.
- At various outlets on property (restaurants, spas, etc.): Email addresses captured to reserve dining or appointment times can also be used when sending interest-based marketing pieces.
- The sales team: Email addresses collected by your sales teams at conferences and conventions are also a great lead to begin nurturing with digital marketing.

## Best Practices Email Marketing

A number of factors need to be considered prior to launching any email campaign.

- TARGETING: To whom will you mail? Past customers tend to be most responsive (assuming a generally positive past stay experience). It is better to have a smaller, well-targeted list. Determining where you will obtain your list should be your first step. Does your list comply with opt-in compliance?
- COPYWRITING: What will your subject line say to entice your targeted list? What will you be selling primarily? What will your offer be?
- DESIGN: Visually, how will you support your message? Is there a photograph that showcases the element of your property that would be particularly appealing to your targeted audience?
- DELIVERY AND DEPLOYMENT: How will you send the email? Will you use a software company like Constant Contact or ExactTarget? What links will you have back to your website? What action will you be asking your audience to take? Are the links working and landing pages operational?
- MEASUREMENT: Start with a goal – opens, clicks, revenue produces – and then measure your results to that goal. If you fell short, at what point along the way did you miss the target? Was it the wrong list? Was it the wrong offer?
- TESTING: Each element of your email can have a dramatic impact on your success, so always test and verify results. Try new subject lines, change your offers, or change the visuals. Repeat successes and learn from failures.

Additional best practices include the following:

- Plan your email marketing campaigns the same way you plan any other quarterly or yearly marketing schedule. Start with a purpose, and make sure your emails are purpose-driven and will support your other marketing efforts to attain specific goals.
- Every email should be planned in advance so that timing is taken into consideration on a large scale, with each email having a goal or specific purpose behind it. Do not send emails just to send emails. It will end up decreasing your response rates for future campaigns when you actually have something of value to offer or mention.
- Segment your email lists by market and customer type (meeting planner, leisure traveler, business traveler, etc.) and tailor your marketing messages to target consumers strategically.
- Consolidate past guest email addresses from your Property Management System, booking engine, and past customer relationship management databases.

- Segment the data you have from your Property Management System not only to target customers by market or customer type but also by their past purchasing behavior (booking date, stay dates, amount spent, rooms stayed in, etc.) to even better tailor your messages.
- Each message should present a concrete offer, available only for a limited time to create urgency. Include a direct and easy-to-follow booking link or instructions.
- Ensure the landing page you are driving your customers to is congruent with the creative, the message, and the call to action that is in your email to provide the best customer experience.
- Design your pieces so that they are responsive to whichever device, email software, or browser they are viewed in, automatically optimizing the piece to be viewed and responded to from any device.
- Strong and short subject lines are key.
- Create clean, enticing designs, in line with other branding and marketing efforts, so that the guests are able to associate the offer with your property.
- Be concise. In email marketing less is more, driving deliverability rates upward as well as increasing the likelihood of response and action on your offer/message.
- Comply with GDPR and the CAN-SPAM Act, respecting customers' privacy and the frequency with which they desire to receive marketing messages.
- After a campaign has been sent, analyze the reporting statistics to see the response to different aspects of the email: day of week it was sent, time it was sent, how many links/materials were included, and bookings generated. Adjust aspects of your future emails based on the information learned from previous campaigns. It is all part of the process to determine what works best for your specific audiences and property.
- On property, request guests' business cards or contact information upon check-in or via in-room questionnaires to build your email databases.
- On the hotel's website, an email sign-up widget should be present on the Home page so that email addresses can be collected from people who have an interest in receiving your email. Also, have a dedicated Stay Connected page.
- Your Facebook page should also have a Stay Connected widget which will allow people to submit their email addresses directly to your database.

## Be Aware of GDPR

Hoteliers would be wise to ensure compliance with GDPR (General Data Protection Regulation) guidelines. GDPR was established by the European Parliament, the Council of the European Union, and the European Commission in 2016, but became enforceable in 2018.

GDPR requires all organizations and businesses collecting, storing, and sharing their customer data to be more transparent with the use of the data.

Hotels that collect, store and use customer's personal data should document what personal data they hold, where it came from and with whom it is shared. Personal data includes an individual's name, phone number, email, address, reservation number, IP address or any relevant information that allows them to be uniquely identified.

This all applies to any hotel that targets customers from the EU. Many hotels globally have taken precautions to follow the GDPR rules regardless of their customer base.

Hoteliers must also ensure that all rules they follow must also be adhered to by the software company in order to be compliant. Every vendor that receives personal data from a hotel must share a Data Processing Agreement (DPA) with the hoteliers to confirm that the vendor is compliant with the GDPR rules.

Hotels should review current privacy notices and put a plan in place for making any necessary changes if not done so already. Review how all personal data is captured and stored; and finally, manage the consents and implementing all required changes needed to be compliant.

This is not an exhaustive explanation of GDPR and all the requirements that hotels must follow but instead is touched on to ensure that the reader understands the importance of compliance. Non-compliance with the rules of GDPR can result in hefty fines for hotels. Customer data capture and email marketing is often a discussion that involves the revenue person at the hotel. Therefore, it is a very important topic to ensure is covered as it relates to this section.

# PART THREE:
# EMERGING ELEMENTS IMPACTING REVENUE STRATEGY

**By the time this book goes from the editor to the printer, it is likely that some new development will crop up presenting all new challenges to hoteliers.**

This section highlights three of the emerging elements in the industry that are having a significant impact today, and that all revenue professionals should pay attention to.

For ongoing updates from HSMAI regarding new developments impacting revenue optimization (and sales and marketing), become a member for access to cutting edge insight and thought leadership on the most important issues facing hoteliers. www.hsmai.org/join

## Alternative Accommodations

The growing popularity of alternative accommodations – home rentals – shows no sign of slowing down, and is contributing to the complexity of revenue optimization for hotels. Before diving into the key areas causing the complexity, it is best to understand the history of alternative accommodations and where they are today.

"After World War II, a vacation system in Europe became

popular which involved 'vacation home sharing.' European families would buy a vacation cottage/villa jointly and have exclusive use of the property for one of the four seasons. Each family rotated seasonally so all enjoyed the prime seasons equally. This concept was mostly utilized by families related to each other because of the trust factor involved in joint ownership and no property manager.

"However, few families vacationed for an entire season at a time so owners found ways to monetize vacant periods, leading to the birth of the vacation rental and timeshare markets we know today.

"The idea of vacationing in homes became widely accepted in the United States in the 1960's. By the 1970's and early 1980's many property management companies emerged, largely as a by-product of real estate companies identifying additional revenue streams and securing client loyalty."[36]

By 1985, the vacation rental industry needed more formal support and The Vacation Rental Management Association (VRMA) was formed. Ten years later, in 1995, the first online listing of a vacation rental property came on the scene. An official web presence for vacation rental properties was born, and Vacation Rental By Owner (VRBO.com) launched.[37]

Historically, travelers using vacation rental properties had traditions of vacationing at the same destination summer after summer, or they would repeat the same trip to the same home holiday after holiday. The process to book these homes was extremely manual. In 1995 and 1996 with the launch of VRBO.com and other similar sites like PerfectPlaces.com, travelers could more easily shop and book other destinations or homes.

Leading up to 2010, consumer travel trends began changing at a more rapid pace. Consumers no longer wanted the same, repetitive place to stay for leisure or work, and the internet and mobile devices made change feasible. A cookie-cutter hotel or experience was not as desirable, boutique hotels had gained enormous share, and now travelers wanted even more curated, personalized experiences. Instead of visiting the same place year after year, people wanted to explore.

The "experience economy" was changing travel. In 2011, Airbnb came onto the scene with real investment interest. What started just four years earlier as a few roommates who needed extra cash and decided to rent an air mattress in their apartment (breakfast included), became an entire market in and of itself. Along the way, both the traditional lodging channels like Booking.com and Expedia also expanded their offerings to include alternative lodging. The internet has removed some of the friction involved in booking non-traditional lodging. Today, the ease of booking a yurt or treehouse is as easy as booking a luxury home. In some ways it is even as easy as booking a traditional hotel.

Alternative accommodations are not a new option, but advancements in technology will continue to influence the space. For years the alternative accommodations industry mostly existed as a separate space from traditional lodging operators. Today the lines are blurring.

Large hotel chains are showing interest in expanding their offerings, and many developers of luxury and upscale hotel developments now include residential homes as part of mixed-use developments. In these types of projects, the developer creates a hotel AND for-sale-housing that will eventually become part of the hotel's inventory. This trend has important implications for revenue optimization technology, practices, and measures.

New players continue to enter the market from technology, operations, and marketing angles. Though the two worlds (traditional and alternative lodging) may be overlapping, it is important to recognize that differences remain. There are different zoning laws, owner and management company factors, cleaning and maintenance hurdles, and other fees and services to consider. The overall lodging sector will continue to evolve and it is exciting to look ahead at what the future will bring.

There are three key implications for hoteliers as it relates to managing the complexities introduced by alternative accommodations.

### Demand Forecasting

Typically, hotel inventory is fixed and rarely changes over time. In the home rental space the inventory is far more dynamic with home owners having dynamic windows to make inventory available for sale. This causes challenges in creating and managing demand forecasts and requires the ability to be able to segment room types for demand in addition to other forms of segmentation.

Inventory availability can be limited with many distinct product types which further complicate accurate demand forecasting (think about distribution too). RMS solutions must be able to address this need by ensuring demand forecasting is completed at a room-type level in addition to other segmentation schemas.

### Determining Optimal Pricing

Often the home-product type and service offering can vary significantly from the hotel product requiring the revenue professional to have a clear pricing strategy dedicated to the residential home rental unit. This includes understanding a different competitive landscape such as other home owners and online home rental sites.

The other important challenge is that profit motivations vary across these different competitors and within the hotel/rental business unit. Understanding these profit considerations are critical to establishing the optimal price point for your hotel rooms versus home-rental and online competitors.

## Obtaining Market Intelligence

The inventory of tools supporting hotel demand and competitive results is quite robust for the traditional hotel segment. However, for the home-rental market they are in the early development stage. There are no products that can give you clear understanding of your competitive price position and market share since much of the market is not managed by hotel companies but rather by individual owners and online home-sharing sites. Monitoring pricing and competitive position requires a decidedly more manual process.

As this model continues and home sharing sites continue to expand, the implications to revenue optimization will continue to need new solutions to manage this very complex business model.

## Understanding the Consumer Experience

In addition to understanding the implications for revenue optimization, it is also helpful to understand the differences for the consumer. Today, the lines are being blurred among different accommodation types.

For the consumer there are many options available for booking through the multitude of online channels. A traditional hotel, timeshare, vacation rental, or even a treehouse can be easily booked by consumers. Though the consumer booking experience may be more seamless, the arrival, stay, departure, fee structure, and loyalty program components can be very different.

The arrival experience for alternative accommodations typically includes self-serve requirements, a secondary location to access entry to a home, or a personalized host greeting. Very rarely is there a "front desk."

Onsite, maintenance may not be available on the spot and the quality of furnishing and fixtures may not be backed by a brand promise. This can make the stay experience either more of an adventure or higher risk, depending on the customer's perspective. Daily housekeeping may or may not be available, and other amenities also vary.

The departure may also vary with requirements of the guests to tidy the rental or complete a different checkout process to return the key or lock the property.

Alternative accommodations also have different fee requirements. A separate cleaning fee and damage waiver or deposit are common. Cancellation policies are typically stricter as well, with a non-refundable full prepayment in advance or reservations may only be cancellable up to 30-60 days prior to arrival. Because of this financial commitment, the reservation process typically includes an option to purchase trip insurance.

## The Owner and Operator Experience

Alternative lodging is a more fragmented space compared to the traditional hotel space, but global consolidation and distribution is beginning to occur. Like an independently branded single hotel, local alternative accommodations operators are considering the need to join a global platform to ensure survival.

Owners and operators also have differing experiences and differing legal requirements and regulations, and are challenged with different branding opportunities.

Property systems are typically legacy systems unable to support rapidly changing technology needs of the business, though this is changing with new entrants into the space.

There are little or no official governing bodies for property classification or market data, and this area, too, is ripe for improvements.

Local zoning laws are rapidly changing, and keeping up and enforcing these laws can be daunting. Very specific criteria may exist depending on whether the unit is shared, the number of bedrooms, or if the parking spaces meet requirements.

The ability for a local owner and operator to join a larger, global brand to strengthen loyalty and trust was not an option in the past. As traditional hoteliers enter the space and new entrants evolve to include hotel-like offerings, these differences from the traditional hotel space are also changing.

## Resort and Urban Fees

In the United States in particular, an emerging issue revolves around resort and urban fees. This issue does not apply in the European Union where it is illegal to charge or advertise any type of mandatory fees that are not included as part of the total room rate.

For most travelers in the United States, the idea of paying a resort fee when staying at a true resort hotel is generally accepted without question. Things like beach and pool towels, use of the resort pool, use of the resort gyms, and some specialty exercise classes such as yoga are often covered by a resort fee.

Today the concept of charging a resort fee has extended well beyond resorts. More non-resort hotels are imposing mandatory "urban fees" or "facility fees" on guests. Many consumers do not like this approach and feel they are being charged for every little item or service versus the previous practice of included general amenities in the room rate. The consumer often does not always see the value for what is included; especially if the urban fee covers amenities that the consumer is not using.

While these fees do cover real expenses in resorts such as offsetting services at the pool or beach, it is not necessarily doing the same at urban hotels. Instead, it is revenue added to the bottom line which is positive for an operator's P&L. And, with the rising costs of acquisition, imposing resort or urban fees is a way to recoup some of those costs in a different way.

However, the practice can have a negative impact on service scores. The consumer expects something very tangible for the urban fee. If they are not satisfied with what is covered by the fee, they often feel the value received is not worth the value paid. This can often lead to negative reviews and it becomes a challenge for hoteliers to manage expectations.

Often, the negative impact shows up on consumer review sites. In today's digital world, the consumer can tell everyone what they liked and what they did not like at a hotel. Many are taking to online reviews and rating hotels in a different way when considering the urban fee.

Hoteliers should weigh the benefits and the associated risks of charging these fees. Will the revenue upside outweigh the consumer frustration?

Also consider the potential for a hotel to differentiate itself from others with a fee. Is there an opportunity to turn that distinction into a competitive advantage? Can you use the fact that your competitor charges a fee and you don't as a competitive advantage?

If your hotel adds a fee – resort, urban, or other – fully disclose it up front and clearly to the consumer at the time of booking. Be sure to list the fee very clearly on all booking channels and include it in all written confirmations. It would be very wise to put together a list of all the inclusions as a reference for the consumer to see. Share it on brand.com, with the reservation confirmation, and in the key packet. It can make conversations with customers much easier for reservations and the front desk.

One thing is clear. The fees will continue to increase as do other prices each year. And it seems more and more hotels are adding this as another revenue stream.

## The Consumer

It is no secret that when it comes to shopping for hotel stays consumers are more educated and savvier today than ever before. The transparency of information that is available to the consumer makes it much easier for them to find what they are looking for. It can also make them much more demanding...even before they arrive.

Rates, reviews, user-generated photos (both good ones and bad ones), and the plethora of options for the consumer to book hotels make it easier for consumers to know what they will be getting even before they get there.

The younger generation of travelers are leading the growth of using all types of sites to compare and choose their travel products.

All of this is pushing the hotel industry into a more consumer-centric space. Knowing what the consumer wants before they want it, and serving specific offers or experiences to them based on their search criteria and history, is quickly becoming expected and will soon be the new normal.

Data about the consumer (interests, preferences, and more) is critical to success when it comes to personalization. Understanding the data that is available through Google Analytics helps to show more about search activity, demand and booking patterns, specific needs of the consumer, and so much more. It is a way to dive much deeper than customer segmentation ever allowed.

More sophisticated technology is available allowing different types of direct communication with the guest before they arrive, while on property and throughout their stay – both offsite and onsite. This provides an opportunity to connect on an entirely new level and have a two-way dialogue with them. Whatever your tactics, be sure to understand and comply with GDPR (General Data Protection Regulation).

Hoteliers now know more about the customer than ever before. Combing this knowledge and data allows hoteliers to make personalized recommendations to the consumer, making it easier and more convenient for the traveler than ever before.

A host of new technologies – including facial recognition, biometric sensors, augmented reality, and brainwave readers – will eventually allow hoteliers to customize the guest experiences based on a deeper, more authentic understanding of the guest. This deeper level of personalization will mean even more choices for the consumer.

The consumer is willing to share information with trusted sources if it benefits them in the end. Hoteliers that can figure out the right data collection and application, and turn that data into personalized offers, will have an edge on the competition.

Hoteliers who make travelers' decisions easier, simpler, and more convenient will win with future consumers.

# APPENDIX A:

## REVENUE TEAM MEETING SAMPLE AGENDA

### Purpose:

The revenue team meets weekly to review the next full 1 - 3 months** in detail with regards to group, transient, and catering pricing. The focus is on maximizing revenues over high-demand periods and maximizing occupancy over low-demand periods over the course of a one-year booking horizon. The team will include additional projects that address the overall revenue strategy of the hotel within all outlets.

** Depending on your hotel's booking window, you may want to extend this out to 6 months.

### Historical:

- Follow-up items and minutes from previous week's meeting
- Review prior week's strategy and critique opportunities in all sales and operational areas
- Review the hotel's market share performance in the last week's STR report
- Review any group turndowns for last week to determine if different decisions could have been made
- Cumulative assessment of how the hotel is performing thus far vs. last year, budget, and projection predicting how hotel will finish the month

### Future:

- Review pace detail (on the books vs. same time last year) at the highest level, by major market segment [group and transient could be examined at the minor market segment level (retail, OTA, discount, etc.)]
- Highlight opportunities for changes in transient pricing depending on hotel and market demand for the next 1-3 and potentially further out
- Review future group sales strategies and tools to ensure consistent rate quoting for overall revenue optimization strategy
- Review potential changes to catering free-sell strategies
- Competition update to include: rate shops, reader boards, competitors' group pace, citywide events, sales manager conversion of leads
- Review transient and group restrictions for next 3 months with focus on next 30 days. Make changes to restrictions as needed. Discuss need times and overbooking philosophies.

- Review high demand dates to ensure appropriate strategy exists across all distribution channels
- Special promotions tracking: wins/losses
- Examination of demand indicators — web traffic, reservation conversion, call volume, turn-aways, city-wide bookings

### Long Range:

- STAR report review and comp set forecast (if applicable)
- Convention center booking pace (TAP reports)
- Proactive pricing philosophies for next two quarters (seasonal pricing, special events, promotions)
- Trend analysis: mix shifts, STAR data trends, segmentation changes, channel shifts
- Review forward-looking market intelligence data to understand market or comp set trends
- Review YTD weekday/ weekend P&L by segment

### Misc:

- Weekly training topic (e.g., package production, channel contribution, digital marketing efficiencies, room type sales, market forecasts)
- YTD Recap
- Issues from: Front Office, Sales, Catering/Events, Reservations

# APPENDIX B:
## *SWOT ANALYSIS EXAMPLE*

| | Hotel A | Hotel B | Hotel C |
|---|---|---|---|
| Year built / last full room renovation | 1972 / 2016 | 2010/ n/a | 1984 / 20011 |
| Number of rooms/suites | 315 | 403 | 298 |
| Number of meeting rooms | 14/11 (flexible) | 12 | 10 |
| Meeting room square footage | 21,000<br><br>Ballroom=5,000 | 17,000<br><br>Grand Ballroom=6,000 | 12,000<br><br>Palace Room=3,000 |
| Restaurants and capacity | Prince of Wales / 100 / breakfast, lunch, dinner<br><br>Limehouse Pub / 50 / bar, dinner<br><br>24-hour room service | Oak Terrace / 130 / breakfast, lunch<br><br>The Camelia House / 60 / fine dining<br><br>24-hour room service | Avenue One / 90, breakfast, lunch, dinner<br><br>The Lantern Room / 30 / bar, appetizers in the evening<br><br>24-hour room service |
| Other facilities | Exercise room, small business center | Spa with pool and fitness room, business center | Exercise room, discounted access to spa next door, business center |
| Parking | Valet parking in nearby garages | Valet parking in own garage | Valet parking in nearby garages |
| STRENGTHS | High name recognition within the city<br><br>Most flexible meeting space<br><br>Good location for leisure guests<br><br>Experienced banquet and sales team<br><br>Unobstructed lake views<br><br>Large guestrooms and bathrooms<br><br>Easy access from street, lobby/bar visible from outside | Chain affiliation with access to largest loyalty reward program<br><br>Very popular bar<br><br>Parking in own garage<br><br>Spa with pool<br><br>Fine dining restaurant<br><br>24h business center | New product, state-of-the-art equipment in both guest rooms and meeting space<br><br>Next door access to spa<br><br>Largest guest rooms/bathrooms<br><br>Good location for both leisure and business |
| WEAKNESSES | Guest rooms need renovation<br><br>Small bathrooms<br><br>Lack of brand affiliation / name recognition outside of the city<br><br>Valet parking in nearby garages often causes long waits<br><br>No spa or pool | Confusing meeting room setup on 3 different levels<br><br>Change of ownership last year resulted in high staff turnover, especially in sales<br><br>Low visibility from street level due to side entrance<br><br>Perceived as too expensive, especially for meetings<br><br>Location not ideal for both leisure and business | Chain / brand name still not well known in U.S.<br><br>Obstructed views on 3 sides<br><br>Inexperienced staff<br><br>Limited meeting space<br><br>Lobby / front desk not on street level |

| OPPORTUNITIES | Decision to drastically raise prices for SMERF segment lowered group base and should open up more opportunities to take high rated business over high demand dates and citywide conventions<br><br>New two-way interface between PMS and CRS should greatly increase guest satisfaction, decrease reservation labor costs<br><br>City to host the largest number of conventions since 1998 | Expected increase in international travel will favor hotels with international presence / brand recognition<br><br>Newly installed CRM system is now operating. This should further help the current strong marketing and brand position<br><br>City to host the largest number of conventions since 1998 | If merger talks with a large U.S. chain succeed it would give them a much larger guest base and better name recognition and distribution channels<br><br>With staff gaining more experience they should be able to better sell their superior product and location and become a stronger competitor<br><br>City to host the largest number of conventions since 1998 |
|---|---|---|---|
| THREATS | Construction of a new high rise next to the hotel will increase traffic congestion and valet parking problems, noise complaints<br><br>Tentatively planned start of room renovation in October—while necessary—would greatly decrease results in Q4; some of the biggest conventions will take place during that time | Large number of low rate airline crew contracts will work against them in the next year with a lot more citywide compression<br><br>Biggest corporate account will have no new store openings next year (after 7 last year) which will greatly reduce their room night production | New hotel of similar size and style will open in March only 2 blocks away and will compete for the same market<br><br>Might lose several of their key corporate accounts following intense price competition with Hotel A |

# APPENDIX C:
## REVENUE OPTIMIZATION TOOLS

This appendix provides examples of companies available to support the hotel industry's revenue management needs. It is not an endorsement of companies, nor is it exhaustive. HSMAI invited industry partners to self-report what products and services they offer as of 2018. Most of these companies offer additional products and services beyond the categories examined here.

| Company | Revenue Management System (RMS) | Channel Manager | Forecasting Tools | Rate Shopping | Central Reservations Management | Business Intelligence | Direct Booking Strategies | Social Networking & Media Tools | Web Analytics Tools | Other |
|---|---|---|---|---|---|---|---|---|---|---|
| Duetto | • | | • | • | | • | • | | | |
| Expedia, Inc. | | • | • | • | | • | • | | | |
| Focal Revenue | | | | | | • | | | | |
| GroupRevMax | | | | | | | • | | | Group & Event Revenue Management |
| HEBS Digital | | | | | | | • | • | • | |
| HotelIQ Business Intelligence | | | • | | | • | | | | |
| Hotelsoft Inc. | • | | • | • | | • | | | | |
| IDeaS — A SAS COMPANY | • | | • | | | | | | | |
| Infor | • | | • | | | • | | | | Marketing Resource Management, Offer Management, Marketing Automation, Customer Relationship Management |
| iVvy Pty Ltd | | • | | | • | | • | | | |
| Kalibri Labs | | | • | | | • | | | • | Evaluation and prediction of revenue performance net of acquisition costs |
| Knowland | | | • | | | • | | | | Insights into group meeting and event activity to guide positioning strategies and align sales efforts with revenue maximization policies |
| NAVIS | | | | | • | • | • | | | CRM |
| Nor1 | | | | | | • | | | | |
| OTA Insight | | • | | • | | • | | | | |
| The Rainmaker Group | • | | • | • | | • | | | | |
| RateGain | • | • | | • | | • | | | | Online Reputation Management |

| Company | Revenue Management System (RMS) | Channel Manager | Forecasting Tools | Rate Shopping | Central Reservations Management | Business Intelligence | Direct Booking Strategies | Social Networking & Media Tools | Web Analytics Tools | Other |
|---|---|---|---|---|---|---|---|---|---|---|
| RedAwning | | • | | | • | | | | | |
| ResortPass, Inc. | | • | | | • | • | • | • | | |
| Revinate | | | | | | • | | | | Marketing automation |
| Sabre Hospitality Solutions | | • | | | • | • | • | • | • | Call Center and Digital Marketin |
| Sojern | | | | | | | • | | | |
| STR | | | | | | • | | | | |
| Tambourine | | • | | | • | | • | • | • | Booking Engine, eCommerce, Advertising |
| The Guestbook | | | | | | | • | | | Loyalty |
| Total Customized Revenue Management, LLC | | • | • | | • | • | • | | | Revenue Management Services |
| Travel Outlook Premium Voice Reservations | | | | | • | | | | | |
| Travel Tripper | | • | | • | • | • | • | | • | |
| TravelClick | | • | • | • | • | • | • | • | • | Customer Relationship Management, Central Reservation System |
| TrustYou | | | | | | | • | • | • | |
| Vertical Booking USA | | • | | • | • | • | • | | • | Spa & Merchandising Booking Engine, Destination Management System |

## Merging the Revenue Optimization and Marketing Disciplines for Higher Return

This is a case study of a luxury resort in Cabo San Lucas. All 161 rooms, suites, and villas have 100% views of the Sea of Cortez and the famed El Arco rock formation. The resort boasts a spa; a signature restaurant whose executive chef is arguably the most renowned chef in Mexico, having made a name for himself in the U.S. with restaurants in New York and Los Angeles; the most exclusive oceanfront rooftop lounge in Los Cabos; an oceanfront infinity pool with swim-up bar; and two additional lounges and restaurants. The team at this property has won awards from Condé Nast Traveler and TripAdvisor users for its services.

## The Challenge

It had been a rough year for the team at the resort. It opened its doors the prior summer in a well-established luxury market, in the low season for the market. The twelve months that followed proved to be difficult.

In order to shore up owner confidence, the management team resolved to audit, and change as necessary, its revenue generation practices to achieve an aggressive Q4 room revenue budget. While there was opportunity to take advantage of the key U.S. market holidays of Thanksgiving, Christmas, and New Year's Eve, several challenges plagued the team going into the quarter, including:

■ Ramping up the hotel's pace to achieve the expected goals. There was a lot of pick up needed and not a lot of time to get there.
■ The booking window for the majority of guests was over 30 days. About 90% of the resort's guests come from the U.S., and naturally the booking window is longer for international travel.
■ There was already lower-rated business on the books for peak demand holiday dates in November and December.
■ The team had very little time to plan a comprehensive leisure marketing campaign and needed to move quickly and efficiently.

## The Planning Stage

The hotel engaged a consultant to assist in achieving the goals.

Understanding the landscape from the perspectives of both marketing and revenue optimization was the first priority. Marketing and revenue professionals must be aligned to achieve the goal of developing and optimizing a successful marketing campaign for the greatest return. Marketing cannot effectively optimize a campaign's true potential if that campaign is not rooted in an understanding of the hotel's current revenue needs, the booking behaviors of its guests, and current market conditions.

In this case, the team needed to drive short-term business, so the consultant sought answers to the following questions to develop a strategy to target the right audience with the right message at the right time:

■ What are the revenue goals we're trying to achieve? Will we get there through driving occupancy, length of stay, increasing ADR, etc.?
■ Where do the guests who booked in-the-quarter-for-the-quarter in the prior year live? And/or how might this differ from the property's key feeder markets the rest of the year? What was their booking window and length of stay?
■ From which cities does Los Cabos see direct flights in the fourth quarter and how do they overlap with fourth quarter key feeders?
■ What does availability look like over the time period we're trying to impact?
■ In which accommodation types does the property currently have the most availability and/or trouble booking? Where is the opportunity for the highest ADR in terms of room types to promote?
■ Are there any macro-economic outliers for the market as a whole that should be taken into consideration?
■ What are the main activities and events in the market and at the property that appeal to guests traveling into market specifically in fourth quarter?
■ What upsell initiatives are currently in place with the reservations and/or front desk teams?
■ What offers does the competitive set currently have in the market?

Finally, knowing that the management company also had a robust CRM program in place, the consultant reached out to the home office team to provide additional insights to help round out a more robust profile of not only past guests, but also people who identify with — and book — with the overall hotel brand in all markets where it operates. Doing so allowed the consultant to build a look-alike profile for an acquisition strategy. Additional information gathered that would help further define the campaign's audiences included:

■ People who travel internationally for leisure
■ Household income
■ Age range
■ Marriage status
■ Occupation
■ People who drive luxury cars
■ Children in the household
■ Media consumption habits
■ Discretionary income habits

From this information-gathering period, the two-person Revenue + Marketing team identified two key initiatives. Following are the marketing strategies and tactics for each.

## Strategy #1: Drive Overall Leisure Room Revenue with One Go-To-Market Offer

The team determined to put the effort and budget behind one offer that was simple enough to appeal to a broad audience. In order to achieve the revenue goal for the quarter, the team had to drive both occupancy and ADR — it was not enough to just drop the rate to drive demand. The offer needed to be:

■ Quick and easy for the revenue director to build in systems
■ Easy to communicate and easy for the guest to understand the value proposition
■ Easy to build from for leisure sales marketing opportunities
■ Easy to flex the rate as needed based on pace without having to constantly update creative executions
■ Perceived as a better value than the rest of the competitive set's offers

The team determined that the go-to-market offer would be an extra night free. It was not the sexiest or most earth-shattering offer ever created, but it accomplished all of the points above. The consultant would rely on visual assets and copy to create the sexy and set it apart.

*Side note: While the team was building out creative executions for launch, it also audited and updated the existing packages to better meet the revenue needs of the resort while giving guests easier access to the amenities that were most popular.*

*Another side note: When the consultant looked at all the guests who had booked in-the-quarter-for-the-quarter prior year, she found that city and occupation were quite different from the broader past guest. While most of the resort's guests hail from LA, Dallas/Houston, New York, or Chicago, and fit a finance/business management occupation profile, the guests booking short term for fourth quarter stays were mostly tech execs out of Silicon Valley. The San Francisco/San Jose area continued to have direct flights to Los Cabos during fourth quarter. And with the weather getting cooler faster in northern California than LA and Dallas/Houston (and being much closer than New York or Chicago), she added this group into the targeting mix.*

### Marketing Strategy and Execution Planning

Having gathered the details needed, the consultant considered all the channels and assets at her disposal to effectively promote the offer.

Reviewing internal resources helped determine the media mix strategy and creative considerations for the budget that would optimize direct bookings (excluding OTA channel and GDS promotional executions).

### Internal Resources

■ Resort's website
■ All applicable online listings (TripAdvisor Business Listing, etc.)
■ Resort's social media network
■ Resort's emailable database
■ Resort's PR team already on retainer (for short lead offer placements)
■ Brand level communication channels: brand.com, a broader emailable database, use of social media channel outreach, participation in company-wide initiatives like Cyber Monday promotion, and collaborating with brand-level partners whose audiences share an affinity for the type of luxury offerings provided
■ Leisure sales manager outreach to consortia and travel agent partnerships

## External Resources Needed (including but not limited to)

- Targeted pay per click in key feeder markets, both brand and non-brand terms
- Targeted display ads
- Retargeted display ads
- Targeted TripAdvisor banner ads
- Email acquisition list targeting
- Social media ad targeting and holiday/event visual content for boosted posts
- Creative design for pdfs and digital ads that would help promote the ad and activities and events for the time period

The consultant worked with the revenue director, digital team, social media manager, leisure sales manager, and the PR team to outline what the messaging would be by audience and channel, as well as the timeline for each execution through December 31. The execution campaign calendar was shared with everyone to keep everyone in step throughout the lifecycle of the campaign.

This calendar was also provided to the reservations team leader in order to staff accordingly to accommodate the influxes of calls when emails would drop. Copies of each eblast were also provided to the reservations team so it would have them in hand to reference as needed for people calling in to book.

Throughout the course of the campaign, the consultant provided feedback on wins in PPC and online media ROI increases over prior year, how much revenue the executions were generating, etc. Attendance at all weekly revenue calls for the property was also critical to stay abreast of pick up and any changes that may have been needed to optimize spikes in demand.

Important Note: Before any communication was deployed, all of the details for any event or activity that the team would be promoting to help drive room nights over peak demand holidays were added to the website so the digital creative could link to more information. Being able to provide these details in the creative helps inform the audience's decision to book a stay and/or how many days to book. These details included days and times of events, prices, menus, entertainment, etc., for Thanksgiving, Christmas, and the New Year's Eve party.

## Strategy #2: Drive Awareness and Demand for the Villa Product

The resort offers guest rooms, suites, and villas. Of these three accommodation types, the villas were the most difficult for the property team to book. There was a lot of opportunity here. The resort's villas are stunning in design, equipped with full kitchens with state-of-the-art appliances, large oceanfront terraces with their own infinity pools, and fire pits, offer 1-3 bedrooms and additional personalized services. Some come with pool tables, media rooms, etc. With all these extras, the villas can command a much higher ADR compared to other room types.

A quick audit of the resort's website and OTA channels revealed areas of opportunity to promote the villas. Images were limited to only 1-2 per room type, and there was so much more to show in a villa. Also, the villa bedrooms look very much like a regular guest room, and this was one of the only images used to promote these room types, so the value of what the guest received for his/her money was not being conveyed properly.

Also, the villas were buried in the accommodations section of the website. The resort needed to make them more visible, and the team found a few different on- and offline opportunities to drive more awareness and bookings for the villas.

## Marketing Tactics

1. Draw more visibility to the villas in the accommodations section of the website by
   a. Giving them more real estate in that section
   b. Developing enhanced copy describing the additional amenities and personalized services
   c. Adding more images for each of the villa room types that show off their design, amenities, and views
2. Deploy eblasts to those in the past guest database who had booked villa stays in the past, but didn't have a future reservation, utilizing the extra night free offer.
3. Utilize more villa images in all online listings (TripAdvisor, OTA channels, leisure sales, etc.)
4. PR team to pitch a package specifically built for villas to luxury lifestyle feeder market publications for short lead opportunities

5.  Utilize awards and accolades the accommodation type had garnered since opening in all online messaging (social media, PPC, website, etc.)
6.  Develop an upsell initiative for the reservations team to convert guests who were looking to book other room types into villa guests
7.  Work villa messaging and promotion into the current PPC budget promoting accommodations for groups of friends, family gatherings, weddings, and special events in Los Cabos

## The Results

The team began the fourth quarter with a reach to forecast exceeding $900,000 and ended the quarter by exceeding revenue promised to ownership by over $265,000. Marketing channels for the property drove the following increases over prior year:

■  Revenue from PPC increased 125% over same time prior year with ROI increasing 68% over prior year
■  Revenue from online media generated over $428,000 at an average ROI of 16:1
■  Revenue from internal eblasts generated over $60,000
■  Brand Website and Voice Direct channels drove over 20% more revenue than same time prior year combined, while ADR for these channels increased 8%
■  Revenue for the villa bookings increased 37% over same time prior year

**Revenue Director**
**Reports to: General Manager**

## Overview

The revenue director is focused on driving the optimal revenue performance for their hotel. This includes a focus on optimal business mix through the most profitable channels leading the hotel to optimal revenue profit and market share results.

## Responsibilities

- Understand hotel competitive market and defined set; relevance to hotel based on market segments, location, price point, and positioning within the set.
- Responsible for ensuring that effective strategies are in place, accurately executed and being adhered to by revenue generating departments. (Shared responsibility with DOSM)
- Responsible for driving hotel performance to achieve optimal results.
- Partner with sales team members to achieve optimal revenues through sales leads, bookings, placement, etc.
- Responsible for achievement of monthly key metrics: Budget, Forecast Accuracy, RPI. (Shared responsibility with DOSM)
- Responsible for determining the optimal segmentation and channel mix and the achievement of both. (Shared responsibility with DOSM)
- Drive development and execution of a strategic, demand-based pricing philosophy for all room categories.
- Responsible for management of positive relationship with all OTA, FIT, and call center partners.
- Ensure regular internal education on revenue management and how each department impacts.
- Lead the charge to ensure a focus on total hotel revenue optimization.
- Create and implement appropriate programs specific to hotel needs, market needs, and/or seasonal needs – examples include but not limited to: suite sales/conversion initiatives, call center conversions, front desk upsell programs, walk-in capture improvement.
- Drive the development of annual budget for top-line revenues, along with strategies to achieve. (Shared responsibility with DOSM)
- Responsible for all inventory management to optimize hotel results – room type stay patterns and sell-through ability, group blocks, etc.
- Responsible for forecasting – day by day, segment by segment based on home office guidelines and hotel needs (e.g., 90 days, monthly).
- Forecast demand/understand demand time periods.
- Develop and implement effective transient & group pricing and selling strategies.
- Facilitate communication among all revenue team members to ensure all perspectives are considered and strategies understood.
- Achieve relevant certifications: HSMAI's CRME (Certified Revenue Management Executive)
- Ensure all relevant hotel departments and members of the sales team are adhering to all standard work.

- Contribute to and support all strategic business planning and related hotel concerns.
- Optimize and expand distribution partnerships.

## Tasks & Accountability (Primary, Contributory, or Shared)

- Utilize all tools available to assist with optimizing the hotel's yield such as subscription-based marketing intelligence reports. (Shared with DOSM)
- Utilize all tools available to evaluate the hotel's position with respect to competition. (Shared with DOSM)
- Complete a 30-60-90 day-by-day forecast each month. (Primary)
- Maintaining all relevant system related tools such as PMS, CRS, GDS, OTAs, RMS, Channel Connect - to ensure timely information, rates, room types, etc., are up to date and accurate at all times. (Primary)
- Consistently evaluate revenue optimization tools and processes for accuracy and appropriate parameters in the following areas: inventory, rates, transient demand, group forecast, and group potential. (Primary)
- Anticipate the need for, and utilize, promotions during "need" periods. (Contributory to DOSM & Marketing Manager)
- Educate all staff members on revenue optimization philosophy. (Primary)
- Provide monthly reporting on historical activity, as well as future data to be used for strategic decisions. (Primary)
- Chair weekly Revenue meetings (ensure conversation revolves around maximizing all revenues). (Primary)
- Attend weekly Sales meetings. (Contributory to Sales Team)
- Participate in company's Revenue conference calls/meetings. (Primary)
- Continuous open communication with Reservations department. (Primary)

## Measurement

- RevPAR, and non-room revenue actuals versus forecast and budget.
- Actual to Forecast variance of no more than +/-4%.
- Market share index growth.
- All team members have the same understanding of revenue philosophies and strategies.
- Ensure data quality, accurate tracking, accuracy of rate loading and respective validity dates, accuracy of group block maintenance, and utilization of group analysis procedures.
- CRS, PMS, and Internet sites are running properly and matching the hotel's strategies on a daily basis.
- Participating member of the hotel's Executive Committee.

# GLOSSARY

As the silos in hotel organizations continue to erode, revenue optimization professionals are increasingly expected to engage at a higher level with asset managers and owners (not to mention GMs, sales teams, and marketing).

In those interactions, revenue leaders must demonstrate their knowledge of their own discipline AND all of the hotel's operations and functions that run parallel with it. This kind of business acumen validates your proficiency and shows those colleagues and stakeholders that they can trust you and rely on your performance.

One easy way to brush up on your business acumen is to sharpen your understanding of the acronyms, jargon, and terminology used in and around the business of hotels. It will strengthen your skills, build your reputation as a knowledgeable team member, and form the foundation for your future success.

For a thorough overview of digital marketing terminology, see *Hospitality Digital Marketing Essentials: A Field Guide for Navigating Today's Digital Landscape*, the study guide for HSMAI's Certified Hospitality Digital Marketer (CHDM) certification. Learn more at www.hsmai.org/chdm.

| | |
|---|---|
| Addendum | Additional document added to a contract with further terms and conditions. |
| ADR | Average Daily Rate<br><br>ADR = Actual Daily Room Revenue / Total # of Rooms Sold |
| ADR Index | A measure of a hotel's ADR performance relative to a group of hotels. An ADR Index of 100 equals fair share of ADR, compared to the group of hotels. An ADR Index greater than 100 represents more than a fair share of the group's ADR performance. An ADR Index below 100 reflects less than a fair share of the group's ADR performance.<br><br>ADR Index = (Hotel ADR / Group of Hotels' ADR) x 100 |
| ALOS | Average Length of Stay |
| Amortization | An accounting term that refers to the process of allocating the cost of an intangible asset over a period of time. It also refers to the repayment of loan principal over time.<br><br>When a hotel amortizes expenses, it helps tie the cost of the asset with the revenues it generates. For example, if a hotel sales office buys a ream of paper, it writes off the cost in the year of purchase and generally uses all the paper the same year. Conversely, with a large asset like a building, the owner reaps the rewards of the expense for years, so it writes off the expense incrementally over several years.<br><br>A related term, depreciation, refers to tangible assets. |
| Ancillary Revenue | Revenue generated from goods or services that differ from or enhance the main services or product lines of a company. For example, spa and wellness treatments, mini bar, transportation, etc. |
| Attrition | A contract clause that outlines the client's commitment to pay for a specific number of rooms/meeting space and, should the room/meeting space number decrease, this reduction of numbers may require a payment as a penalty. |
| Average Daily Rate (ADR) | Metric derived by dividing actual daily room revenue by the total number of rooms sold.<br><br>ADR = Actual Daily Room Revenue / Total # of Rooms Sold |
| Average Length of Stay (ALOS) | Metric derived by adding the total number of nights and dividing by the total number of bookings.<br><br>ALOS = Total # of nights / Total # of bookings |
| B2B | Business to Business |
| B2C | Business to Consumer |
| BAR | Best Available Rate |

| | |
|---|---|
| Best Available Rate (BAR) | The non-qualified, publicly available rate that serves as the baseline for comparison between hotels. This rate serves as the benchmark and typically drives discount and package pricing based on a percentage or dollar amount above or below this rate. BAR replaced Rack Rates as revenue management evolved and became more dynamic. |
| BT | Business Travel |
| Cancellation Clause | This contract clause summarizes the fee owed by a group if its event does not take place. There is often a sliding scale that indicates the fees owed based on when the meeting cancels. |
| CapEx | Capital Expenditure. Money spent by a company to upgrade or acquire physical assets such as buildings or equipment. |
| Capitalization Rate | A ratio that can be used to estimate the value of income-producing properties. Put simply, a cap rate is the net operating income of an asset divided by its sales price or value expressed as a percentage. A cap rate is determined by evaluating the financial data of similar properties which have recently sold in a specific market. For example, a US$1-million sale price of an apartment building that produces an annual net cash flow of US$90,000, results in a calculated capitalization rate of 9 percent. [90,000/1,000,000 = .09][38] |
| Chain Scales | Chain scale segments are a method by which branded hotels are grouped based on the actual average room rates. Independent hotels, regardless of their average room rates, are included as a separate chain-scale category. The chain-scale segments are:[39] <br><br> • Luxury <br> • Upper Upscale <br> • Upscale <br> • Upper Midscale <br> • Midscale <br> • Economy <br> • Independents |
| CHDM | Certified Hospitality Digital Marketer. The professional certification awarded by HSMAI to those who demonstrate proficiency in digital marketing for hotels. www.hsmai.org/chdm |
| Class | An industry categorization which includes chain-affiliated and independent hotels. The class for a chain-affiliated hotel is the same as its chain scale. An independent hotel is assigned a class based on its ADR, relative to that of the chain hotels in its geographic proximity.[40] |
| Closed to Arrival (CTA) | A room inventory control function. Indicates that a reservation cannot be confirmed for arrival on this date. |
| CMM | MBA-level executive education program for meeting professionals with more than seven years of experience, including a minimum of three years in management positions. |
| CMP | Certified Meeting Professional. The Events Industry Council (formerly CIC) launched the CMP program in 1985 to enhance the knowledge and performance of meeting professionals, promote the status and credibility of the meeting profession, and advance uniform standards of practice. |
| Commission | A charge that a hotel pays to a third party (e.g., travel agent, OTA) for selling its hotel rooms. It is usually a fixed percentage of the room rate. |
| Comp Set | Competitive Set. Comparable hotels that compete for guests. |
| Concession | Cost or consideration given by a seller to motivate the buyer to complete the purchase. |
| Cost of Acquisition | All costs associated with acquiring a new customer. |
| CRMA | Certified Revenue Management Analyst. This HSMAI certification recognizes students for their understanding of the application of revenue optimization concepts. www.hsmai.org/crma |
| CRM | Customer Relationship Management. Refers to practices, strategies, and technologies that companies use to manage and analyze customer interactions and data throughout the customer lifecycle, with the goal of improving business relationships with customers, assisting in customer retention, and driving sales growth (e.g., Salesforce) |
| CRME | Certified Revenue Management Executive. The professional certification awarded by HSMAI to those who demonstrate proficiency in revenue optimization for hotels. www.hsmai.org/crme |
| CRO | Central Reservations Office |
| CRS | Central Reservation System |
| CTA | Closed To Arrival |

| Customer Relationship Management (CRM) | Refers to practices, strategies, and technologies that companies use to manage and analyze customer interactions and data throughout the customer lifecycle, with the goal of improving business relationships with customers, assisting in customer retention, and driving sales growth (e.g., Salesforce). |
|---|---|
| DDR | Daily Delegate Rate |
| Demand Indicators | Factors such as behaviors or events that will have a direct impact — either positive or negative — on the demand in a market and/or for a hotel. |
| Displacement Analysis | Compares the value of different pieces of business to identify the one that brings the most value to the hotel. For instance, use a displacement analysis to calculate the value of a group sale by contrasting it to transient business that it would displace. |
| DMC | Destination Management Company. A locally based, for-profit tourism business that provides (mostly) groups with travel, meeting, and entertainment needs. |
| DMO | Destination Marketing Organization. Similar to Convention & Visitors Bureaus (CVB). An organization that promotes a town, city, region, or country in order to increase the number of visitors to it. |
| DOM | Director of Marketing |
| DORM | Director of Revenue Management |
| DOS | Director of Sales |
| DOSM | Director of Sales and Marketing |
| Dynamic Packaging | The ability of a consumer to create their own packages by choosing individual components as they shop. The component prices are not shown to the consumer, just the total package price. |
| EBITA | Earnings Before Interest, Taxes, and Amortization (EBITA) refers to a company's earnings before the deduction of interest, taxes, and amortization expenses. |
| EBITDA | Earnings Before Interest, Tax, Depreciation, and Amortization is a measure of a company's operating performance, and is often used to value a property or company. |
| External Analysis | Provides hoteliers with a view of what is happening within the market. This includes consumer trends (demand) and competitors (supply). |
| F&B Minimum | The total dollar amount of catered events (not including service charge and sales tax) required by the hotel, based on the meeting space and dates being held. |
| Fair Share | Fair share can be thought of as the subject hotel's "piece of the pie" in the market. For example, if the subject hotel's ADR is $50 and the ADR of its competitive set is $50, the subject hotel's index would total 100. If the subject hotel's ADR totaled $60, its index would be 120, indicating the hotel has captured more than its fair share. If the subject hotel's ADR totaled $40, its index would be 80, indicating the hotel has captured less than its fair share. |
| FFO | Funds From Operation. Used by REITs to define cash flow from overall operations; includes deductions for depreciation and amortization.[41] |
| FIT | Foreign Independent Tour or Flexible Independent Travel or Free Independent Traveler. It describes a type of travel or tourism that is customized by a travel professional but typically does not involve a packaged tour. |
| Fixed Cost | A cost the hotel incurs regardless of the total number of rooms occupied. |
| Force Majeure | This contract clause removes liability for natural and unavoidable catastrophes that interrupt the expected course of events and restrict participants from fulfilling obligations. Commonly referred to as an "act of God" or "impossibility" clause, it is often used during natural disasters that make it impossible for the guests to travel either out of their city or to the hotel's city. |
| Forgone Potential of Group Revenue (FPGR) | If one group takes up too much space for the rooms booked, the hotel is unable to book another group requiring meeting space "on top of it" and optimize the hotel's revenue. |
| FPGR | Forgone Potential of Group Revenue |
| Free-sell | A short-term booking window in which the hotel will take any business to fill open meeting rooms in the near future (Function-Only Business or Event-Only Business). |
| FY | Fiscal Year |
| GDP | Gross Domestic Product |

| GDPR | General Data Protection Regulation. A legal framework that sets guidelines for the collection and processing of personal information of individuals within the European Union (EU). The GDPR sets out the principles for data management and the rights of the individual, while also imposing fines that can be revenue-based. The General Data Protection Regulation covers all companies that deal with data of EU citizens, so it is a critical regulation for corporate compliance officers at banks, insurers, and other financial companies. GDPR came into effect across the EU on May 25, 2018.[42] |
|---|---|
| GDS | Global Distribution System |
| Global Distribution System (GDS) | Computerized reservation networks through which users — travel agents, airline employees, or travelers — view data on a wide range of travel services, including air, hotel, auto rental, and the like. Several GDSs provide their services to users worldwide (e.g., Amadeus, Sabre) while others provide regional or national coverage. |
| GM | General Manager |
| GOP | Gross Operating Profit |
| GOPPAR | Gross Operating Profit Per Available Room |
| Gross Domestic Product (GDP) | GDP is the total of all goods and services produced in an economy. As it measures the market value of all final goods and services produced by a nation, it is a fundamental indicator of an economy's performance. GDP is highly correlated with personal incomes and standard of living. It can be looked at as a true measure of the value added by an economy. |
| Gross Operating Profit Per Available Room (GOPPAR) | GOPAR = (Revenue — Expenses) / Number of available rooms |
| Group Ceiling | The maximum number of rooms at a hotel that will be allocated to groups each night. |
| GTD | Guaranteed |
| HSMAI | Hospitality Sales & Marketing Association International |
| Indemnification | A contract clause in which one party (the group or the hotel) agrees to be financially responsible for specific damage or loss incurred by the other party. Indemnification clauses in hotel contracts should be reciprocal and should make each party responsible for their own negligence. |
| Index | Measures a hotel's performance relative to an aggregated grouping of hotels (e.g., competitive set, market, submarket). An index of 100 means the hotel is capturing its fair share. An index of more than 100 means it is capturing more than its fair share. An index lower than 100 means it is capturing less than its fair share. |
| Internal Analysis | Provides hoteliers with an understanding of what is happening within their own hotel or company that can influence their position within the market. |
| JTFR/JTR | Joint Travel Regulations. Regulations for per diem, travel and transportation allowances, and relocation and other allowances that apply to members of the Uniformed Services of the United States, Department of Defense (DoD) civilian employees, and civilians who travel using DoD funding. |
| KPI | Key Performance Indicator. A measurable value that demonstrates how effectively a company is achieving key business objectives. |
| Last Room Availability | LRA. An agent's ability to book the last available room in a hotel. |
| LRA | Last Room Availability. An agent's ability to book the last available room in a hotel. |
| LTV | Loan-To-Value. The percentage of the loan to the overall property value. The value may be the purchase price, the development cost, the appraised value, or the current value + renovation costs; typically between 60% and 70%; = loan ÷ value.[43] |
| Market | Set of actual and potential customers. Also defined as a specific geographic area. |
| Market Penetration | The ratio comparing a hotel's total occupied rooms with the total occupied rooms of a competitive set.<br><br>Market Penetration = Total occupied rooms in hotel / Total occupied rooms in competitive set |
| Market Share | The percentage of the market for a product or service that a company supplies. In the case of hotel's, it is the total number of rooms in a hotel as a percentage of total rooms within a competitive set.<br><br>Market Share = (Total # of rooms in hotel / Total # of rooms in competitive set) x 100 [results in a percentage] |

| Mark-Up | The difference between the cost of a product and its selling price. |
|---|---|
| Maximum Length of Stay | A room inventory control function. Indicates that a reservation for arrival on a particular date may not extend past a certain number of days. |
| Minimum Length of Stay | A room inventory control function. Indicates that a reservation for arrival on a particular date must be for a minimum number of nights (two or more). |
| MTD | Month-To-Date |
| Multi-Channel Distribution | Channel management which includes the techniques and systems used by a hotel in line with its distribution policy. This management method includes content management as well as data reconciliation in various distribution channels. It involves the updating of hotel information, room rates, and availabilities across all distribution channels, such as the hotel's website, third parties (OTAs, IDS, ADS), and the CRS/GDS. |
| Net Operating Income | NOI. A company's operating income after operating expenses are deducted but before income taxes and interest are deducted. If this is a positive value, it's referred to as net operating income, while a negative value is called a net operating loss. NOI often is viewed as a good measure of company performance. Some believe this figure is less susceptible than other figures to manipulation by management.<br><br>Hotel industry example: A hotel's net operating income percentage is most closely tied to its occupancy, although it is also influenced by average daily rate, market segment, property's age, and brand affiliation.[44] |
| Net RevPAR | Net Revenue Per Available Room. A hotel's daily revenue after removing sales and marketing expenses divided by the total number of rooms at that hotel.<br><br>Net RevPAR = Net revenue / Total # of available rooms in hotel |
| NOI | Net Operating Income |
| OBT | Online Booking Tool |
| OCC (Penetration) Index | An index designed to measure a hotel's share of the segment's (comp set, market, tract, etc.) demand (demand = rooms sold).<br><br>(Hotel Occupancy / Segment Occupancy) x 100 = Occupancy Index<br><br>Fair share can be thought of as the subject hotel's "piece of the pie" in the market. For example, if there are 1,000 rooms in the competitive set and the subject hotel has 100 rooms, the subject hotel's fair share is 10.00%. If the subject hotel accounts for 10.00% of the room nights generated within the competitive set in a given time period, the subject hotel's actual share equals its fair share, giving it an occupancy index of 100%.[45] |
| Occupancy | The percentage of available rooms that were sold during a specified period of time. Occupancy is calculated by dividing the number of rooms sold by rooms available.<br><br>Occupancy = Rooms Sold / Rooms Available[46] |
| Online Travel Agency (OTA) | Website that specializes in the sale of travel products to consumers. Some agencies sell a variety of travel products including flights, hotels, car rentals, cruises, activities, and packages. Examples include Expedia and Booking.com. |
| Onward Distribution Channels | Commonly referred to as third-party distribution channels, onward distribution channels are intermediaries that facilitate a hotel's ability to sell itself to the traveling consumer. |
| OTA | Online Travel Agency |
| Overbooking | Also called overselling, this is the practice of accepting more reservations for a particular day than there are actually rooms in the hotel. It is usually done strategically and carefully, with decisions based on the history of no-shows and last-minute cancellations. |
| PMS | Property Management System |
| PPC | Pay-Per-Click |
| Price Discrimination | Occurs when a business charges different groups of consumers different prices for what are, more or less, the same products or services. |
| Price Parity | To ensure an even playing field of pricing or rates across all channels based purely on the price points. Also referred to as Rate Parity. |
| Product Parity | To ensure an even playing field of pricing or rates across all channels based on products and fences around rates. |

| | |
|---|---|
| Profit per Available Room (ProPAR) | Profit earnings for each room available in the hotel. ProPAR is based on operating profit, which accounts for movements in both revenues and expenses. Often confused with Net RevPAR which only takes into account distribution costs.<br><br>ProPAR = [Revenue – All Operating Costs] / number of available rooms |
| ProPAR | Profit Per Available Room |
| Property Improvement Plan (PIP) | A requirement by hotel brands that owners undertake renovations and upgrades to meet current chain standards. PIPs are generally required when a hotel joins a brand system, when a branded hotel is sold, or when a franchise or membership agreement comes up for renewal.[47] |
| Property Management System (PMS) | The computer system in a hotel that contains information about available and occupied guestrooms, historical and future reservations, and guest charges. |
| Rack Rate | The official or advertised price of a hotel room, on which a discount is usually negotiated. |
| Rate Parity | Ensures an even playing field of pricing or rates across all channels based purely on price points. Also referred to as Price Parity. |
| Rebooking Clause | In the case where a financial penalty is owed the hotel, this contract clause enables a portion or all of the penalty to be applied to a future meeting or meetings. |
| REIT | Real Estate Investment Trust. A special type of corporate entity that invests in real estate (on the debt or equity side). This type of company has special tax benefits (e.g., a lower tax rate), but has certain restrictions and is required to distribute 90% of its profits to shareholders.[48] |
| Revenue Generation Index (RGI) | RGI is a ratio of the hotel's RevPAR divided by the RevPAR of the competitive set. Formerly known as RevPAR Index (RPI).<br><br>RGI = Hotel's RevPAR / Competitive Set RevPAR |
| Revenue Optimization | The science of managing a limited amount of supply to maximize revenue and profits, by dynamically controlling the price and quantity offered by distribution channel. Often used interchangeably with "revenue management." |
| RevPAG | Revenue per Available Guest. Total revenue divided by the total number of guests in the total. |
| RevPAR | Revenue Per Available Room. The daily revenue of a hotel divided by the total number of available rooms at that hotel. Daily hotel revenue / Total # of available rooms in hotel. |
| RevPAS | Revenue Per Available Space. A measurement of efficiency of utilization of meeting space. Similar to RevPAR, the higher the occupancy of the meeting rooms and the higher the average check, the higher the RevPAS.<br><br>RevPAS = Total Catering Revenue Generated / Total Available Square Footage of Meeting Space |
| RevPASH | Revenue per Available Seat Hour.<br><br>RevPASH = Total Outlet Revenue / (Available Seats x Opening Hours) |
| RevPATT | Revenue Per Available Tee Time. |
| RFI | Request for information |
| RGI | Revenue Generation Index. RGI is a ratio of the hotel's RevPAR divided by the RevPAR of the competitive set. Formerly known as RevPAR Index (RPI).<br><br>RGI = Hotel's RevPAR / Competitive Set RevPAR |
| RMS | Revenue Management System. The system a hotel uses as a tool to assist with the maximization of revenue. The system typically contains information on the hotel's availability, room types, stay patterns (future and historical), ALOS, etc. A system can be automated or manual. |
| ROH | Run of House |
| ROI | Return on Investment |
| SAM | Strategic Account Management |
| SEO | Search Engine Optimization. The primary purpose of SEO is to position your hotel in the highest placement possible in the organic search engine results for relevant, popular keywords. A key SEO metric involves the visibility (e.g., top 10, top 30) for important keywords relative to your competitors. |

| | |
|---|---|
| SGR | Space to Group Room Ratio |
| SMM | Strategic Meetings Management is a disciplined approach to managing enterprise-wide meeting and event activities, processes, suppliers, and data in order to achieve measurable business objectives that align with the organization's strategic goals/vision, and deliver value in the form of quantitative savings, risk mitigation, and service quality. |
| Space to Group Room Ratio (SGR) | The amount of meeting space a group requires compared to the number of hotel rooms the group will need.<br><br>SGR = Total Square Footage / Sleeping Rooms for that Day |
| STAR Report | The STAR program from STR is used by the global hotel industry as a vital revenue optimization tool. The report benchmarks a hotel's performance against its competitive aggregate and local market. The STAR program tracks and delivers monthly, weekly, and daily data. |
| STR | STR, formerly known as Smith Travel Research, is an American company based in Hendersonville, Tennessee, that tracks supply and demand data for multiple market sectors, including the global hotel industry. |
| TA | Travel Agent |
| Third Party | A person or company involved in a purchase that is neither the purchaser nor the provider of the goods or services. In the hotel industry, third parties may be contracted to assist, in whole or in part, in the arrangements of customer meetings, events, conferences, and/or exhibitions. Third parties also include OTAs, GDS, and more. |
| TMC | Travel Management Company (AmEx, CWT) |
| TO | Tour Operator |
| Transient | Guests who book individually rather than with a group. |
| TRevPAR | Total Revenue Per Available Room. The sum of net revenues from all operated departments plus rentals and other income per available room for the period divided by the total available rooms during the period.[49] |
| Unconstrained Demand | The amount of demand for a hotel in the absence of any pricing and inventory constraints. |
| Upgrade | To provide a guest with a more expensive or luxurious accommodation than the customer reserved, without charging more. |
| Upsell | To encourage a customer or guest to purchase a more expensive room (or other item). |
| USALI | Uniform System of Accounts for the Lodging Industry. USALI is the guide for hotel owners, managers, and other parties for reporting and presenting hotel financial statements. The resulting standardization established by the USALI permits internal and external users of financial statements to compare the financial position and operational performance of a specific hotel with similar types of hotels in the lodging industry. |
| Variable Cost | Variable costs are incurred when a hotel room, or service, is sold. Variable costs will change, and are dependent on the total number of additional sales. An example is an additional housekeeper who is scheduled to work only after a certain number of rooms are sold. |
| Wash | The difference between a group's contracted room block and what the hotel expects will actually materialize, considering the hotel's estimate of no-shows, cancellations, and early departures. |
| YOY | Year Over Year |
| YTD | Year To Date |

Kathleen Cullen is Senior Vice President of Preferred Hospitality Solutions, a division of PHG Consulting, which is a sister company to Preferred Hotels & Resorts.

Kathleen brings more than 25 years of diverse experience in the hospitality industry. Previously, her responsibilities ranged from holding strategic senior leadership positions in the corporate offices of dynamic, fast-paced, global hotel companies and owning her own consulting firm to authoring professional publications and working in varied operational departments on the property level. Leading change management has been a major factor in her success over the years, and in her new role with Preferred Hospitality Solutions, Kathleen will leverage her astute ability to understand individual's strengths and line them up with hotels' needs, while demonstrating her strong sense of when and how to respond quickly to changes needed to guarantee a hotel's success.

Prior to joining Preferred Hospitality Solutions, Kathleen was Senior Vice President of Revenue & Distribution for Two Roads Hospitality. In that role, she was responsible for the overall revenue strategies and increasing hotel market share for a portfolio of more than 75 hotels, as well as optimizing the company's revenue management foundation for all brands, including organizational set up, expert human resources and deployment, technology platform, tools, and connectivity. During her tenure Two Roads Hospitality, she was a key leader and held cross-discipline responsibilities for all new hotel openings and transitions.

Kathleen has been an active member of HSMAI since 2005, serving as the Chair for the Revenue Management Advisory Board in 2014 and 2015. She is also the author of the industry's first and best-selling revenue publication, Defining Revenue Management: Top Line to Bottom Line, which was published by HSMAI in 2006, as well as two editions of Evolving Dynamics of Revenue Management, published in 2010 and 2015, and the third edition of Evolving Dynamics of Revenue Optimization in 2019. These publications serve as the official study guide for the industry-recognized revenue optimization certification offered by HSMAI — CRME, and are also used as the curriculum in Universities such as Cornell University, NYU, and Michigan State University.

Kathleen attended Fitchburg State University in Massachusetts, and has received certificates in both "Hotel Yield Management" from Horand Vogel and Associates, and "E-Business Strategy" from the University of Chicago. A mother of three, she resides with her family in the San Francisco Bay Area.

# ACKNOWLEDGEMENTS
## ECONOMICS AND ITS ROLE IN REVENUE MANAGEMENT

This book would not have been possible without the help, insights, and contributions of many in the travel industry. This includes the sponsors who funded it because they recognize the importance of the overall discipline of revenue optimization, and the importance of elevating the understanding of and education on this topic throughout the industry. It also includes multiple revenue professionals, hotel executives, and industry consultants who were called upon for their insights, best practices, case studies, and feedback to the author along the way. Their knowledge and perceptions were invaluable to the writing and editing process

**Veronica Andrews, CRME**
*Director, Digital Data Solutions*
STR

**Christian Boerger, CRME, CHDM, CHBA**
*Revenue Strategist and Digital Marketing Expert*

**Andressa Chapman**
*Consultant*
Trigger Hotel Marketing

**Sara Fults**
*Vice President Distribution*
MGM Resorts International

**Eric Gravelle, CRME**
*Vice President of Revenue Management, North America*
Diamond Resorts International

**Linda Gulrajani, CRME**
*Vice President, Revenue Strategy & Distribution*
Marcus Hotels

**Mehernosh "MJ" Jehangir**
*Corporate Director of Revenue Management*
Loews Hotels & Co

**Juli F. Jones, CAE**
*Vice President*
Hospitality Sales & Marketing Association International (HSMAI)

**Flo Lugli**
*Principal*
Navesink Advisory Group LLC

**Chris Nixon, CRME, CHDM**
*AVP of Revenue Optimization*
Ashford

**Heather Richer**
*Chief Marketing Officer*
Red Awning

**Andrew Rubinacci**
*SVP, Revenue & Distribution*
Omni Hotels & Resorts

**Jim A. Struna, CRME**
*Regional Director of Revenue Management*
Rosewood Hotel Group

**Kathleen Tindell**
*Program Director, HSMAI University*
Hospitality Sales & Marketing Association International (HSMAI)

**Paul Van Meerendonk, CRME**
*Director, Global Advisory Services*
IDeaS - A SAS COMPANY

**David Warman**
*Senior Vice President Hotel Marketing and Revenue Management*
Four Seasons Hotels & Resorts

**Tim Wiersma**
*Vice President, Revenue Management*
Red Roof Inns, Inc.

**Stefan Wolf**
*Key Account Director - Asia Pacific*
Snapshot GmbH

# ENDNOTES

[1] Noone, B. M., Enz, C. A., & Glassmire, J. (2017). "Total hotel revenue management: a strategic profit perspective." Cornell Hospitality Report, 17(8), 3-15.

[2] Cross, Robert G. Revenue Management: Hard-Core Tactics for Market Domination. Orion Business, 1998.

[3] O'Hanlon, Maureen. "Prescriptive Analytics and Machine Learning for Revenue Management Leaders." HSMAI, June 15, 2017, http://www.hsmai.org/knowledge/article.cfm?ItemNumber=34354. March 1, 2019.

[4] Haley, Mark, Hoare, Mark, Xuereb, Monica. "What to Look for in a Hotel Revenue Manager." HospitalityUpgrade.com, https://www.hospitalityupgrade.com/_magazine/MagazineArticles/What-to-Look-for-in-a-Hotel-Revenue-Manager.asp, June 18, 2018. February 19, 2019.

[5] Noone, B. M. (2017). ""Bridging the Revenue Management Talent Gap." HotelExecutive.com. http://www.hotelexecutive.com/business_review/5407/bridging-the-revenue-management-talent-gap. February 18, 2019.

[6] Noone, B. M. (2017). ""Bridging the Revenue Management Talent Gap." HotelExecutive.com. http://www.hotelexecutive.com/business_review/5407/bridging-the-revenue-management-talent-gap. February 18, 2019.

[7] Slembeck, Tilman. "Principles of Economics". http://www.slembeck.ch/principles.html, October 1, 2006. March 1, 2019.

[8] HNN Editorial Staff. "Hotel Industry Terms to Know." Hotel News Now, http://www.hotelnewsnow.com/Articles/6217/Hotel-Industry-Terms-to-Know, January 26, 2018. March 1, 2019.

[9] Sowell, Thomas. Basic Economics: A Common Sense Guide to the Economy, 3rd edition. Basic Books, April 3, 2007.

[10] Watkins, Ed. "5 changes coming in hotel financial reporting." Hotel News Now, August 20, 2014. http://www.hotelnewsnow.com/articles/23556/5-changes-coming-in-hotel-financial-reporting. November 8, 2018.

[11] McGuire, Kelly A. Hotel Pricing in a Social World: Driving Value in the Digital Economy. Wiley and SAS Business Series, October 26, 2015.

[12] Enz, C. A., Canina, L., & Lomanno, M. (2004). Why discounting doesn't work: The dynamics of rising occupancy and falling revenue among competitors [Electronic article]. Cornell Hospitality Report, 4(7), 6-25.

[13] Canina, L., Enz, C. A., & Lomanno, M. (2006). Why discounting doesn't work: A hotel pricing update [Electronic article]. Cornell Hospitality Report, 6(2), 6-20.

[14] G. Cross, Robert & Higbie, Jon. (2009). Revenue Management's Renaissance: A Rebirth of the Art and Science of Profitable Revenue Generation. Cornell Hospitality Quarterly - CORNELL HOSP Q. 50. 56-81. 10.1177/1938965508328716.

[15] Thompson, G. M., & Sohn, H. (2008). Accurately estimating time-based restaurant revenues using revenue per available seat-hour [Electronic article]. Cornell Hospitality Report, 8(9), 6-15.

[16] Tetreault, Allie. 'How to Use a Menu Engineering Worksheet." Toast, January 29, 2016. https://pos.toasttab.com/blog/restaurant-menu-engineering-worksheet-free-menu-template. February 7, 2019.

[17] Kimes, S. E. (2000). Revenue management on the links: Applying yield management to the golf-course industry [Electronic version]. Cornell Hotel and Restaurant Administration Quarterly, 41(1), 120-127. Retrieved February 7, 2019, from Cornell University, School of Hospitality Administration site: http://scholarship.sha.cornell.edu/articles/463/.

[18] Kimes, S. E., & Schruben, L. W. (2002). Golf course revenue management: A study of tee time intervals [Electronic version]. Retrieved [insert date], from Cornell University, SHA School site: http://scholarship.sha.cornell.edu/articles/846

[19] Clough, Rodney G. "2018 HVS Performance Report: Spa Department." HVS, November 20, 2018. https://hvs.com/article/8392-2018-HVS- Performance-Report-Spa-Department.

[20] 2017 Trends in the U.S. Hotel Industry. CBRE Hotels' Americas Research.

[21] Mandelbaum, Robert. "How the Composition of RevPAR Growth Impacts Changes in Profits." Lodging, November 2017. http://www.cbrehotels.com/EN/Research/Pages/How-the-Composition-of-RevPAR-Growth-Impacts-Changes-in-Profits.aspx. February 25, 2019.

[22] Estis Green, Cindy and Mark V. Lomanno. Demystifying the Digital Marketplace: Spotlight on the Hospitality Industry, Part 1. Kalibri Labs, 2016.

[23] Estis Green, Cindy and Mark V. Lomanno. Demystifying the Digital Marketplace: Spotlight on the Hospitality Industry, Part 1. Kalibri Labs, 2016.

[24] "New Research Shows Consumers Spend $5.2 Billion Annually in Fraudulent and Misleading Hotel Booking Transactions." AH&LA, May 3, 2018. https://www.ahla.com/press-release/new-research-shows-consumers-spend-52-billion-annually-fraudulent-and-misleading. February 12, 2019.

[25] Jackson, Kate. "Landmark UK ruling ends misleading OTA practices." AccomNews, February 10, 2019. https://www.accomnews.com.au/2019/02/landmark-uk-ruling-ends-misleading-ota-practices/. March 6, 2019.

[26] "Hoteliers Encourage Congress to Stop Online Booking Scams." Hotel News Resource, October 1, 2018. https://www.hotelnewsresource.com/article101868.html. March 6, 2019.

[27] "Hotel Distribution Technology." Snapshot, 2017. https://blog.snapshot.travel/hubfs/Hotel%20Distribution%20Technology%20Chart%20v2.pdf. February 13, 2019.

[28]Estis Green, Cindy. (2017). "Time to Take Action: Data Analysis to Drive Revenue." Asian American Hotel Owners Association (producer). [Webinar].

[29]"Kalibri Labs Net Revenue Metrics." https://www.kalibrilabs.com/metrics/. February 14, 2019.

[30]Estis Green, Cindy, Mark V. Lomanno, and Matt Carrier. Demystifying the Digital Marketplace: Spotlight on the Hospitality Industry, Part 3. Kalibri Labs, 2018.

[31]"Cindy Estis Green on Optimizing Your Distribution." HSMAI. https://www.hsmai.org/knowledge/summary.cfm?ItemNumber=5041. February 14, 2019.

[32]Hoisington, Alicia. "Revenue Management Data helps hotels drive revenue, reduce customer-acquisition costs." Hotel Management, December 19, 2017. https://www.hotelmanagement.net/revenue-management/how-to-use-data-to-drive-revenue-at-hotels. February 14, 2019.

[33]www.hotelmanagement.net, a division of Questex, "Data helps hotels drive revenue, reduce customer-acquisition costs," Alicia Hoisington, 12/19/17.

[34]Significant portions of this chapter have been repurposed from HSMAI's book, Hospitality Digital Marketing Essentials: A Field Guide for Navigating Today's Digital Landscape, the study guide for the CHDM certification. The complete publication is available from www.hsmai.org/chdm.

[35]"Important mobile booking stats for hotels in 2018." Travel Tripper blog, February 6, 2018. https://www.traveltripper.com/blog/important-mobile-booking-stats-for-hotels-in-2018/. February 22, 2019.

[36]Hinote, Amy. "How Vacation Rental Marketing Has Changed." VRMA Blog, May 9, 2013. http://www.vrma.org/p/bl/et/blogaid=1015. February 25, 2019.

[37]Martinelli, Kristen. "Everything You Need to Know About the Vacation Rental Industry | Part 2." Futurestay. https://www.futurestay.com/read/vacation-rental-history/industry-pt-2/. February 25, 2019.

[38]Lesser, Daniel. "Hotel capitalization rates: Caveat emptor." Hotel News Now, December 7, 2009. http://www.hotelnewsnow.com/Articles/4551/Hotel-capitalization-rates-Caveat-emptor.

[39]HNN Editorial Staff. "Hotel Industry Terms to Know." Hotel News Now, January 26, 2018. http://www.hotelnewsnow.com/Articles/6217/Hotel-Industry-Terms-to-Know. March 1, 2019.

[40]HNN Editorial Staff. "Hotel Industry Terms to Know." Hotel News Now, January 26, 2018. http://www.hotelnewsnow.com/Articles/6217/Hotel-Industry-Terms-to-Know. March 1, 2019

[41]HNN Editorial Staff. "Hotel Industry Terms to Know." Hotel News Now, January 26, 2018. http://www.hotelnewsnow.com/Articles/6217/Hotel-Industry-Terms-to-Know. March 1, 2019

[42]General Data Protection Regulation (GDPR). Investopedia, February 10, 2019. March 5, 2019.

[43]HNN Editorial Staff. "Hotel Industry Terms to Know." Hotel News Now, January 26, 2018. http://www.hotelnewsnow.com/Articles/6217/Hotel-Industry-Terms-to-Know. March 1, 2019

[44]HNN Editorial Staff. "Hotel Industry Terms to Know." Hotel News Now, January 26, 2018. http://www.hotelnewsnow.com/Articles/6217/Hotel-Industry-Terms-to-Know. March 1, 2019

[45]HNN Editorial Staff. "Hotel Industry Terms to Know." Hotel News Now, January 26, 2018. http://www.hotelnewsnow.com/Articles/6217/Hotel-Industry-Terms-to-Know. March 1, 2019

[46]HNN Editorial Staff. "Hotel Industry Terms to Know." Hotel News Now, January 26, 2018. http://www.hotelnewsnow.com/Articles/6217/Hotel-Industry-Terms-to-Know. March 1, 2019

[47]HNN Editorial Staff. "Hotel Industry Terms to Know." Hotel News Now, January 26, 2018. http://www.hotelnewsnow.com/Articles/6217/Hotel-Industry-Terms-to-Know. March 1, 2019

[48]HNN Editorial Staff. "Hotel Industry Terms to Know." Hotel News Now, January 26, 2018. http://www.hotelnewsnow.com/Articles/6217/Hotel-Industry-Terms-to-Know. March 1, 2019

[49]HNN Editorial Staff. "Hotel Industry Terms to Know." Hotel News Now, January 26, 2018. http://www.hotelnewsnow.com/Articles/6217/Hotel-Industry-Terms-to-Know. March 1, 2019

[50]Chaykowski, Kathleen. "Number Of Facebook Business Pages Climbs To 50 Million With New Messaging Tools." Forbes. December 8, 2015. https://www.forbes.com/sites/kathleenchaykowski/2015/12/08/facebook-business-pages-climb-to-50-million-with-new-messaging-tools/#171436de6991. January 10, 2018.

[51]"Why Brands Should Embrace Instagram Instead of Facebook." selfstartr. https://selfstartr.com/why-brands-should-embrace-instagram-instead-of-facebook/. January 10, 2018.

[52]Zenn, Jacqueline. "9 Ways to Measure Your Brand's Social Media Health." Mashable. June 11, 2012. http://mashable.com/2012/06/11/social-media-brand-data/#qL895kx0TqqJ. January 10, 2018.